WITHDRAWN

The Compass of Irony

Mr Matthew Arnold. To him, Miss Mary Augusta, his niece: 'Why, Uncle Matthew, oh why, will not you be always wholly serious?'

(from *The Poets Corner* by Max Beerbohm)

The Compass of Irony

D. C. MUECKE

METHUEN & CO LTD

11 NEW FETTER LANE LONDON EC4

First published 1969 by Methuen & Co Ltd
11 New Fetter Lane, London EC4
© *1969 by D. C. Muecke*
Printed in Great Britain
by Richard Clay (The Chaucer Press), Ltd
Bungay, Suffolk

DISTRIBUTED IN THE U.S.A. BY
BARNES & NOBLE INC.

TO MY WIFE

CONTENTS

PREFACE

The first part of this work consists of a general account of the formal qualities of irony and a classification, in detail and with examples, of the more familiar kinds. The second part is designed both to introduce the less familiar, because more recently developed, kinds and to relate their emergence to the gradual dislodgement of the old 'closed world' view of life by the new 'open universe' view. The two parts are not discontinuous, but the second is necessarily at a different level since it deals less with the forms of irony and more with its functions, its topics, and its cultural significance.

While some (still employed) forms of irony are as old as Western civilization – to be able to be ironical is perhaps part of the definition of our civilization – we shall see that in the Romantic and post-Romantic period irony becomes the expression of an attitude to life or more accurately a way of organizing one's response to and coming to terms with a world that seems to be fundamentally at odds with mankind. I shall try to show that this increasingly 'philosophical' use of irony is intimately related to the development of European thought, more specifically to the growth of scepticism, relativism, liberalism, and positivism and to the emergence of the scientific attitude and its (in part) complementary opposite, romanticism. Nor is it by chance or out of mere personal interest that religion and the question of free will are recurrent topics in this work. Any similar work, any representative history of irony, would find itself obliged to give them as much attention.

Chapter I begins in a cloud of unknowing, with the acknowledged conceptual vagueness of irony, continues with a sketch of the present state of 'ironological' studies, and illustrates the need

for further work even beyond what is attempted here. The reader
will find in Chapter II a general analysis of irony into its essential
elements, and in Chapters III–V a classification of the principal
forms, grades, and modes. Up to this point at least, he will be on
quite familiar ground. I have, however, tried to introduce more
order and argument into the classification than one readily finds
elsewhere. Relatively little, considering its importance, has been
said here about Dramatic Irony, but this is because it is the one
form of irony which has been adequately treated in English.

Chapter VI opens Part II with a distinction between 'Specific
Irony' and 'General Irony', the former signifying the class of
ironies of which any of us may be so uncircumspect as to become
a victim, the latter the class of ironies of which we are all inevitably victims, the ironies based upon apparently fundamental and
inescapable contradictions of the human condition. What is
called Cosmic Irony is a form of General Irony.

In Chapter VII I try to present a more sympathetic account of
Romantic Irony than is commonly found in English or American
works. The principal theorist of Romantic Irony, Friedrich
Schlegel, is attracting more and more attention; his anticipations
of Thomas Mann's explicit and implicit 'ironology' and of the
New Critics' theory of irony have been pointed out by Erich
Heller and René Wellek respectively; some of Alain Robbe-
Grillet's views on the novelist's need to be in his novels a theorist
of the novel may be found in Schlegel; a recent lecture of Michel
Butor's (Melbourne, 1968) seemed to me to be pure Romantic
Irony both in theory and in practice. What is needed, of course,
is an English translation of Schlegel's earlier works.

The contemporary importance of irony as a literary and cultural phenomenon necessarily attracts attention to the position of
the ironist himself. My last chapter discusses the complementary
relationship between the ironist and the victims of irony and the
questions this raises as to the morality of irony.

I take the opportunity formally to thank Professor Ivan Barko,
Mr Dennis Douglas, Mr Tony Hassall, Professor A. King, and
Mr John Radvansky, who read the work in manuscript, and
especially Professor Brian Medlin, whose very critical reading of
Part I did it a lot of good, and Professor Leslie Bodi, without whose

constant advice, criticism, and encouragement this work would have been another *Key to All the Mythologies.*

I should like also to express my gratitude to the French Embassy in Australia for procuring a grant from the French Government that enabled me to work for some months in Paris.

D. C. MUECKE

ACKNOWLEDGEMENTS

The author and publishers would like to thank the following for permission to use material from the below-mentioned sources:

Citadel Press Inc. for extracts from *The Poetry and Prose of Heinrich Heine*, edited by Frederic Ewen; J. M. Dent & Sons and E. P. Dutton & Co. Inc. for an engraving by Eric Gill from the New Temple Shakespeare edition of *Hamlet*; Faber and Faber Ltd and Harcourt, Brace & World Inc. for extracts from *The Cocktail Party* by T. S. Eliot; William Heinemann Ltd and Dodd, Mead & Co. for the drawing of Matthew Arnold from *The Poets Corner* by Max Beerbohm; Macmillan & Co. Ltd and the Trustees of the Hardy Estate for an extract from *The Dynasts* by Thomas Hardy; Mr Elder Olson for the poem entitled 'Prologue to his Book' from *Collected Poems* (1963); A. D. Peters & Co. and Alfred A. Knopf Inc. for an extract from 'Godolphin Horne' from *Selected Cautionary Verses* by Hilaire Belloc; Martin Secker & Warburg Ltd and Coward-McCann Inc. for extracts from *A Man Without Qualities* by Robert Musil, translated by Eithne Wilkins and Ernst Kaiser; Mr Saul Steinberg for a drawing from *The New World*; and the University of Chicago Press for extracts from *The Rhetoric of Fiction* by Wayne C. Booth.

Part One

I

IRONOLOGY

Banks fou, braes fou,
Gether ye a the day,
Ye'll no gether yer nieves fou.

Getting to grips with irony seems to have something in common
with gathering the mist; there is plenty to take hold of if only one
could. To attempt a taxonomy of a phenomenon so nebulous that
it disappears as one approaches is an even more desperate adventure. Yet if, upon examination, irony becomes less nebulous, as it
does, it remains elusively Protean. Its forms and functions are so
diverse as to seem scarcely amenable to a single definition: Anglo-
Saxon understatement, eighteenth-century raillery, Romantic
Irony, and schoolboy sarcasm are all forms of irony; Sophocles
and Chaucer, Shakespeare and Kafka, Swift and Thomas Mann
are all ironists; for Socrates irony was a standpoint, the governing
principle of his intellectual activity; to Quintilian irony was a
figure in rhetoric; to Karl Solger irony was the very principle of
art; and to Cleanth Brooks irony is, 'the most general term we
have for the kind of qualification which the various elements in a
context receive from the context'.[1] Irony may be a weapon in a
satirical attack, or a smokescreen concealing a retreat, or a device
for turning the world or oneself inside out; irony may be found
in words and attitudes, in events and situations; or we may find
nothing on earth and quite certainly nothing in heaven that is not
ironic.

There is enough here to suggest how agreeable it would be if
one could get it all properly sorted out, and enough to suggest the
improbability of ever succeeding. There seems, however, to be no
difficulty in finding explanations for the conceptual fogginess of
irony, and it is perhaps with these explanations that one should
begin. First of all there are the related points that the several forms

of irony may each be approached and therefore defined from many different angles, and that in practice instances of irony are usually complicated by other factors which may then illegitimately enter into definitions of irony. Secondly, there is the feeling that 'irony' should mean 'good irony', that is, the feeling that irony ought to be qualitatively defined, and this means running into the same sorts of difficulties as one meets in attempting to define 'Art' or 'Pure Poetry'. And thirdly, there is the fact that the concept of irony is still in the process of being developed so that almost everyone may be dismayed by the narrowness of some definitions and outraged by the looseness of others.

In seeking to define irony or distinguish its several kinds one can quite legitimately look at it from many different angles. But it is precisely this that explains the chaos which the terminology of irony presents. One has only to reflect for a moment upon the various names that have been given to 'kinds' of irony – tragic irony, comic irony, irony of manner, irony of situation, philosophical irony, practical irony, dramatic irony, verbal irony, ingénu irony, double irony, rhetorical irony, self-irony, Socratic Irony, Romantic Irony, cosmic irony, sentimental irony, irony of Fate, irony of chance, irony of character, etc. – to see that some have been named from the effect, others from the medium, others again from the technique, or the function, or the object, or the practitioner, or the tone, or the attitude. Clearly, there could be several mutually independent (and separately inadequate) classifications of the 'kinds' of irony, each based upon a different point of view; but merely to go on inventing and using as occasion requires such a scatter of terms as I have listed will ensure that one never sees any ordered relationship between the kinds and consequently never gets a clear picture of the whole range or compass of irony.

Again, since we find in literature not just irony but the irony of Ariosto and Molière, Hardy and Proust, the tasks of distinguishing the kinds and detecting the essential qualities of irony are complicated by the natural desire to describe as accurately as possible the personal quality of each author's irony. But obviously, Byronic irony is not a kind of irony that any other writer may practise at will. The difference between, let us say, Chaucer's irony and

Thomas Mann's irony is not entirely a matter of different ironical techniques and strategies nor this difference compounded by the difference between an Englishman's fourteenth-century and a German's twentieth-century outlook; it consists partly of the difference between Chaucer and Thomas Mann. Their ironical manners reflect their personalities – *le style ironique est l'homme même*. This implies a distinction, for practical purposes, between an ironologist and a literary critic analogous to the distinction between an academic depth-psychologist and a practising psycho-analyst. It would be the business of the critic but not of the irono-logist to give a complete account of the differences between the irony of one writer and that of another. It is the business of the ironologist to prepare the ground for a complete account; he is permitted therefore to simplify and generalize. To the ironologist, Chaucer's irony will not mean all that it might mean to a critic or a reader of Chaucer. This is not to say that the ironologist will find himself able to dispense with the skills of the literary critic.

The concept of irony is also obscured by the frequent and close conjunction of irony with satire and with such phenomena as the comic, the grotesque, the humorous, and the absurd. As a result there is a tendency to define irony in terms of the qualities of these other things, some of which defy definition even more success-fully than irony. But irony is not essentially related to satire, and when it is related in practice it is a relationship of means to end; and although irony is frequently found overlapping with the ab-surd or the comic it may also be found overlapping with the tragic.

As a subject for discussion irony is more than a set of conceptual and methodological problems. To deal with irony even from a theoretical point of view is to be dealing with an art or, if one is thinking of the ironies of life, at least with very striking *objets trouvés*. One has some sympathy, therefore, with the desire to de-fine irony so as not to ignore what it is that characterizes effective or successful irony even though this should mean weighing the imponderable and objectifying the subjective. What can be said, putting it very simply, is that the art of irony is the art of saying something without really saying it. It is an art that gets its effects from below the surface, and this gives it a quality that resembles

B

the depth and resonance of great art triumphantly saying much more than it seems to be saying. And yet one must also say of irony that it is an art closely related to wit; it is intellectual rather than musical, nearer to the mind than to the senses, reflective and self-conscious rather than lyrical and self-absorbed. Its virtues are those of fine prose rather than those of lyric poetry. No one will need to be reminded how many of the great writers of prose were also great ironists, nor that the Age of Prose and Reason was also the period in which the art of irony (and of the novel) developed so rapidly.

It would be too simple to say that prose tends to be ironical and poetry tends not to be; poetry was often ironical before and during the Age of Prose as well as afterwards, and prose is by no means typically characterized by irony. The distinction is between that kind of writing which, largely by means of syntax, exploits the possibilities of wittily ordering ideas while neglecting or subordinating other possibilities and that other kind of writing which, largely by means of 'music', metaphor, and elevated diction, exploits the possibilities of evoking moods and feelings. Among earlier poets we may compare Chaucer, the sophisticated 'Southren' man rejecting the strong rhythms of the alliterative line and practising the run-on couplet and the throw-away rhyme, with 'our sage and serious' Spenser who reverted to alliteration and devised a remote poetic diction and a highly musical stanza for his *Faerie Queene*. In later ironical poetry a reflective or a self-conscious quality (both words attest the inherent duality of irony) is manifested in the mock-heroic poems of the Enlightenment, the anti-climactic element in Byron and Heine, and the sly juxtapositions and *sous-entendus* of Eliot. Here the contrasts would be with *Paradise Lost* (which is not, however, entirely unironical), with Keats, and with Dylan Thomas.

Prose-writers too may be compared along these lines; Harvey Gross in his *Sound and Form in Modern Poetry* compares the opening sentences of *Pride and Prejudice* and *Ulysses* in terms that are completely apropos though he is not thinking of irony:

[Jane Austen] fashions a prosody of wit. The movement of her language is quick with 'the feel of thought' – the powers of abstraction, of generalization, of perceiving and confronting ideas. Joyce's language moves on different principles. His prose is dense with heavy stresses, alliterative effects, and a careful placing of long and short vowels. He is not concerned with the witty presentation of an idea but with *things* and arrangements; and, as we learn from the context, symbols. The rhythm of Joyce's prose is determined by the weight and shape of the words; Jane Austen's rhythm is determined by the shape of her syntax formed by the energy of her mind.[2]

But these are only hints towards a poetics of irony, a large subject and one that is outside the scope of the present work.

Even without bringing into consideration the fact that the concept of irony is still evolving, we can see that the diversity of the forms of irony multiplied by the diversity of approaches to irony – the attempts to define it in terms of motivation, function, aesthetic quality, or response – and the difficulty of distinguishing it from the satiric, the comic, and so on might themselves explain why there has not been any adequate classification of irony. They might also explain why there is no history of irony in European literature, or even the outline of a history. So far as I know, there is no complete history of irony in any of the principal European literatures. J. A. K. Thomson's *Irony: An Historical Introduction* (1927) is restricted to classical literature. An article by Earle Birney briefly and with disabling omissions covers English irony before Chaucer. F. McD. C. Turner's book *The Element of Irony in English Literature* (1926) omits Chaucer and Shakespeare and is eccentric in other ways. Beda Allemann's *Ironie und Dichtung* (1956) covers Germanic literature from Schlegel to Musil. Morton L. Gurewitch has written a doctoral thesis on 'European Romantic Irony'.

The history of the concept of irony is in rather better shape. Otto Ribbeck's 'Über den Begriff des εἴρων' (1876) is the classical study of *eironeia* in Greek literature of the fifth and fourth centuries. G. G. Sedgewick's Harvard dissertation of 1913 traced the history of the word through classical Greek and Latin to Medieval Latin. Norman Knox, in his *The Word IRONY and its Context 1500–1755* (1961), has carried the history of the semantic development of the English word from its first appearance down to the date of Dr Johnson's dictionary. And I think one could safely assume that in 1755 the concept of irony in other European countries had not become significantly more complex than it had in England.

It was, however, *after* 1755 that the word 'irony' began to take on several quite new meanings, though less rapidly in England and France than in Germany. In 1755 Dr Johnson apparently recognized only one kind of irony, defined in his dictionary as: 'A mode of speech in which the meaning is contrary to the words.' Though he was somewhat behind the more knowledgeable of his contemporaries (*vide* Knox) in a theoretical acquaintance with irony – a precedent seized upon by subsequent lexicographers and encyclopaedists – not even the most knowledgeable had more than a glimmering recognition of dramatic irony as a form of irony. The *force* of dramatic irony had of course long been felt, and by story-tellers as well as dramatists. I raise later the question of how explicitly it was felt and by what other names it was referred to. The concept of dramatic irony was introduced into English by Connop Thirlwall in 1833, but, as Sedgewick notes, the term was not universally acceptable even as late as 1907. Bradley in his *Shakespearean Tragedy* (1904) uses the term 'Sophoclean irony' but felt the need to define it and distinguish it from 'irony in the ordinary sense'. So far as I can discover the position was no better in France or Germany (see page 40).

A. W. Schlegel's unwillingness to admit the presence of irony in tragedy was owing in part to his not having a clear idea of dramatic irony and in part to his inability to separate irony and satire (which connotes the comic).

> No doubt, wherever the proper tragic enters everything like irony immediately ceases; but from the avowed raillery of Comedy, to the point where the subjection of mortal beings to an inevitable destiny demands the highest degree of seriousness, there are a multitude of human relations which unquestionably may be considered in an ironical view, without confounding the eternal line of separation between good and evil.[3]

His brother Friedrich's concept of irony, as we shall see later on, was much more advanced and unorthodox than this.

It was, however, the German Romantics who first recognized Shakespeare's objectivity as a kind of irony, objectivity in the sense of a free critical detachment from, and fully conscious power over, one's own creations. And it was they who invented Romantic Irony with the startling claim that irony is the very principle of art. The history of the concept of Romantic Irony from Friedrich Schlegel to Kierkegaard has been written by Ingrid Strohschneider-Kohrs, *Die romantische Ironie in Theorie und Gestaltung* (1960).

With minor exceptions (Thirlwall, I. A. Richards, and the 'New Criticism', for example), the *theory* of irony has been in the hands of the Germans or of those with a Germanic education, like Kierkegaard and the Swiss Amiel in the nineteenth century and Vladimir Jankélévitch in the twentieth century.

There is a great deal of work waiting to be done on irony: on the history of irony, on the concept of irony (especially in England and France in the later eighteenth and the nineteenth centuries), on the psychology of irony (both the motives to irony and the response to irony), and on the relationship of irony to intellectual and literary history in general and to satire and literary theory in particular.

Much work has been done, and most of it quite recently, at the level of literary criticism. At that level one can certainly speak of irony as a fashionable topic. *The International Index to Periodicals*, admittedly a somewhat rough and ready guide in this matter, records five articles under the heading Irony between March 1946 and February 1952, twelve in the next six years, thirty-two in the following six years, and thirty-three in the following *four* years (to March 1968); nearly all of these are articles on irony in this or that work or author. Irony as a topic for literary criticism is in some respects clearly a profitable new vein to be worked until it gives out or another, more profitable, is discovered.

This increase in critical work on irony, books as well as articles, has a three-fold explanation: (*a*) literature itself is more ironical than it used to be; (*b*) critics are not only more interested in but also more sensitive to irony than they used to be; and (*c*) the concept of irony has been enlarged to cover situations, attitudes, and ways of writing that formerly would not have been thought ironical at all.

These developments, of which we are now feeling the cumulative impact, can be traced back for two hundred or two hundred and fifty years and cannot of course be explained either separately or in purely literary terms. The development of irony, of the interest in irony, and of the concept of irony are closely related not only to each other but also to other shifts and trends in the intellectual history of Europe. No general treatment of irony can avoid being in some degree historical.

Saying that literature is more ironical than it used to be is not simply saying that the proportion of ironical to non-ironical works has increased but rather that irony now pervades literature, obliterating very largely this distinction of ironical and non-ironical. Nowadays only popular literature is predominantly non-ironical.

For most 'serious' writers, whether poets, novelists, or dramatists, irony is now much less often a rhetorical or dramatic strategy which they may or may not decide to employ, and much more often a mode of thought silently imposed upon them by the general tendency of the times. With a certain temperament, or a certain insensitivity to changes in the climate of thought, they may not feel this pressure, or may feel it very slightly. They may consciously resist it. Or they may find it congenial. But whatever their response to this pressure, it is there as it cannot be said to have been even in the eighteenth century.

To this silent pressure there is to be added the influence of the explicit views; (a) that 'modern' literature *must* be ironical and (b) that all *good* literature is by definition ironical. Both these views are as old as German Romanticism. Friedrich Schlegel, investigating the principles of modern art and the conditions under which it developed and recognizing that in many respects it was the antithesis of classical art – objectivity *v.* subjectivity, rational *v.* irrational, *Naiv* v. *Sentimentalisch*, absolute *v.* relative, and so on – argued, as did others of his time, that the only solution, since it was unthinkable to jettison the values of classical art, lay in the attempt at a reconciliation, if only by recognition and acceptance, of irreconcilable opposites. 'Every good poem must at the same time be wholly conscious and wholly instinctive.'[4] The names given to this attempt were (German) Romanticism and (Romantic) Irony. Kierkegaard sees them as the same thing in his *Concept of Irony*:

> Throughout this discussion I use the expressions: *irony* and the *ironist*, but I could as easily say: *romanticism* and the *romanticist*. Both expressions designate the same thing. The one suggests more the name with which the movement christened itself, the other the name with which Hegel christened it.[5]

To the extent that the above antitheses remain unreconciled today, the need to write ironically also remains.

It is the second of these views, the one without overt historical implications, which has commended itself to English and American critics. Though perhaps owing something to the eighteenth-century dictum that ridicule is the test of truth, in its modern form it derives from I. A. Richards and was developed by several of the American 'New Critics'. I quote, however, from an Australian: 'Perhaps all good poetry is to some extent ironical, in that it is more complex and paradoxical than mere statement can be.'[6]

This and the quotation from Schlegel imply that the kinds of irony dominant in current literature are not those dominant in earlier centuries. Modern literature is not only more ironical but also ironical in different ways. To be, for the moment, brief and general, modern irony is less satirical and more subjective, less rhetorical and more 'atmospheric', less aggressive and more defensive. In post-eighteenth-century literature we commonly find the complex ironizing the simple, the ambiguous the clear-cut, the uncertain the certain, and the relative the absolute.

It is also true that critics have, quite recently, become more sensitive to irony and consequently have been busily detecting it everywhere in the literature of the past, from *Beowulf* to 'Tears, Idle Tears'. It was not until the middle of the twentieth century that we were invited to see *Juvenal 13* as a mock *consolatio*,[7] Swift as being ironical at the Houyhnhnms' expense,[8] and *Moll Flanders* as an ironical 'placing' of Moll and her muddled morality.[9]

But we should distinguish here between, on the one hand, a greater willingness to suspect (rightly or wrongly) the intended presence of irony of a traditional kind behind Juvenal's apparent sympathy or Swift's apparent praise or Defoe's apparent straight reporting and, on the other hand, that increased awareness of and sensitivity to oblique effects and subtle implications which has extended the meaning of irony beyond anything that the authors of *Beowulf* and 'Tears, Idle Tears' would have called irony. If Swift's praise of the Houynhnhnms had been ironically intended, it would have been so in a sense of the word acceptable both to Swift and to modern critics; it would not be inconceivable that a letter from Swift should turn up in which he complained that his irony had not been seen. If his praise had not been ironically intended, the moderns would have been in error, seeing irony where none was intended. But the fact that Tennyson would have been indignant if he had been told that his poem was ironical does not necessarily mean that he would have denied that it had the qualities and characteristics that led Cleanth Brooks to call it ironical.[10]

How rapidly the word 'irony' has developed one of its most recent meanings may be seen in the following account. In 1921 T. S. Eliot set himself the task of defining the quality of Marvell's wit. Though he was himself an ironical poet, in a tradition going back through Laforgue and Gautier (whom he quotes in his essay), though he discussed Marvell's wit in terms that I. A. Richards and the 'New Critics' were later to apply to irony, and though the word 'irony' appears in this essay, Eliot did not say and, we can be fairly certain, did not then think that irony was a quality of Marvell's wit.

Only three years later I. A. Richards, in his *Principles of Literary Criticism*, classed Marvell's 'The Definition of Love' among those poems which are characterized by irony; irony in Richards' sense 'consists in the bringing in of the opposite, the complementary impulses'.[11] Since then every critic of Marvell has spoken of his irony and often, latterly, without feeling any need to define or justify their use of the word. For example, in writing of 'A Dialogue between the Resolved Soul and Created Pleasure', a poem which the common reader would assume to be a perfectly straightforward expression of orthodox morality, F. W. Bradbrook takes the line that 'the attitude of the poet towards his subject is ironical',[12] and does so with an air of stating the inherently probable. There is now (1965) Harold E. Toliver's book, with a title, *Marvell's Ironic Vision*, which would have been inconceivable forty years, perhaps even thirty years earlier.

In his *Principles of Literary Criticism* Richards classed 'Rose Aylmer' among those limited poems which, not being themselves ironical, 'will not bear an ironical contemplation'. In 1942 Robert Penn Warren demonstrated that 'Rose Aylmer' was ironical in a refinement of Richards' sense, 'tensions' replacing 'opposites'.[13] By a somewhat different and further refinement of Richards' 'irony', Cleanth Brooks persuaded himself that all poetry, even 'Tears, Idle Tears', is ironical. He took the view that the modification or qualification of any one part of a poem by the rest, that is, by the context in which it appears, is a kind of irony, or in other words, that the very way language is used in poetry (in contra-distinction to the way it is used in mathematics) ensures that all poetry is ironical. By taking this view he has done his best to finesse the word 'irony' out of useful existence. We cannot go on meaningfully saying that *Don Juan* and *Psalm 23* are both ironical. 'Ironical' without distinguishing qualifications is now in danger of being as uninformative a term in literary criticism as 'realistic'. One thing Cleanth Brooks has made clear, though it was not his intention to do so, is that the concept of irony is eminently in need of clarification.

II

THE ELEMENTS
OF IRONY

1 · *Defining Irony*

It might perhaps be prudent not to attempt any formal definitions. Since, however, Erich Heller, in his *Ironic German*, has already quite adequately not defined irony, there would be little point in not defining it all over again. I shall therefore hazard something like a definition begging the reader to remember, even though I should fail to do so myself, that I am writing primarily as an ironologist and only secondarily if at all as a literary critic, that I have no brief and simple definition that will include all kinds of irony while excluding all that is not irony, that distinctions from one angle may not be distinctions from another, and that kinds of irony theoretically distinguishable will in practice be found merging into one another.

⌈Let us then take the plunge, first remarking from the comparative safety of the diving board or the plank we have forced ourselves to walk that irony, like beauty, is in the eye of the beholder and is not a quality inherent in any remark, event, or situation. We might be able to define the *formal* requirements of an ironical remark or an ironic situation, but we should still have to ask of a remark, *Was it meant ironically?* and of a situation, *Do you see it as irony?* or, more exactly perhaps, *Do you feel it as irony?* To be sure, in ordinary discourse we ignore this and talk of irony, as we do of beauty, as if it were an objective quality or phenomenon, and generally we may rely upon having enough in common, a sufficient intersubjectivity, to be able to talk meaningfully of heavy or subtle, tragic or comic, bitter or playful or striking irony.⌉

While irony and beauty resemble one another in that both need to be subjectively vouched for, they bear to one another a closer relationship than resemblance. An ironical remark or work, an ironic event or situation, must have, beyond its formal requirements, certain minimal aesthetic qualities, lacking which, it fails to affect us as irony. An ironist, therefore, is not just *like* an artist, but *is* an artist, governed by the artist's need for perfection of form and expression and all 'the nameless graces which no methods teach'. The art of the ironist is most like the arts of the wit and the raconteur; and not only because irony runs the same risks of failure through being too laboured or too subtle, too brief or too long drawn out, mistimed in the telling or ill-adapted to audience or occasion.

The ironic events and situations which life itself presents are more or less effective according to how they exhibit the balance, economy, and precision of a work of art. And to have a sense of irony, to be able to see the ironic potential of a situation or state of affairs, is to have, among other qualities, something analogous to the artist's ability to see what would make a good picture or the writer's ability to see how an event could be turned into a good story. I mention this necessary aesthetic quality of (effective) irony so that it may henceforth be taken for granted along with the equally necessary subjective quality. The degree to which specific instances of irony are effective is a matter for the literary critic; my concern is elsewhere.

At this point it would be proper to set before the reader some examples of irony. I could not exemplify every distinguishable variety in less compass than a small volume, but a few brief quotations will remind the reader of the range of irony which any general definition must cover. The examples set out below are presented simply as a collection, and not arranged on any taxonomic principle, since our present purpose is to see what they have in common, not what distinguishes one kind from another.

1 Mutton cooked the week before last is, for the most part, unpalatable. (Ezra Pound)
2 LADY MACBETH: A little water clears us of this deed.
3 When all was over and the rival kings were celebrating their victory with Te Deums in their respective camps . . . (Voltaire, *Candide*)

4 When phoning for seats, be sure to have all your family and friends around you, because the box-office clerk has only you to attend to, and likes to hear you consult them all.

(From a circus programme)

5 In the School of Political Projectors I was but ill entertained, the Professors appearing in my Judgment wholly out of their Senses, which is a Scene that never fails to make me melancholy. These unhappy People were proposing Schemes for persuading Monarchs to chuse Favourites upon the Score of their Wisdom, Capacity and Virtue; of teaching Ministers to consult the Publick Good; of rewarding Merit, great Abilities and eminent Services; of instructing Princes to know their true Interest by placing it on the same Foundation with that of their People: Of chusing for Employments Persons qualified to exercise them; with many other wild impossible Chimaeras, that never entred before into the heart of Man to conceive, and confirmed in me the old Observation, that there is nothing so extravagant and irrational which some Philosophers have not maintained for Truth.   (Swift, *Gulliver's Travels*)

6 The town of Göttingen, famous for its sausages and university . . . I do not at this moment recall the names of all the students; while among the professors, many as yet have no name.

(Heine, *Reisebilder* (1830))[1]

7   Also I prey you to foryeve it me,
          Al have I nat set folk in hir degree
          Here in this tale, as that they sholde stonde.
          My wit is short, ye may wel understonde.

(Chaucer, *Canterbury Tales*)

8   Miss Nancy Ellicott smoked
          And danced all the modern dances;
          And her aunts were not sure how they felt about it,
          But they knew that it was modern.

(T. S. Eliot, 'Cousin Nancy')

9 A professor scribbles inept abuse in the library copy of a rival's book. The librarian feels that the professor ought to be formally admonished for defacing university property, but feels also, the professor having a degree of eminence, that the book ought now to be re-catalogued as an association copy of some bibliographical interest.   (Actual situation, somewhat modified)

10 It was a period when writers besought the deep blue sea 'to roll'.

(Henry James)

11 OEDIPUS: And it is my solemn prayer
That the unknown murderer, and his accomplices,
If such there be, may wear the brand of shame
For their shameful act, unfriended, to their life's end.

(Sophocles)

12   I repeat,
The Count your Master's known munificence
Is ample warrant that no just pretence
Of mine for dowry will be disallowed;
Though his fair daughter's self, as I avowed
At starting, is my object. Nay, we'll go
Together down, Sir! Notice Neptune, tho',
Taming a sea-horse, thought a rarity,
Which Claus of Innsbruck cast in bronze for me.

(Browning, 'My Last Duchess')

13 [Mrs Ferrars's] complexion was sallow; and her features small, without beauty, and naturally without expression; but a lucky contraction of the brow had rescued her countenance from the disgrace of insipidity, by giving it the strong characters of pride and ill nature.   (Jane Austen, *Sense and Sensibility*)

14 A little boy and a little girl were looking at a picture of Adam and Eve.

'Which is Adam, and which is Eve?' said one.

'I do not know,' said the other, 'but I could tell if they had their clothes on.'   (Samuel Butler, *Note-Books*)

15   O Lord! yestreen, thou kens, wi' Meg –
Thy pardon I sincerely beg;
O! may't ne'er be a livin' plague
      To my dishonour,
An' I'll ne'er lift a lawless leg
      Again upon her.

Besides I farther maun allow,
Wi' Lizzie's lass, three times I trow –
But, Lord, that Friday I was fou,
      When I cam near her,

Or else thou kens thy servant true
Wad never steer her.

May be thou lets this fleshly thorn
Beset thy servant e'en and morn
Lest he owre high and proud should turn,
        That he's sae gifted;
If sae, thy hand maun e'en be borne,
        Until thou lift it.
                        (Burns, 'Holy Willie's Prayer')

16 It gratified my self-conceit when I was told by Hegel that it was
not He who dwelt in heaven, as my grandmother had supposed, but
I myself, who dwelt here on earth, who was the Lord God. This
foolish pride did not, however, have a pernicious influence on me.
On the contrary, it awakened in me a heroic spirit, and I made such
a display of generosity and self-sacrifice at that time, that it certainly
must have eclipsed the most distinguished and noble deeds of the
good Philistines of virtue, who practised virtue merely from a sense
of duty and obedience to the laws of morality. Was I not in my own
person the living embodiment of moral law, and the fountainhead
of all justice and authority? I was primal virtue; I was incapable of
sin; I was purity incarnate. The most notorious Magdalens were
cleansed by the purifying and expiating power of my love-flames;
and they emerged from the embraces of the god as pure as lilies and
blushing like chaste roses – virgin once more. I must admit that this
rehabilitation of damaged Magdalens sometimes taxed my strength.
                        (Heine, *Confessions*)[2]

17 [Rameau's nephew in Diderot's work of that name tells his story of
the renegade who works his way into friendship with an innocent
and worthy Jew for the purpose of robbing him. Our sympathy is
of course with the Jew. Then the narrator adds] The stroke of
genius in his evil-doing is that he himself was the informer who
denounced his good friend the Jew to the Inquisition, which seized
him that morning and made a bonfire of him a few days later. Such
is the way the renegade came to peacefully enjoy the wealth of the
accursed descendant of those who crucified our Lord.
                        (Diderot, *Rameau's Nephew*)[3]

18 A blind god sitting by a stream takes up a handful of mud,

moulds it into a ball, and rolls it from one hand to the other. Aeons pass. Minute beings form themselves on the ball of mud warmed by the god's protecting hands. In the course of evolution, these busy creatures discover the god and so deduce a religion and a morality. Further investigations reveal that the god is blind and totally ignorant even of the existence of his creatures. From this they conclude that their morality is pointless. One day the god inadvertently drops the ball of mud back into the stream in which it dissolves. 'I must be more careful next time,' he thought. And, stooping down, he gathered up a fresh handful of mud and moulded it into form, and once more started rolling it.

(Summary of Laurence Housman's *The Blind God*)[4]

19 Impunity, *n.* Wealth.

(Ambrose Bierce, *The Devil's Dictionary*)

20 (see page 103) the illustration by Eric Gill.

21 (see page 168) the illustration by Steinberg.

In all instances of irony we can distinguish three essential elements. These we might, though loosely, call the formal requirements of irony as distinct from the subjective and aesthetic requirements mentioned above. Though theoretically distinguishable, they are closely interdependent.

In the first place irony is a double-layered or two-storey phenomenon. At the lower level is the situation either as it appears to the victim of irony (where there is a victim) or as it is deceptively presented by the ironist (where there is an ironist). This alternative anticipates Chapter III, Section 2, in which a distinction is drawn between victimizing situations of which we may say, 'It is ironic that . . .' and ironies of which we may say, 'He is being ironical.' At the upper level is the situation as it appears to the observer or the ironist. The upper level need not be *presented* by the ironist; it need only be evoked by him or be present in the mind of the observer. Nor need it be more than a hint that the ironist does not quite see the situation as he has presented it at the lower level (Example 8) or that the victim does not see the situation quite as it really is.

In the second place there is always some kind of opposition between the two levels, an opposition that may take the form of

contradiction, incongruity, or incompatibility. What is said may
be contradicted by what is meant (Example 5); what the victim
thinks may be contradicted by what the observer knows (Example 2). It is, however, by no means uncommon for there to be
a further opposition and generally a more striking one between
two elements both at the lower level. Example 3 is an instance of
this: the rival kings in *Candide* both claim the victory. None the
less, there is still an opposition between the upper and lower levels,
though it may be less apparent; the victory that is claimed on the
lower level is incompatible with the fact that both sides adequately
destroyed each other as well as the countryside round about. It is,
I think, profitable to distinguish 'Simple Irony', in which the opposition is solely between levels, and 'Double Irony' (Empson's
term), in which there is also a more obvious opposition within
the lower level.

In the third place there is in irony an element of 'innocence';
either a victim is confidently unaware of the very possibility of
there being an upper level or point of view that invalidates his
own, or an ironist pretends not to be aware of it. There is one
exception to this; in sarcasm or in very overt irony the ironist
does not pretend to be unaware of his real meaning and his victim
is immediately aware of it. The most that we can say is that the
victim is at a mental disadvantage with respect to the ironist.
Self-irony looks as if it would be another exception since the
victim is also the ironical observer or the ironist and, strictly
speaking, cannot either be or pretend to be an 'innocent'. But self-
irony implies a 'splitting of the ego' and hence an ability to see
and to present oneself as an 'innocent'.

Simple Irony 'comes into being' in one of three ways. An ironist presents or evokes a duality of opposed 'valid' and 'invalid'
levels, at the same time pretending, more or less covertly, not to
be aware of the 'valid' level (Example 13). A person with a sense
of irony sees in some situation or some accidental sequence or
concurrence of events a contradiction of some kind, at the same
time perceiving some other person to be confidently unaware of
it (Example 14). A person consciously opposes in his mind one
situation or event or idea with another which invalidates it, at the
same time being aware that there are those to whom such an in-

validating confrontation would not occur. An example of this would be Housman's story, *The Blind God*, at the moment of its conception. Double Irony is more complex in that there is a double opposition and sometimes a double unawareness.

If the preceding paragraphs may be regarded as a definition of irony, their adequacy as a definition may partly be tested by their power to differentiate irony from other phenomena which have something in common with it: metaphor, symbol, myth and allegory, lies and hypocrisy, hoaxes and illusions. There is one familiar definition of (verbal) irony – saying one thing and meaning another – which is clearly defective since it is no more than the etymological sense of 'allegoria'.

A set of variations on a theme may be used to distinguish irony from these other phenomena. If I say, 'Miss Smith is a butterfly,' my statement may be accounted for in a number of ways. I may think she is actually a lepidopter, in which case I am certainly insane or suffering from an hallucination; I am not being ironical if only because I am not pretending I don't know better. Whether in saying Miss Smith is a butterfly I have put myself in an ironic position depends upon further circumstances. If I were an eminent lepidopterist or if I ridiculed or rejected with pitying contempt the suggestion that Miss Smith was only Miss Smith I think I should then appear to be in an ironic situation because the observer would feel that I made a mistake I ought not to have made or that I had voluntarily put myself in the wrong. If, on the other hand, the overriding impression upon the beholder were that I was not at the time a free and responsible person, I think I should not appear a victim of irony. So that 'confident unawareness' where applied to a victim of irony implies a kind of moral judgement.

In saying 'Miss Smith is a butterfly', I may mean that I think her a gay and giddy creature, in which case I am speaking metaphorically, and not ironically, since my real meaning parallels my ostensible meaning; it does not oppose and invalidate it. To be ironical, my real meaning would have to be that Miss Smith was certainly not a butterfly but something more like a sausage. I should be in an ironic position if, confidently but quite mistakenly, I asserted that she was metaphorically a butterfly. What is

c

said here of metaphor is true also of symbol, myth, and allegory; the elements of the duality, however dissimilar they may appear, are not really in opposition as in irony. There are some compositions which are both allegorical and ironical. *Gulliver's Travels* is an allegory because Lilliput and Laputa correspond to England, the great whore or putta. It is an irony because Swift pretended his book was the true narrative of Gulliver, a ship's surgeon, and by so doing pretended there was no concealed import.

I may think Miss Smith to be like a sausage and yet assure you she is a butterfly for the mere fun of seeing you discomfited when you act upon my misrepresentation of her. In this case I am hoaxing you. I should not call it lying because I deceive only for a time and only for amusement's sake: I should not call it being ironical since I am not trying to take you down a peg: you have not invited a moral or intellectual judgement by setting yourself up as being unhoaxable or a judge of female character. None the less, of all these phenomena, the hoax is the closest to irony: perhaps what distinguishes them is that a hoax is entirely self-regarding whereas irony draws attention to the vulnerability of the victim. If I were simply lying I should have put myself in bondage either to my lie or to the truth; I should be *forced* either to go on lying or to retract and so be discomfited myself. Neither the hoaxer nor the ironist is so firmly bound to his misrepresentation. Just as the 'confident unawareness' of the victim of irony implies a free and responsible person, so the ironist's 'pretence' implies freedom, the responsible irresponsibility of the artist.

If, while thinking Miss Smith to be like a sausage, I behaved towards her as if I approved of her being like a butterfly, I could be hoaxing her for the fun of seeing her trying in vain to adopt a role somewhat beyond her. I should be ironizing her if I thought that she was vain enough to imagine she was like a butterfly. I should be a hypocrite, which is a kind of liar, if my behaviour put me in bondage to the future, so that I was *forced* to go on being hypocritical either indefinitely or until I was *forced* to stop.

What I have said here of the essential requirements of irony stands in need of some further enquiry, particularly as regards the duality of irony, the element of 'innocence', and the victim.

2 · *The Duality of Irony*

The more familiar kind of irony is Simple Irony, in which an apparently or ostensibly true statement, serious question, valid assumption, or legitimate expectation is corrected, invalidated, or frustrated by the ironist's real meaning, by the true state of affairs, or by what actually happens. In the example of verbal irony which Johnson invented for his dictionary – 'Bolingbroke was a holy man' – an assertion as of a fact confronts and is corrected by our prior knowledge of Bolingbroke's impiety. We could say much the same of Ezra Pound's understatement (Example 1), the instance of dramatic irony in *Macbeth* (Example 2), Swift's praise disguised as blame (Example 5), and most of the other examples. In Musil's *Man without Qualities* we read, in the light of our knowledge of subsequent European history, of the committees set up in Vienna in 1913 to organize the celebration of the seventieth anniversary of the Emperor Francis Joseph (1848–1916), 'our Emperor of Peace'; 1918 was to be a whole year of jubilee, not principally because of the great esteem in which, naturally, the emperor was held, but rather because the seventy years would not be up until December of that year, and it was thought desirable both to forestall and to eclipse the celebrations with which those upstarts, the Germans, were already proposing to mark merely the thirtieth anniversary (in July 1918) of the Kaiser Wilhelm.

Simple Ironies always function quite openly as correctives. One term of the ironic duality is seen, more or less immediately, as effectively contradicting, invalidating, exposing, or at the very least, modifying the other. In the light of greater awareness, or of prior or subsequent knowledge (sometimes supplied by the ironist himself), an assumed or asserted fact is shown not to be true, an idea or a belief to be untenable, an expectation to be unwarranted, or a confidence to be misplaced. To ironize something (in this class of irony) is to place it, without comment, in whatever context will invalidate or correct it; to see something as ironic is to see it in such a context. We see Henry James's fragment of literary history – 'It was a period when writers besought the deep blue sea "to roll" ' – as ironical because he evokes, through the petitionary 'besought', the contrary image of the sea's indifference. It is ironic that the last of the Roman emperors in the West was called Romulus Augustulus because he turned out to be so unlike those his names recall, those for whom he was so confidently and ambitiously named, the first Romulus and Augustus, the first emperor.

We have an interesting variant of Simple Irony when the invalidating term of the duality is in turn invalidated in a second duality. Hofmannsthal's essay on *The Irony of Things*[5] presents instances of this in the form of a long ironic sorties, so to speak; the 'reality' that ironizes an 'appearance' is in turn ironized by a higher 'reality': the bold upright hero by the prudent sapper who survives him; the relatively helpless private by the organized regiment; the regiment in turn by the amorphous mass; the mass by the national spirit or by 'the temporary omnipotence of a few individuals who somehow got their hand on the wheel'; these by the realities beyond their control, for example, the coal-shortage; and so on.

The less familiar kind of irony is Double Irony in which the dominant feature is an opposition at the lower level. French ironists seem to be fond of a form of irony in which two equally invalid points of view cancel each other out. I have already cited (Example 3) the passage from *Candide*:

> When all was over and the rival kings were celebrating their victory with Te Deums in their respective camps . . .

There is also the well-known opening of Chapter Four of Book Five of *L'Île des Pingouins*:

> Les Pingouins avaient la première armée du monde. Les Marsouins aussi.

Flaubert's *Dictionnaire des idées reçues* has the following:

> Étranger – Engouement pour tout ce qui vient de l'étranger, preuve de l'esprit libéral.
> – Dénigrement de tout ce qui n'est pas français, preuve de patriotisme.

In each of these cases the contradiction and mutual destruction directs us to the ironist's real meaning. This variant of Double Irony also functions as a corrective.

We have a second variant of Double Irony when there is a single victim to whom both terms though contradictory seem equally valid. The librarian in Example 9 holds in his hand a book whose value has been enhanced through being impaired – or the other way about. A less trivial instance would be one of those heroic dramas in which Honour inexorably commands the hero to do what Love categorically forbids: both, he feels, must be obeyed. Or we might instance Kafka's *The Castle* in which the hero is presented as involved in a series of what seem to be exasperatingly futile actions (though one cannot be quite certain) set in motion accidentally (though perhaps after all not accidentally) by an unapproachable 'authority' at the head of which stands a figure whose existence there are never quite sufficient grounds for affirming or denying.

Ironies of this kind which take the form of paradoxes, dilemmas, or what we call 'impossible situations' would still function quite clearly as corrective ironies if the ironic point were simply that the victim was confidently unaware of being in a dilemma or if he only thought he was in a dilemma when in fact he was not. The case is somewhat different when the ironist or the ironical observer himself feels the paradox or dilemma as a real one. The ironist may feel no less than the victim that Love and Honour are absolutes. A common view of *Don Quixote* sees Cervantes as using Sancho Panza's realism to ironize Don Quixote's idealism and at the same time using Don Quixote's idealism to ironize Sancho Panza's realism. Idealistic and realistic behaviour are both right and both wrong. Without Don Quixote Sancho Panza would appear neither so gross nor so sensible; without Sancho Panza Don Quixote would appear neither so noble nor so foolish.

Ironies of this kind do not function as simple correctives. It is not these ironies that we find in satire or comedy or wherever else it is desired simply to correct absurdities of opinion or behaviour. Simple corrective irony is effective at the point at which we pass from an apprehension of the ironic incongruity to a more or less immediate recognition of the invalidity of the ironist's pretended or the victim's confidently held view. Psychic tension is generated but rapidly released. In this other kind, however, the psychic tension generated by the ironic contradiction is not released or not

entirely released by any element of resolution since the ironist or
the ironical observer remains, to some extent, involved in the
irony.

Haakon Chevalier, in his *Ironic Temper*, tells us that 'the basic
feature of every Irony is a contrast between a reality and an appearance'.[6] We shall probably agree with this very readily if we
are thinking of such things as Swift's pretended defence of nominal Christianity which is really an attack upon it or of Lear's belief that Cordelia loves him least when in fact she loves him most.
But it needs to be said that there are instances of irony in which
one is left in doubt which is the reality and which the appearance.
One such instance is Anatole France's *Le Procurateur de Judée*
which Chevalier himself discusses though not as modifying his
statement.

In this story we see Pontius Pilate, who is now living in retire-
ment, sitting with a friend and talking over old times. The friend
recalls the crucifixion, twenty years earlier, of a young Galilean
miracle-worker, Jesus the Nazarene. Pilate, who has claimed earlier
on that his memory is in no way enfeebled by age, casts his mind
back, but in vain: 'Jesus? . . . Jesus the Nazarene? I don't recall.'
What makes this so strikingly ironic is that Pilate should have forgotten precisely the one name which has made his own name so
unforgettable, precisely the one historical event which has secured
his own place in history, not to mention fiction. Clearly we see
Pilate at a disadvantage, as confidently unaware of the possibility
of any other view of world history but his own. We see the striking disparity between the insignificance of the event in Pilate's
eyes and its enormous significance in ours. But is it so certain that
the irony ends there, or works only in that one direction? Might
it not be that the strength of our shock at Pilate's 'I don't recall' is
the measure of *our* confident unawareness of the fact that in different circumstances, those so clearly presented in this story, the crucifixion of God really was as forgettable as the crucifixion of any
other obscure trouble-maker in a distant province? If indeed the
story invites us to take Pilate's view (it is by no means certain
that it does) the irony is reversed, reality becomes appearance
and appearance reality.

These ironies which are not simply corrective are both more

'philosophical' and more modern than the others; more 'philoso-phical' because their subject matter is frequently the basic contra-dictions of human nature and the human condition, more modern because they are more self-conscious, more tentative (lacking the element of resolution), and more open to dialectic exposition. It is not surprising, therefore, to find some critics regarding irony of this kind as the one true irony. The German Romantics, for example, were inclined to disparage corrective or mocking Verbal Irony (*Spott*), even that of Swift. In this they were followed by Hegel and Kierkegaard, and later by English and American critics. A. H. Wright in his *Jane Austen's Novels* says that *Jonathan Wild* 'is not an ironic work, despite the author's free use of rhetorical irony' because, 'Fielding's commitment is wholly to the values of Heartfree'. 'But in *Billy Budd* there is genuine irony. . . . the story displays, with painful clarity, the unresolvable conflicts be-tween justice and mercy, experience and innocence, noble anger and devilish calculation.'[7] Similarly, Morton Gurewitch in *European Romantic Irony*:

> Perhaps the fundamental distinction between irony and satire, in the largest sense of each, is simply that irony deals with the absurd, whereas satire treats the ridiculous. The absurd may be taken to symbolize the incurable and chimerical hoax of things, while the ridiculous may be accepted as standing for life's corrigible deformities. This means that while the manners of men are the domain of the satirist, the morals of the universe are the preserve of the ironist.

> Irony, unlike satire, does not work in the interests of stability. Irony entails hypersensitivity to a universe permanently out of joint and unfailingly grotesque. The ironist does not pretend to cure such a universe or to solve its mysteries. It is satire that solves. The images of vanity, for example, that litter the world's satire are always satis-factorily deflated in the end; but the vanity of vanities that informs the world's irony is beyond liquidation.[8]

The distinction these two critics make is perfectly legitimate and what is more, useful and important. But the terms in which they make it – 'genuine' and 'so-called' irony, irony and satire – are so contrary to common English usage that the distinction itself may seem absurd. Nothing is gained by denying the name of irony to the corrective irony of *Jonathan Wild*, and certainly nothing by confusing corrective irony with satire, which need not even employ irony. Moreover, it would be wrong to accept this distinction, important as it is, as a distinction between two absolutely different kinds of irony. Ironies which do not function simply as correctives are nevertheless not without an element of 'correction'. Their dominant feature may be the opposition, at the lower level, of equally valid terms, but this only obscures the existence of an upper level, it does not imply its absence. It is true that the victim of ironies of this latter kind is primarily seen not as being simply in the wrong but as being in an inescapable and usually unhappy position, caught between love and honour, mercy and justice, soul and body, or in some similar predicament, situations in which we all may find or have found ourselves. Yet even though the victim is everyman, even though Kafka may see himself or us in the same impossible position as K., the very fact that the victim is being seen with irony and not simply with bewilderment or compassion preserves a distance between him and the ironist or observer.

An ironist who sees a paradox or an 'impossible situation' as ironic (and not simply as puzzling or as a case for compassion) must be aware of a victim's confident unawareness even though he sees himself as the victim. For example, he might believe with the hero of the play that the demands of love and honour are equally absolute, but if he is to look upon the hero and himself with irony he would have to see that there has been a certain unwarranted trust in the impossibility of impossible situations, an assumption, gratuitously though understandably made, that society ought not to have been so unjustly organized. As victim he feels the injustice: as ironist he does not expect justice this side of doomsday, or even then. So even in such cases as these irony is corrective though correction is not its *raison d'être*. We can say, at least, that it is heuristic. The distinction remains, however, and I shall return to it under the heading of General Irony (see Chapters VI and VII).

Since in this section I am speaking only of the formal characteristics of irony, I cannot dwell upon what is none the less of the

highest importance – the observer's sense of intellectual and emotional, or quasi-emotional, shock at the incongruity or disparity
between the two levels of irony. The most familiar ironic confrontations are those in which one of the confronting 'realities' is
revealed as or discovered to be only an appearance. But there
would be no irony unless the appearance were convincingly present as a reality. As Allan Rodway says in an article ,'Terms for
Comedy', 'Irony is not merely a matter of seeing a "true" meaning beneath a "false", but of seeing a double exposure (in both
senses of the word) on one plate.'[9] Oedipus was mistaken in thinking he had escaped his fate; but his sense of the situation as he saw
it was real. Swift did not really think it a good idea to market
infants' flesh; but his modest proposer makes out a plausible case.
Unless it were so we should not have had the clash and shock as
of two co-existing but irreconcilable, irrelatable 'realities'. Our
minds which naturally seek to relate and synthesize are affronted.

The same is true of the grotesque; but whereas it is part of the
definition of the grotesque that the terms of the opposition – the
organic and the inorganic, the ridiculous and the frightening, the
meaningful and the meaningless, the beautiful and the hideous,
the orderly and the violent – remain disturbingly irrelatable, in
irony the tension, if not relieved by the recognition that one of the
'realities' is only an appearance, is at least transcended by an ironic
acceptance of contradiction as normal. One might add that the
grotesque is usually, perhaps essentially, more emotional and
irony usually, perhaps essentially, more intellectual.

3 · The Element of 'Innocence'

The first formal requirements of irony are that there should be a
confrontation or juxtaposition of contradictory, incongruous, or
otherwise incompatible elements and that one should be seen as
'invalidating' the other. We need, however, more than this. It is
not being ironical merely to place a bucket of water alongside a
fire even with the intention of eventually extinguishing it. We
have the formal requirement of opposing elements; we need in
addition an ironic intention, that is, a pretence that one has no

sinister designs upon the fire. The pretence may be designedly quite transparent. As a reply to someone who has announced his intention of sitting all night by the fire, the bringing in of a bucket of water may be a pointed way of saying, 'We'll see about that.' Nevertheless there is a pretence that this reply has not been made. The ironist always pretends, even though transparently as in sarcasm, to be innocent of his real meaning or intention.

Similarly, it is not in itself ironical when we notice that a writer through some oversight has said something which he did not intend to say (for example, the pun in the last paragraph) or something which contradicts what he has said in a previous sentence. We have, in this second instance, the formal requirement of an invalidating contradiction; we need in addition to be aware of some degree of *confident* unawareness or impercipience in the victim, an innocent but *positive* assumption that nothing is wrong. The writer in question might, for example, have drawn attention to a contradiction in a book by someone else and done so in a contemptuous, malicious, or condescending way thus indicating that he thought himself *immune* from error.

The typical victim of an ironic situation or event is essentially an innocent. Just as scepticism depends upon belief – we can be sceptical only of what someone believes or has believed or might believe – so the irony of most ironic situations cannot exist without a complementary alazony. The alazon or victim is the man who blindly assumes or asserts that something is or is not the case, or confidently expects something to happen or not to happen; he does not even remotely suspect that things might not be as he supposes them to be, or might not turn out as he expects them to. This should not imply that the victim is always so arrogantly confident or so wilfully blind that we feel he deserves what he gets. All that is necessary is the merest avoidable assumption on the part of the victim that he is not mistaken. For one of the odd things about irony is that it regards assumptions as presumption and therefore innocence as guilt. Simple ignorance is safe from irony, but ignorance compounded with the least degree of confidence counts as intellectual hubris and is a punishable offence. One cannot even express confidence that the sun will rise tomorrow, for, as in Leopardi's fable, the sun may decide for a change not to rise but to call upon Copernicus to persuade the earth to bestir itself and turn upon its axis. One cannot, like Pontius Pilate, carelessly forget a single incident in one's life for this may be the one incident that preserves the memory of one's own existence. The only shield against irony, therefore, is absolute circumspection, a shield no man can lift.

If this seems to put the ironist at an altogether unfair advantage it has to be observed that the ironist is equally vulnerable, for the very act of being ironical implies an assumption of superiority, an assumption one cannot make without forgetting either that the tables may be turned, as they were upon Wilberforce when he tried to make a monkey out of Huxley, or that one may be subject to irony from a level higher than one's own, as exemplified in Morgenstern's 'Vice Versa' (which is here rather freely translated):

> Washing herself upon the green
> Miss Hare believes she can't be seen;
>
> And yet with sly binoculars
> That take down her particulars
>
> A man, from hill contiguous,
> Peeps unawares at pretty puss.
>
> And yet to him it never occurs
> To think how God must view voyeurs.

The ironist, therefore, is faced with the same need to be universally circumspect and with the same chance of success. And even though he should practise continual self-irony, he is trapped by that irony of the infinite regressiveness of irony which was one of Friedrich Schlegel's important discoveries.

What makes expectation ironic can perhaps be made clearer by a brief examination of the Irony of Events. To begin with, if I expect something not to happen it is ironic if it does, and the stronger my expectations or the flimsier their basis the more striking the irony. The merely unexpected event, on the other hand, is not ironic however unlikely it is. I do not expect to meet a tiger in the streets of Melbourne and it would not be ironic if I did. At least it would not have been ironic yesterday; but now that I have formulated and raised to consciousness my non-expectation, changing it in effect from a 'not-expecting' to an 'expecting-not', my meeting a tiger would be ironic. In fact I should now think it ironic if I were to read in this evening's paper of someone's meeting a tiger in the streets of Copenhagen. For the unexpected to be ironic, then, it seems that there must be some stress upon or some positive assumption of its unlikeliness. And this confident unawareness can even be *imputed* to the victim; it would, I think, be ironic if a professional tiger-hunter met a tiger in the streets of Melbourne, a professional hunter being a man whom we presume to have positive expectations about the likelihood or unlikelihood of meetings tigers in Melbourne.

The case is similar with the mere non-fulfilment of an expectation. It is not in itself ironic if a man fails to get the promotion he expects, but it would be if he had expressed his confidence of being promoted and still more if he had anticipated his promotion by buying a new car. To give another example: in 1814 Johanna Southcott actually prophesied in print and persuaded her followers to believe that she would shortly be giving birth to the Prince of Peace. His non-appearance was clearly an ironic non-event.

But if what happens is the *contrary* of what is expected and not merely a contradiction of it a slighter degree of confidence seems to be sufficient for irony. If the man who expected promotion had been demoted instead, his expectation alone would be sufficient to make him a victim of irony: though he has not actually expressed himself as confident of promotion he has by merely expecting promotion shown himself as confidently unaware of the possibility of demotion. Similarly, though it was ironic that, after all the publicity, Johanna Southcott did not give birth to the Prince of Peace, it would still have been ironic if, with less publicity beforehand and less confidence, she had given birth to the Prince of Darkness instead.

Perhaps there is a rule here which can be generally applied: to maintain the same level of irony the degree of disparity between the ironic opposites should be in inverse proportion to the degree of confident unawareness felt by the victim or pretended by the ironist. Or putting it another way, the irony may be made more striking either by stressing the ironic incongruity or by stressing the ironic 'innocence'.

In the following instance we see Gibbon employing the former method: assuming that an event which sufficiently outrages a deep-rooted sense of the fitness of things will be thought ironic even if this sense has not been formulated as a confident expectation that God would not allow such things to happen, Gibbon stresses the ironic incongruity by concluding his brief account of the career of a certain iniquitous bacon-contractor and arch-bishop with this sentence:

> The odious stranger, disguising every circumstance of time and place, assumed the mask of a martyr, a saint, and a Christian hero; and the infamous George of Cappadocia has been transformed into the renowned St George of England, the patron of arms, of chivalry, and of the Garter.[10]

It would scarcely be necessary to present evidence of Gibbon's skill as the pretended innocent. Shakespeare, on the other hand, is more likely to be found presenting his characters as real innocents. Such are the two labourers in Jack Cade's army in *Henry VI, Part II*:

> – The nobility think scorn to go in leather aprons.
> – Nay, more, the king's council are no good workmen.
> – True; and yet it is said, 'labour in thy vocation'; which is as much to say as, 'let the magistrates be labouring men', and therefore should we be magistrates.
> – Thou hast hit it.

In presenting these two innocents Shakespeare does not explicitly draw attention to their absurdities. And so with other ironists: they present us with a contradiction or an incongruity; they put us in the way of seeing the incompatible elements of an ironic duality, arranging them so as to make a sharper or more striking contrast, but the fact of there being a pair of incompatible elements is never asserted. In other words, while the victim really is 'innocent' and confidently assumes nothing is wrong, the ironist only pretends 'innocence' and writes or behaves *as if* nothing were wrong. It would, no doubt, be misleading to speak of a 'deceptively innocent manner' where, as in sarcasm, the pretence is quite transparent or conventional; sarcasm, however, is generally recognized as only minimally ironical. But where an ironist achieves a degree of subtlety and convincingly adopts a tone of gravity or ingenuousness we can see that he is, as regards the art of irony, at the beginning of a development which may result in the creation of an ironic *persona* such as one finds in Chaucer. A personified pretence of innocence such as 'Chaucer the pilgrim' does in fact closely resemble the truly 'innocent' victim of irony. Once a *persona* is created, the ironist is no longer simply being ironical but being ironical by means of the ironic situation in which he has placed his 'innocent' *persona*.

4 · *Victims of Irony*

The previous section has left us with little to do under this heading but to distinguish the various ways in which one may be a victim of irony. We might begin by distinguishing between the object and the victim of irony. The object of irony is what one is ironical about. When Ambrose Bierce, in his *Devil's Dictionary*, defines Absurdity as, 'A statement or belief manifestly inconsistent with one's own opinion', the object of his irony is that aspect of human self-assurance which justifies his definition. When Samuel Butler, in one of the most brilliant touches in *Erewhon*, makes his hero say, after a narrow escape from drowning, 'As luck would have it, Providence was on my side,' the object of his irony was the doctrine of Special Providence. When Johnson wrote, 'Bolingbroke was a holy man,' Bolingbroke, though a person, was the object of his irony. It would be a blurring of distinctions to call him the victim of Johnson's irony but it would not spoil one's day. The object of irony may be a person (including the ironist himself), an attitude, a belief, a social custom or institution, a philosophical system, a religion, even a whole civilization, even life itself.

The victim of irony is the person whose 'confident unawareness' has directly involved him in an ironic situation. If someone were to take Johnson's remark about Bolingbroke seriously he would be a victim of irony. If Bolingbroke were discovered to be a 'holy man' after all, Johnson would be a victim of irony. To the extent that Butler is presenting the hero of *Erewhon* not as being ironical but as being unconscious of the implicit contradictions in his statement, he is presenting him as the victim of irony. It not infrequently happens in novels and plays that one cannot be certain whether an ironical author is presenting a character as an ironist or a victim of irony though the object of the irony may be perfectly clear.

There are some ironies in which there seems to be neither an object nor a victim of irony. Ezra Pound's understatement, 'Mutton cooked the week before last is, for the most part, unpalatable,' can hardly be regarded as irony at the expense of the mutton, and there would be an air of desperation in the claim that there is always a hypothetical victim, the person who might conceivably take the statement seriously. Ezra Pound, of course, pretends to be speaking seriously, as all ironists do, and so might be called a pseudo-victim. The concept of the pseudo-victim becomes more interesting and useful when an ironist like Chaucer not only pretends to be serious but also presents himself in the character of a typical victim of irony.

We can now perhaps see in what different ways one may be a victim of irony.

I · THOSE WHO, STRICTLY SPEAKING, ARE OBJECTS OF IRONY

These divide into two classes:

(a) *Those to whom one speaks ironically:* Satan addresses the fallen angels ironically in Book I of *Paradise Lost*:

> or have ye chos'n this place
> After the toyl of Battel to repose
> Your wearied vertue, for the ease you find
> To slumber here, as in the Vales of Heav'n?
> Or in this abject posture have ye sworn
> To adore the Conquerour?

The fallen angels know they are the victims of Satan's irony since they react appropriately:

> They heard and were abasht.

(b) *Those of whom one speaks ironically:* In *Northanger Abbey*, after
a scene in which Isabella Thorpe is presented as a victim of irony
hypocritically expressing her disdain for men in general and for
two young men in particular, Jane Austen makes her the object
of irony:

> and therefore, to shew the independence of Miss Thorpe, and her
> resolution of humbling the sex, they set off immediately as fast as
> they could walk, in pursuit of the two young men.[11]

In Evelyn Waugh's *Helena* the Christian apologist, Lactantius,
is made to say:

> 'You see it is equally possible to give the right form to the wrong
> thing, and the wrong form to the right thing. Suppose that in years
> to come, when the Church's troubles seem to be over, there should
> come an apostate of my own trade, a false historian, with the mind
> of Cicero or Tacitus and the soul of an animal,' and he nodded
> towards the gibbon who fretted his golden chain and chattered for
> fruit.[12]

II · THOSE WHO ARE IN AN IRONIC SITUATION WITHOUT KNOWING IT

This is a large and varied class which may roughly be divided
into:

(a) *Those unable to recognize they have been ironically addressed:*
When Mr Bennet in *Pride and Prejudice* speaks ironically his victims are frequently unaware of it:

> 'What say you, Mary? for you are a young lady of deep reflection
> I know, and read great books, and make extracts.'[13]

Had she been more perceptive or Mr Bennet more openly ironical she would, like the fallen angels, have heard and been abashed.
As it is we are told she 'wished to say something very sensible, but
knew not how'. She is therefore both an object, in Sense I(*a*), of
her father's irony and a victim of an ironic situation – her failure
to see the real meaning of his words, her assumption that he was
not being ironical. Madame de Tourvel in *Les Liaisons Danger-*

euses is in a slightly different position since her inability to recognize that the letter sent her from Paris by the Vicomte de Valmont is a continued *double entendre* is not owing to any obtuseness on her part. She reads his words:

> Never have I taken more pleasure in writing to you; never have I felt in doing it so sweet and yet so lively an emotion. Everything seems to enhance my rapture; the air I breathe is all ecstasy; the very table on which I write, never before put to such use, has become in my eyes an altar consecrated to love. How much dearer will it be to me now that I have traced upon it a vow to love you forever! Forgive, I beg you, these unruly feelings. I should perhaps not yield so far to transports which you cannot share. But I must leave you for a moment to calm an excitement which mounts with every moment, and which is fast becoming more than I can control.[14]

But she does not know and could not know what he has told the Marquise de Merteuil:

> I have been using [Émilie] for a desk upon which to write to my fair devotee – to whom I find it amusing I should send a letter written in bed, in the arms, almost, of a trollop (broken off, too, while I committed a downright infidelity), in which I give her an exact account of my situation and my conduct.[15]

Here, unless after all it is only a hoax and not irony, we might also place Charles Lamb's story of the Oxford scholar who puzzled a porter whom he met carrying a hare by asking him: 'Prithee, friend, is that thy own hare, or a wig?' The porter's predicament is that he cannot comprehend this nonsensical fusion of a pertinent and not unexpected question, 'Is that thy own hare?' and a sensible though quite irrelevant one, 'Is that thy own hair, or a wig?' Thinking to be able to answer the first as he hears it, he is thrown off balance by the way it continues, though he can't see why.

(b) *Those unable to recognize irony not directed against them:* For an example we can go to Mark Twain's *Pudd'nhead Wilson:*

> For some years Wilson had been privately at work on a whimsical almanac, for his amusement – a calendar, with a little dab of ostensible

D

philosophy, usually in ironical form, appended to each date; and the Judge thought that these quips and fancies of Wilson's were neatly turned and cute; so he carried a handful of them around, one day, and read them to some of the chief citizens. But irony was not for those people; their mental vision was not focussed for it. They read those playful trifles in the solidest earnest, and decided without hesitancy that if there had ever been any doubt that Dave Wilson was a pudd'nhead – which there hadn't – this revelation removed that doubt for good and all.[16]

They fail to see Wilson's irony, as Mary Bennet fails to see her father's, but since it is not directed against them they are not its victims. The irony they *are* victims of is an irony of their own making; they are too confident of their wisdom and too ignorant of their ignorance. Of course a great deal of verbal irony is calculated not to be immediately apparent; but the ironist who strengthens the force of his irony by momentarily misleading his readers can hardly be said to make victims of them. Though when, as sometimes in Swift for example, misleading the readers becomes an ironic attack upon them as well as or instead of an attack upon someone or something else, they will be victims in Sense I(*a*) (when they see it) or in Sense II(*a*) (when they fail to see it). Butler's *Fair Haven* 'victimizes' Christianity in Sense I(*b*), and also, in Sense II(*a*), the Christians whom he calculated would fail to recognize his irony.

(c) *Those unable to recognize that they are victims of circumstances or intrigue:* One hardly needs to exemplify so familiar a class; the names 'Oedipus' and 'Othello' will suffice. See Chapter V, Section 3, however.

(d) *Those unable to recognize that their own words betray them:* This too is a large and familiar class. Those who have no looking-glass need only recall Polonius or Aunt Norris, who never suspect how they condemn themselves out of their own mouths. See Chapter V, Section 4.

III · PEOPLE WHO KNOW THEY ARE IN AN IRONIC SITUATION

If Oedipus had known who he was and what he had done, if Pentheus had known that the effeminate foreigner he arrested was Dionysus, and if Don Quixote had not forgotten he was only a poor country gentleman, they would not have become victims of ironic situations. None the less, one may be a victim of an ironic situation in spite of knowing it. Imagine a man who has been deprived of all that makes life worth living until at last, when he is 'sans teeth, sans eyes, sans taste, sans everything', he becomes by some unexpected chance wealthy enough to indulge his every sense. But the only sense remaining to him (we shall imagine) is a sense of irony. This will enable him to see himself in an ironic situation. He may of course feel as if God or Life were deliberately mocking him, in which case he would be a victim in Sense I. But he need not feel this. And the stronger his sense of irony the more he will be enabled to detach himself from his situation and become, by a kind of double-think, the ironical observer of himself as victim.

Since, in this preliminary analysis, I have spoken of the victim of irony I ought now to pass on to the ironist and the ironical observer. But I could hardly do so without first entering upon a discussion of such involved and substantial matters as the motives to irony, ironical attitudes, and responses to irony, matters which no one could consider as mere preliminaries. I leave them therefore in abeyance and, in the next chapter, take up the problems of classifying kinds of irony.

III

BASIC CLASSIFICATIONS

1 · *Classifying Irony*

I do not know of any book or article, whether English, American, French, or German, or of any European or American dictionary or encyclopaedia which presents a classification of irony one could regard as adequate. What classifications there are, either are not up to date, or reveal national biases and blindspots, or are too broad to be useful.

There is a general reluctance in the English-speaking world to come to grips with what are vaguely called the 'newer ironies'. One American article seems to suggest that if one ignored them they would get discouraged and go away. The English ignore and the Americans misrepresent Romantic Irony; in both cases, I think, because they find a difficulty in seeing irony in any other terms but that of a reality correcting an appearance as in both satiric and dramatic irony, the kinds most familiar in English literature. The French have tended to neglect Dramatic Irony but have long shown themselves to be aware of the ironic contradictions of life and of the ironical attitudes they generate. The Germans too have neglected Dramatic Irony, but emphasize irony as *Lebensgefühl* and as *schöpferisches Prinzip*. This neglect might be explained by the fact that from the early nineteenth century the German concept of irony was dominated by the many-levelled and multi-directional irony of Goethe whose readers were rather the victims of authorial irony than sharers with the author of the comedy of life or spectators of a tragic destiny. As we shall see, Max Scheler gives the name 'tragic' to what an English-speaking critic would call Irony of Events (see p. 48).

On the other hand, enough is known about irony to make its classification a profitable exercise. I believe also that we have reached a stage in literary criticism where an accurate and systematic survey of the meanings of irony is highly desirable and could be very useful. Such a classification could, of course, only be preliminary to literary discussion. The critical evaluation of actual irony would still have to be done. No classification of irony, no list of all the ironical techniques ever practised, will enable the critic immediately to put a tag on every piece of irony he finds. [But he will perhaps be able to see that irony can take such diverse forms that the word itself is now too general to be informative. And, what is more important, he will perhaps be able to see more quickly that such and such a passage or work combines two or more techniques or forms of irony, or is on the borderline between one technique or form and another, or combines ironical with non-ironical elements.]

For what appears to be an instance of complex or subtle or striking irony frequently turns out to be ironically quite simple but complicated by some other element or coloured by various feelings or by the personality of the ironist. The basis of the following stanza from *Don Juan* is the familiar ironic situation in which fear of dying temporarily restores piety ('Plenty well, no pray; big belly-ache, heap God'):

> The first attack at once proved the Divinity
> (But *that* I never doubted, nor the Devil);
> The next, the Virgin's mystical virginity;
> The third, the usual Origin of Evil;
> The fourth at once established the whole Trinity
> On so uncontrovertible a level
> That I devoutly wish'd the three were four,
> On purpose to believe so much the more.   (XI, vi)

But it is complicated (*a*) by Byron's mere pretence of self-irony – we are meant not to believe a word of it, (*b*) by the irony's being reversed and directed not against the pious man but against the curious things sickness makes him believe – 'the *usual* Origin of Evil', that is, even *that* explanation of evil, and (*c*) by the element of intellectual farce – sickness brings not a pious fear of God but a set of controversial theological dogmas which effortlessly enter the mind with each twinge of pain that attacks the body (and here the irony is directed not at the believer nor at the belief but at

the supposed mechanism of the conversion). But the complexity
is unified by Byron's tone, that of a persifleur being 'a moment
merry'.

2 · 'He is being ironical.' 'It is ironic that . . .'

The most convenient, though most conventional, place to begin
a classification of irony is the dictionary. The *Oxford English
Dictionary* distinguishes between a primary sense of irony ('A figure
of speech in which the intended meaning is the opposite of that
expressed by the words used'), and a transferred or figurative sense
('A condition of affairs or events of a character opposite to what
was, or might naturally be, expected; a contradictory outcome
of events as if in mockery of the promise and fitness of things').

This does not take us far but it gives us a start since it distinguishes the two kinds of irony most familiar to English-speaking people, Verbal Irony and Situational Irony. Moreover,
although the definitions are themselves unsatisfactory, the terms
in which the two kinds are defined do at least serve to draw attention to what basically distinguishes them. Verbal Irony implies an
ironist, someone consciously and intentionally employing a
technique. Situational Irony does not imply an ironist but merely
'a condition of affairs' or 'outcome of events' which, we add, is
seen and felt to be ironic. In both there is a confrontation or juxtaposition of incompatibles, but whereas in Verbal Irony it is the
ironist who presents, or evokes, or puts us in the way of seeing,
such a confrontation, in Situational Irony something which we
see as ironic happens or comes to our notice; we may see a pick-
pocket having his own pocket picked while busy picking pockets.
Should we see this in a play or read about it in a novel, and probably we have met more fictitious than actual ironic situations, the
position is less simple. Now we have an ironist being ironical by
showing us something ironic happening. Strangely enough, when
there is no ironist but simply something ironic happening, we
often speak and feel as if Life or Fate or Chance were an ironist
being ironical.

We are making this same distinction between Verbal or Intentional Irony and Situational Irony when we say on the one hand, *He is being ironical*, and on the other hand, *It is ironic that . . .* Samuel Butler was being ironical in his *Fair Haven*, saying one thing and meaning another. It was ironic that some of the people the work should most have displeased supposed its author to have been 'throughout in downright almost pathetic earnestness'. Take the following elderly anecdote from *Punch*:

FIRST YOUTH: Hullo, congenital idiot!

SECOND YOUTH: Hullo, you priceless old ass!

THE DAMSEL: I'd no idea you two knew each other so well.

If the damsel intended her words to be equivocal, she was being ironical. If she did not realize they had the double meaning they have for us, it was ironic that she did not know, and *Punch* was presenting her too in an ironic situation.

Talking about Verbal Irony means talking about the ironist's techniques and strategies. Talking about Situational Irony means talking about the kinds of situations we see as ironic and also, therefore, about the observer's sense of irony, his attitudes, and responses. As I have said, one way of being ironical is to invent and present ironic situations, but an ironist who presents ironic situations will have much the same sense of irony, attitudes, and responses as the ironic observer. Since ironic situations are found in the world at large they will be found there by dramatists, novelists, and historians with a sense of irony, and we shall therefore find them imitated or presented in literature – in *Ghosts*, *Don Quixote*, *Penguin Island*, and *The Irony of American History*. I should add here that an ironist who, in real life, arranges things so as to lead some victim up the garden path and in this way bring about an ironic situation or event is still an artist though his medium is life. He is 'playing' with an actual person much as an ironical novelist or dramatist plays with his fictitious characters. This basic distinction between an irony that implies both artist and medium and an irony that is essentially a situation or happening in life is sometimes overlooked as, for example, in R. W. Stallman's introduction to *The Red Badge of Courage*.[1]

The OED definition of irony as a figure of speech is obviously quite inadequate, covering only one small area of what we understand by 'Verbal Irony'. But this firmly established term is not much less unsatisfactory. In the first place it designates only one sub-class of a class that has no name, the other sub-classes being Musical Irony, Pictorial Irony, Ironic mimicry, etc., the 'etc.' including, not inconceivably, Architectural Irony and even Culinary Irony (as in *Timon of Athens*, Act III, Sc. vi). Thirlwall would call this last Practical Irony a term not to be discarded though Thirlwall himself in some of his examples confuses it with Situational Irony. I do not know how Thirlwall would have classed Musical Irony. In the second place 'Verbal Irony', as the term is generally used, excludes at least one way of using words to be ironical – the creation or presentation of ironic situations. From a practical point of view this may be no great matter but it can and does lead to confusion. For these reasons I prefer saying, whenever I can, 'being ironical' and I shall speak of ways of being ironical rather than of kinds or forms of Verbal Irony.

The ways and modes of being ironical range from mere figures of speech to the elaborate pretences of a Chaucer or a Swift, from the most passionate to the most objective, from the most transparent to the most opaque, from the merely rhetorical to the fully 'dramatized', from the aggressive to the evasive. As I discuss these ways and modes I shall make distinctions and bestow names, remembering, however, that these various ways and their subdivisions can be distinguished only as we distinguish blue and green while recognizing that by innumerable intermediate shades one merges into another.

We notice in passing that a man is popularly called an ironist whether his irony is the rhetorical irony of a barrister, the self-disparaging irony of a Socrates, or the completely 'dramatized' irony of a novelist or playwright. We call Mr Bennet in *Pride and Prejudice* an ironist because of his frequent, not to say habitual, recourse to irony; and we call Jane Austen an ironist not simply because of her frequent recourse to irony but also because she frequently presents ironic situations. In the following conversation Mr Bennet is seen being ironical at Mr Collins's expense, while Mr Collins, in that he unwittingly convicts himself of folly while imagining he is displaying his talents, is the victim of an ironic situation created and presented by Jane Austen:

'Her [Miss De Bourgh's] indifferent state of health unhappily prevents her being in town; and by that means, as I told Lady Catherine myself one day, has deprived the British court of its brightest ornament. Her ladyship seemed pleased with the idea, and you may imagine that I am happy on every occasion to offer those little delicate compliments which are always acceptable to ladies. I have more than once observed to Lady Catherine, that her charming daughter seemed born to be a duchess, and that the most elevated rank, instead of giving her consequence, would be adorned by her. These are the kind of little things which please her ladyship, and it is a sort of attention which I conceive myself peculiarly bound to pay.'

'You judge very properly,' said Mr Bennet, 'and it is happy for you that you possess the talent of flattering with delicacy. May I ask whether these pleasing attentions proceed from the impulse of the moment, or are the result of previous study?'

'They arise chiefly from what is passing at the time, and though I sometimes amuse myself with suggesting and arranging such little elegant compliments as may be adapted to ordinary occasions, I always wish to give them as unstudied an air as possible.'[2]

Concealed behind the stage Jane Austen pulls the strings that make Mr Collins innocently expose his absurdity. But one frequently finds in fiction a much closer combination than that of puppet and puppet-master. In the following passage from *Middlemarch* George Eliot is clearly presenting Casaubon in an ironic situation but he is not completely dramatized as Mr Collins was:

Mr Casaubon, as might be expected, spent a great deal of his time at the Grange in these weeks, and the hindrance which courtship occasioned to the progress of his great work – the Key to all Mythologies – naturally made him look forward the more eagerly to the happy termination of courtship. But he had deliberately incurred the hindrance, having made up his mind that it was now time for him to adorn his life with the graces of female companionship, to irradiate the gloom which fatigue was apt to hang over the intervals of studious labour with the play of female fancy, and to secure in this, his culminating age, the solace of female tendance for his declining years. Hence he determined to abandon himself to the stream of feeling, and perhaps was surprised to find what an exceedingly shallow rill it was. As in droughty regions baptism by immersion could only be performed symbolically, so Mr Casaubon found that sprinkling was the utmost approach to a plunge which his stream would afford him; and he concluded that the poets had much exaggerated the force of masculine passion. Nevertheless, he observed with pleasure that Miss Brooke showed an ardent submissive affection which promised to fulfil his most agreeable previsions of marriage. It had once or twice crossed his mind that possibly there was some deficiency in Dorothea to account for the moderation of his abandonment; but he was unable to discern the deficiency, or to figure to himself a woman who would have pleased him better; so that there was clearly no reason to fall back upon but the exaggerations of human tradition.[3]

This is a sort of précis of Casaubon's thoughts and feelings suggesting the language in which Casaubon might have expressed to himself his thoughts and feelings. But it is more than a summarized interior monologue; the arrangement and the development of the 'stream of feeling' metaphor are not Casaubon's but George Eliot's. This makes her an ironist in two theoretically distinguishable ways at once; she is presenting Casaubon in an ironic situation of his own making but to the degree that the language is hers and not his she is being overtly if urbanely ironical at his expense.

The order in which the OED presents its two definitions of irony reflects the historical development of the concept of irony: Situational Irony was called irony because, and when, it seemed to resemble Verbal Irony, and this was not until the eighteenth century. But it is obvious that some of the forms of Situational Irony though not named were 'known' and felt very much earlier; and equally obvious that originally Verbal Irony and Situational Irony were quite distinct.

We may imagine, since we can only imagine, that being ironical first developed out of simple deception. A man begins his lie for some practical purpose, to which his lie is strictly subordinated as a means. But should he see that his lie is believed he may go on to lie freely and unnecessarily simply for the lie's sake. It is this freedom of his in relation to his lie that brings him close to irony since the ironist too is free in relation to what he says. Or we may imagine that irony developed, by way of sarcasm and taunting, out of expressions of triumphant scorn: jabbing a spear into your opponent's face, you ask him how he likes that. This we can easily imagine developing into a more adequate expression of concern. Situational Irony, as something felt, is probably no less ancient: perhaps there was paleolithic laughter when some hunter fell into his own too carefully concealed bear-trap. There can be no doubt that Homer and his first audience saw the irony of Ulysses' being present in disguise among the suitors and abiding their insolent derision. By the time of Sophocles and Socrates both kinds of irony had been developed to a high degree of sophistication though neither kind was yet called irony.

According to Sedgewick, '*Eironeia*, as the Periclean Greeks conceived it, was not so much a mode of speech as a *general mode of behaviour*,' and the word, down to Aristotle, was a term of abuse connoting 'sly-foxery' with 'a tinge of "low-bred" '. With Aristotle '*eironeia* came to mean "pretended modesty" (and understatement as well)'[4] and hence the deceptive use of words and irony as a figure of speech. But although classical drama bears witness to a highly developed sense of irony, that is, to a clear recognition of the emotional and dramatic power of ironic situations and events, it was not until the end of the eighteenth century that the name irony was given to them. We can perhaps explain why the irony of the great dramatists from Aeschylus to Shakespeare, Molière, and Racine was not called *irony* until the late eighteenth century; it is puzzling that no language should until then have given it any single name.

Aristotle certainly does not overlook the ironic in his *Poetics* though he does not use the word in this work:

We find that, among events merely casual, those are the most wonderful and striking which seem to imply design: as when, for instance, the statue of Mitys at Argos killed the very man who had murdered Mitys, by falling down upon him as he was surveying it; events of this kind not having the appearance of accident.[5]

The word *peripeteia*, which sometimes appears as 'irony' in trans-
lations of the *Poetics*, might perhaps be regarded as in part supply-
ing the need for a word signifying 'irony of events'. But this kind
of irony is so regularly an ingredient of dramatic action and so
closely connected with the fall of the protagonist that we may suppose that there was no pressing need to distinguish it with a name.

Even today one can find instances of writers preferring 'tragic'
to 'ironic'. One such writer is Max Scheler, in an essay *On the
Tragic* (originally in German, where the word is 'tragisch' not
'ironisch'):

> If we are observing a certain action which is realizing a high value,
> and then see in that same action that it is working towards the under-
> mining of the very existence of the being it is helping, we receive the
> most complete and the clearest of tragic impressions.

> We don't have to talk only of human beings here. An art gallery can
> be destroyed by the very fire that was kindled to preserve the picture.
> The event has a sharp tragic character. The flight of Icarus is tragic.
> The very wax which glued his wings to him melts in the same
> degree as he flies toward the sun.[6]

The popular concept of Fortune's Wheel may also be assumed
to have included the concept of irony of events. In England the
words 'mock' and 'banter' were occasionally used, as we shall see,
in the context of irony of events, but they were not critics' terms.
The word 'humour' was not infrequently used of Situational
Irony. Johnson, for example, commenting on *Henry IV, Part 2*
(V, i, 90–93), uses the word 'humorous' where a modern critic
would probably say 'ironic'.

> There is something humorous in making a spendthrift compute
> time by the operation of an action for debt.

But this is probably no more significant than Miss Burney's and
Mrs Thrale's use of 'drollery' and 'droll' in similar contexts:

> 'But was it not droll,' said she [Mrs Thrale], 'that I should recommend
> it [Miss Burney's anonymously published *Evelina*] to Dr Burney?
> and tease him, so innocently, to read it?'

Butler's coupling of 'humour' and 'irony' in *Life and Habit* (1877) seems to indicate that the concept of unconscious self-betrayal as a kind of irony was by no means familiar:

The most perfect humour and irony is generally quite unconscious.[7]

Knox's very thorough investigations reveal that with three very doubtful exceptions (in the late sixteenth and the early seventeenth centuries) Situational Irony was not recognized as irony before the appearance of the seventeenth number of Fielding's *Jacobite's Journal* in 1748 and Cambridge's *Scribleriad* in 1752, and he provides no evidence for the consistent use before then of any other term. It may be that in other European languages there was a word; if so, I do not know of it.

How then, and why and when did Situational Irony, originally distinct from Verbal Irony and for so long unrecognized as irony, come to be called irony? If we were asked what there is in common between Fielding's irony in calling Mrs Slipslop a fair creature, and the irony of a man's falling into his own bear-trap, we could point to the elements they have in common: the duality, the opposition of the terms of the duality, and the real or pretended 'innocence'. Fielding pretends (though in this case the pretence is only nominal) that his ostensible meaning is his real meaning of which it is the converse. The hunter 'innocently' expects to deceive a bear but his skill deceives himself; the event is the contrary of what was expected. But words are not likely to extend their meaning as a result of an abstract recognition of similarities particularly if there are also recognizable dissimilarities. What is more likely to happen is that the name of one phenomenon will be unconsciously given to another with which it is analogous or actually confused, or which frequently accompanies it, or which has the same emotional effect upon one. There seem to be several routes along which the word 'irony' travelled from simple Verbal Irony to situations and events that formerly were not called ironic.

The best substantiated of these semantic shifts, as it affects the English word 'irony', came about through an intermediate stage at which either such mythological entities as Fortune or Fate or some personified abstraction was regarded as a 'mocker', that is, as

behaving like an ironist who says one thing to our hopes and
expectations and another thing to himself, not unlike Pascal's
Jesuits who held that, 'Promises are not binding, if in making
them one does not intend them to be binding.' The nearest
Shakespeare came to an explicit verbal recognition of the irony of
events is, I think, Troilus's words upon hearing that he must lose
Cressida when he has only just won her: 'How my achievements
mock me!' Using the same word, 'mock', Shakespeare sees
dramatic irony as a joke played upon one by the devil:

> O 'tis the spite of hell, the arch-fiend's mock
> To lip a wanton in a secure couch
> And to suppose her chaste.   (*Othello*, IV, i)

The eighteenth century made a similar use of the word 'banter': in
1714 Bolingbroke wrote to Swift: 'The Earl of Oxford was removed on Tuesday; the Queen died on Sunday. What a world is
this, and how fortune does banter us!' But these uses of 'mock'
and 'banter' were not really accepted for 'irony' until after Thirlwall's essay *On the Irony of Sophocles* in 1833. The next step was to
drop the hypothesis of an ironical personification. We no longer
need to imagine a mocking Chance or Fate to see as ironic the
situation of a hunter who has so effectively concealed his bear-
trap that he falls into it himself. Chevalier, however, seems to
think that the victim does not wholly get rid of the:

> suspicion that . . . there exists a deliberate mockery [at his expense].
> This theoretical imputation of mockery is an atavistic survival of the
> old and enduring consciousness of the 'jealousy of the gods'.[8]

The second route is much more a matter of surmise. Here the
semantic shift was effected through the co-existence, as in a
Socratic dialogue, of Verbal Irony, recognized as such, and of the
ironic situation, recognized but not as irony, of which his oppo-
nents are victims through being confidently unaware of Socrates'
strategy. Although, as Knox puts it, 'the irony of Socrates . . .
was usually referred to during the English classical period as
simply the rhetorical device of blame-by-praise,'[9] any *unspecific*
reference to Socrates' irony necessarily included both kinds of

irony just as the word 'window' came to refer also to the glass that was used to fill the original hole or 'wind-eye'. Until the eighteenth century, the word 'irony' was very largely restricted to the various forms of rhetorical irony and men were principally concerned with the rhetorical force to be achieved through irony. Such irony works by asserting a 'falsehood' and relying upon the reader's or listener's prior knowledge of the truth to contradict it mentally or vocally by an emphatic counter-assertion, this counter-assertion with all its emphasis being the ironist's real meaning. But when, in the eighteenth century, ironical writing became more elaborate, imaginative, and subtle, it was often un-recognized and therefore taken seriously. Sometimes, with a quite radical change of function, irony was *meant* to be taken seriously either temporarily or by the simpler-minded. Really to conceal one's meaning in order to deceive or mislead the unsus-pecting or the slow-witted was one of the meanings of the word 'banter'. So that unspecific references to eighteenth-century irony included instances in which there was both a writer being ironical and a victim confidently unaware of the irony. The way was now open first for the acceptance of an 'innocent' as one of the con-comitants of irony and then for the recognition, as irony, of situations in which there is an 'innocent' even though there is no ironist of a Socratic or Swiftian kind.

A third explanation of the extension of the word 'irony' to include situational irony is to be found in the concept of the ironist as pseudo-victim. In developed Verbal Irony the ironist pretends to hold the views he is really denying and endeavours to give to his pretence every *appearance* of plausibility. He presents himself, perhaps, as an earnest simple fellow who says in all innocence what everyone else knows to be absurd. In short, he pretends to be the same sort of person as the typical ingenuous victim of bantering irony. So when we find an instance of a real simpleton behaving in the same way, with the same combination of innocence, confidence, and wrongness, it will, since it affects us in a similar way, tend to be seen as irony. Or again, just as an ironist says one thing but means another and frequently *by* saying the one in some particular way reveals the other, so any man might, through what he says or does, reveal something quite

different. Thus Squire Western assures Mr Allworthy that Tom
and Sophia could not conceivably be in love:

> 'I never so much as zeed him kiss her in all my life; and so far from
> courting her, he used rather to be more silent when she was in
> company than at any other time; and as for the girl, she was always
> less civil to'n than to any young man that came to the house. As to
> that matter, I am not more easy to be deceived than another; I would
> not have you think I am, neighbour.'[10]

Fielding could quite as easily have been more directly ironical:

> Squire Western asseverated with some warmth that there was no
> question of love between them. But with no more warmth than
> reason, for who could think there was love if there was no kissing?
> And is it to be supposed that a young man in love would fall silent
> when the girl he loved joined the company, or that the girl would
> have cause to appear less civil to him than to another? Nor is it cred-
> ible that a country squire who could fathom the tricks of the most
> cunning fox or poacher would be deceived in so much simpler an
> affair.

The effect of the one will be sufficiently like the effect of the other
for the reader to forget the radical difference, namely, that what
the ironist reveals intentionally the victim reveals inadvertently.
Fielding, according to Knox, was the first clearly to recognize that
the creation of characters who unintentionally betray themselves
was a kind of irony. The next step was simply to extend this
recognition of irony to similar instances of self-betrayal in real life.

3 · Three Grades of Irony: Overt, Covert, Private Irony

The ways of being ironical range from the simple to the complex
and the subtle. Nothing could be simpler than Johnson's 'Bolingbroke is a holy man'. It is not as easy to say what we should put
at the other end of the scale, for complexity and subtlety do not
necessarily accompany each other and a complex or subtle work
need not be complexly or subtly ironical. A complex irony would,
I suppose, be one in which there were ironies within ironies as

there may be clauses within clauses in a complex sentence. For example, Chaucer's *Sir Thopas* is at one level an ironic parody, but at another it is the sort of poem it parodies, naïvely offered by an ironic self-parody of Chaucer and contrary to that *persona*'s expectations condemned, naïvely, by the host.

[In order to be able to say what subtlety means, in relation to being ironical, we need a definition of being ironical. Let us then define irony in this sense as ways of speaking, writing, acting, behaving, painting, etc., in which the real or intended meaning presented or evoked is intentionally quite other than, and incompatible with, the ostensible or pretended meaning. (The 'real meaning' may be the contrary of the pretended meaning or it may be no more than a hinting at a mental reservation. Our definition must likewise be allowed to include not only saying one thing and meaning another but also saying two things and meaning neither.) From the reader's point of view the irony depends upon the felt presence and felt incongruity of both meanings. It is too subtle, occulted, or impenetrable (for him) if the real meaning never appears, and it falls short of irony if the pretended meaning has no force.]Subtlety in irony then will signify the fineness and delicacy with which such ironists as Henry James and Anatole France disclose their real meaning. There is perhaps less scope for an ironist to be subtle when he is depending upon our prior knowledge of something to contradict what he asserts of it; but when, at the same time and in the same words, he says and unsays, beheading his victim but leaving the head in place, it is then that irony can achieve that subtlety or finesse that makes it so wonderful an art.

Complexity and subtlety in being ironical do not lend themselves to theoretical distinctions and may be safely handed over to the literary critic.[But we can usefully divide ways of being ironical into three grades and four modes: into grades according to the degree to which the real meaning is concealed, and into modes according to the kind of relationship between the ironist and the irony. The three grades of irony I call Overt Irony, Covert Irony, and Private Irony. The four modes I call Impersonal Irony, Self-disparaging Irony, Ingénu Irony, and Dramatized Irony.]

OVERT IRONY

In Overt Irony the victim or the reader or both are meant to see the ironist's real meaning at once. The fallen angels heard Satan's irony and immediately were abashed. What makes irony overt is a blatancy in the ironic contradiction or incongruity. No irony could be much more overt than Fielding's calling Mrs Slipslop a 'fair creature' since he calls her this immediately after describing her corpulence, her pimples, her limp, her red face, large nose, small eyes, and 'the two brown globes which she carried before her'. Frequently it is the tone of voice (or its stylistic equivalent) which directs us to disregard the ostensible meaning or indicates the real meaning. The tone in overt irony may be either congruous with the real meaning, and it is then that we have sarcasm or 'bitter irony', or an exaggeration of the tone appropriate to the ostensible meaning, in which case we speak of 'heavy irony'. Spoken overt irony may be accompanied by certain conventional ironical gestures such as a curling of the lip or an 'ironical smile', but the former is perhaps more frequent in novels than in life.

Sarcasm has been called the crudest form of irony. But some sarcasms are not ironical at all and others scarcely or minimally ironical. A teacher who says to a pupil, 'Well, of course I didn't expect *you* to get the right answer,' is being sarcastic but not ironical since the ostensible meaning is the intended meaning. A man who says angrily, 'Well, you've made a fine bloody mess of it, haven't you?' is barely ironical because his tone of voice, and the other words almost totally obliterate both the praise implicit in 'fine' and the syntactical appearance of a question. He might almost as well have said, 'Well, you've made a god-awful bloody mess of it!' According to Lord Macaulay, 'A drayman, in a passion, calls out, "You are a pretty fellow" without suspecting that he is uttering irony.'[11] But it is conceivable that the passionate drayman was right. His abusive 'pretty fellow' in spite of its formal resemblance to a compliment might, in drayman's language, mean exactly the same as the modern 'nice type' which is quite unequivocal when uttered in anger or disgust. If so, it would lack the double meaning essential to irony.

At this point we have to recognize that the law of diminishing returns operates in irony. With every repetition of an ironical expression or device the less effective it becomes as irony. What begins as a genuinely ironical expression, with an incongruity, both intended and felt, between the ostensible and the real meaning, hardens in the course of time into cliché and ordinary language, where, if it is to have any force at all, it will be the force of anger, disgust, or derision and not the force of irony. Obviously, a simple piece of irony like 'Go on!' meaning 'You needn't go on because I don't believe a word of it!' becomes with repetition increasingly ineffective as irony. But by way of compensation it may be pronounced with more and more emotional emphasis passing through all the grades of sarcastic force until finally it becomes the merely derisive 'Garn!' Understatement, on the other hand, tends to be degraded into an emotionally neutral cliché. It is an ironic understatement to say, 'We could do with a drop of rain,' when a hundred thousand square miles of country is crying out for several inches, or to say, 'I'm rather partial to the odd oyster,' when one has just finished eating six or seven dozen; but 'a drop of rain' as a synonym for a light shower (even though a light shower might have half a billion drops) and 'rather partial' as merely implying a decided liking are no more ironical than their synonyms.

An additional distinguishing quality of Overt Irony, especially Overt Irony in which the tone is congruous with the real meaning, is that it may modulate freely and naturally into and out of direct abuse, derision, or reproach, without any feeling of changing gear, since these will employ a similar or even the same tone of voice. And it is the same with 'inverse' irony of an overt kind, such as the abusive endearments mothers offer their children and children their pets:

> 'Oh, you wicked, wicked little thing!' cried Alice, catching up the
> kitten, and giving it a little kiss to make it understand that it was in
> disgrace.

There is certainly an important place in literature for Overt Irony not excluding sarcasm. The great sarcast of English Literature is Milton, and we cannot assume that for his purposes a more subtle or elaborate ironical manner would have been better. For oratory and polemics, where an immediate effect is necessary, Overt Irony will generally be more telling than Covert Irony, though of course in its own way.

COVERT IRONY

The line beyond which Overt Irony will be regarded as having degenerated beyond sarcasm or understatement into direct language will very frequently be a matter of individual judgement. There is another line to be drawn, and the same impossibility of drawing it objectively, between Overt Irony and Covert Irony. What distinguishes Covert Irony is that it is intended not to be seen but rather to be detected. The Covert Ironist will aim at avoiding any tone or manner or any stylistic indication that would immediately reveal his irony. The closer he can get to an 'innocent' non-ironical way of speaking or writing while at the same time allowing his real meaning to be detected the more subtle his irony. He must, of course, run the risk of having his irony go undetected. Much irony does go undetected, as literary history and the correspondence columns of the newspapers inform us; indeed, as Friedrich Schlegel suggested, there may be irony in Shakespeare that has not yet been found out. I should imagine that most Covert Ironists would be rather pleased than otherwise if their irony were not detected by some of their readers. On the other hand, there have been ironists unwilling to take a risk. An early sixteenth-century work (not mentioned by Knox), the 1534 English translation of Laurentius Valla's *Declamation against the Donation of Constantine*, prints in the margin such remarks as 'A bytter Ironie', a procedure made fun of by Artemus Ward's marginal comment on his own work 'N.B. This is rote Sarcasticul'. Equally preposterous is the suggestion made in 1899 by a certain Alcanter de Brahm for a punctuation mark (ᴵ) 'le petit signe flagellateur' to indicate the presence of irony. The only proper comment on his suggested *point d'ironie* is *point d'ironie: plus d'ironie*. Knox has an interesting section on this 'question of clarity'.

How can we tell whether someone is being ironical? I have said several times that a work can be ironical only by intention;

being ironical means deliberately being ironical. It is only events and situations which may be unintentionally ironic (a man may say something which we see as ironic though he does not; but this is not being ironical; it is an ironic happening of which he is a victim). On the other hand, an intention to be ironical does not of itself make a work ironical *for the reader*. Defoe's anonymously published *Shortest Way with the Dissenters* is the standard example. There is nothing in the work itself nor in its relationship with the events of the time which shows it to be ironical (Wayne Booth's *Rhetoric of Fiction* has a passage on this aspect of *The Shortest Way*). And even our knowledge that Defoe intended it to be ironical, though it prevents us from reading it as Defoe's contemporaries did, does not altogether make it an ironical work. I have read, I think in Heine but I have lost the reference, that formerly when a man said something he could be held to it, but nowadays he turns round and says, 'I was being ironical.' He may have been but unless in some oblique manner he has signalled his intentions and we have seen his signal he has not been ironical for us. It is as if a man who missed the target should say he aimed to miss. He may have aimed to miss but how, *post facto*, can he prove it? The Karinthy story (which I quote from memory) is apropos: a colonel, exasperated by the deplorable marksmanship of his troops, snatched a rifle from the nearest soldier, took aim, fired, and missed. 'That's how *you* shoot,' he said. Again he fired and missed. 'And that's how *you* shoot,' he said to the next man in line. At length he scored, and was able to say, 'Now that, that's how *I* shoot.'

According to Quintilian:

[Irony] is made evident to the understanding either by the delivery, the character of the speaker or the nature of the subject. For if any one of these three is out of keeping with the words, it at once becomes clear that the intention of the speaker is other than what he actually says.[12]

Quintilian ought perhaps to have said any *two* of these three. It is not impossible for an apparently ironic 'delivery' to be the result of mere ineptness or inadvertence: to be sure it is not we need to know more of the speaker or his views. Bolingbroke's actual and known impiety is out of keeping with the words, 'Bolingbroke is a holy man', but unless we also know that the writer of these words was himself aware of Bolingbroke's impiety we can only suppose a likelihood of irony. Similarly, the 'character of the speaker' by itself can only raise a presumption of irony, since even known ironists are not invariably ironical.

What suggests to us that someone is being ironical is, to speak generally, the awareness of a contradiction between what is ostensibly the writer's or speaker's opinion, line of argument, etc., and the whole context within which the opinion or line of argument is presented. The 'whole context' comprises (a) what we already know (if we know anything) about the writer and the subject, (b) what the writer tells us (if he tells us anything) about himself and the subject over and above his pretended meaning, and (c) what we are told by the way in which he expresses his opinion, presents his case, or conducts his argument. That is to say, what is ostensibly said may be contradicted or qualified by:

1 our prior knowledge as to,
  (a) its truth, e.g. 'Hitler was kind to the Jews', and/or,
  (b) the author's real opinion, e.g. 'God is good', said by an atheist, and/or,
  (c) the author's real character, if he presents himself as other than he is,

and additionally or alternatively by:

2 what the author says or implies over and above what he seems to be saying. This internal contradiction may be (I select the more important techniques from a list presented in a later section),
  (a) a contradiction of facts or opinions, e.g. Fielding describes Mrs Slipslop as ugly and then calls her a 'fair creature', or,
  (b) a logical contradiction, e.g. 'The Penguins had the finest army in the world. So had the Porpoises,' or,
  (c) a discordant tone in speaking, or,
  (d) any discrepancy between what is ostensibly said and the language in which it is expressed, e.g. an unsuitable metaphor or choice of words, or,

(e) any discrepancy between what is ostensibly said and what is
   revealed of the author's real character.

The method of external contradiction will be employed, obviously, only when the ironist thinks he can rely upon his audience
having the requisite prior knowledge. Where this is lacking some
internal contradiction has to be supplied.
[Overt Irony is best suited for passing remarks and short passages; it would lose its force and become tedious if long continued.
Irony of any length is usually covert since Covert Irony can longer
engage the reader's alert attention.] But even Covert Irony is subject to the law of diminishing returns; should an ironist practise
the same kind of ironical indirection over and over again we
should soon find him tedious, no matter how sly we thought him
at first. It is very probable that Swift recognized this self-exhaus-
tive quality of irony since he not only varies and elaborates his
techniques but also, as F. R. Leavis and A. E. Dyson have shown,[13]
continually shifts his ground precisely so as to keep one step ahead
of the reader who thinks he has caught up with him. When he
wrote (in his 'Verses on the Death of Dr Swift'):

> Arbuthnot is no more my Friend,
> Who does to Irony pretend;
> Which I was born to introduce,
> Refin'd it first, and shew'd its Use.

he was, strictly speaking, claiming more than his due even for
England – Pascal had 'refined' it for France – but certainly he was
the first in modern Europe who 'shewed its use': a complete
manual of the art of being covertly ironical (outside the drama
and the novel) could be compiled almost entirely on the basis of
Swift's writings.

PRIVATE IRONY

[Beyond Covert Irony there is Private Irony, irony which is not
intended to be perceived either by the victim or anyone else.] Jane
Austen's Mr Bennet is a 'private ironist'; he enjoys seeing his wife
or Mr Collins take his remarks at their face value; that is to say,

he enjoys the irony of their being impervious to irony. The passage quoted on p. 45 continues thus:

> Mr Bennet's expectations were fully answered. His cousin was as absurd as he had hoped, and he listened to him with the keenest enjoyment, maintaining at the same time the most resolute composure of countenance, and except in an occasional glance at Elizabeth, requiring no partner in his pleasure.[14]

Even without Elizabeth Mr Bennet indulges in Private Irony, and even with her it is still Private Irony, private in the meaning we give the word when we speak of sharing a private joke. In the *Euthyphro* Plato presents Socrates practising Private Irony. A writer indulging in Private Irony must be either in possession of external evidence available to him alone – he could publicly praise a politician whom he alone knew to be corrupt – or able to rely upon his victim's not seeing an internal contradiction as Mr Bennet and Socrates do. As I have described it, Private Irony may seem very much like hoaxing, and indeed Northrop Frye has called Butler's *Fair Haven* a hoax presumably because Butler seems to have aimed at taking in some of his readers. My own inclination would be to call something a hoax if it seemed to have been undertaken simply for the amusement of deceiving or tricking its victim and if it were a deception against which foresight, perception, or intelligence could not be a safeguard. The boy who cried 'Wolf!' was a hoaxer, until he became a victim of irony and the wolf. The Piltdown Skull case I should call Private Irony. Private Ironists may have several motives. Mr Bennet's was contemplative enjoyment at the expense of fools; for others Private Irony may be a means of release; unable or unwilling openly to express their bitterness or contempt, their anguish or indignation, they find an outlet in 'that hypocriticall figure *Ironia*' as Fulke Greville calls it.[15] Conscious hypocrisy and casuistical 'mental reservations' I should distinguish from Private Irony on the same grounds as lies are distinguished from irony (see p. 22).

4 · *The Four Modes of Irony*

Cutting across this grading of irony as Overt, Covert, or Private is the classification of ways of being ironical into four modes according to the part played by the ironist himself in relation to his irony. Before speaking in detail of these modes I propose briefly to distinguish them.

The first I call Impersonal Irony, a name chosen somewhat *faute de mieux* but intended to indicate, not that this kind of irony is unemotionally expressed, though it very often is, but that in this mode, though we hear the voice of the ironist himself, we are more or less unaware of him as a person. The irony resides more in what he says than in the fact that it is a man of a particular character saying it. We hear someone say, '*The Birdsville Clarion* gives you a very fair coverage of international literary gossip,' and given that the speaker is being ironical (and we should scarcely ask for reassurance), we do not need to know anything about him; his character or personality plays no part in the irony. But the irony of Chaucer's comment on the Monk's view of his duties – 'And I seyd his opinion was good' – depends upon our knowing the sort of person Chaucer presents himself as being. Even in the most impersonal examples of Impersonal Irony the ironist will, by implication at least, claim to be rational, impartial, or objective, but this is a long way from dramatizing himself as a rational man. In more elaborate irony we sometimes find that the ironist's need to present his credentials as a modest, public-spirited, or serious-minded person results in the emergence of a fictitious voice and *persona, still speaking, however, as the ironist.*

At this point the current controversy over the authorial *persona* becomes relevant. Two points might be made. One is that the relationship of the *persona* to the author is a combination of at least two variables: the degree of transparency or opacity of the mask, and the degree to which it resembles or 'dissembles' the face behind it. The various possible combinations suggest something of the rich ironic potential of the authorial *persona*. The other point is that the *persona* has a range of functions some of which are not ironical: it may function only as the almost inevitable accommodation of an author's tone or manner towards his subject or audi-

ence; it may provide a way of putting one's best face forward, a
way of avoiding a merely personal tone, a way of introducing an
additional 'dramatic' role, or a way of concealing or pretending to
conceal one's real attitude. Of these functions only the last need
be ironical.

For our present purposes we need only to distinguish between
two placings of the ironic opposition. The opposition may be between what the ironist (behind a more or less impenetrable mask)
says and what he means, and then we have Impersonal Irony. Or
the opposition may be between the ironist's real opinion and that
expressed by his *persona*. When it is apparent that the pretended
character of the ironist is playing an essential part in the irony we
can talk of a second ironic mode. This mode I call Self-disparaging
Irony; the ironist brings himself on stage, so to speak, in the character of an ignorant, credulous, earnest, or over-enthusiastic person believing, for example, that Bolingbroke was a holy man or
that he could learn from a Euthyphro what holiness is. Self-disparaging Irony is the subjective equivalent of either understatement or overstatement, common varieties of Impersonal Irony;
instead of understating his opinion, saying less than he means, the
ironist understates himself, presenting himself as less intelligent
than he is; or, instead of overstating his opinion, he presents himself as foolishly enthusiastic.

There is a third mode which I call Ingénu Irony following in
part Worcester who speaks of Ingénu Satire in his *Art of Satire*.
Here the ironist, instead of speaking more or less with his own
voice or falsely presenting himself as a simpleton, withdraws even
further and uses, as his mouthpiece only, an ingénu who none the
less sees what the clever ones are blind to, or cannot be brought to
comprehend their sophistries. To keep to our example of Bolingbroke, we might imagine an ironical scene in which a Jesuit's
demonstration of Bolingbroke's essential piety failed to convince
a plain honest Christian. What might appear at first to be an exposure of the latter's intellectual deficiencies is seen in the end to
be an attack upon the former's casuistry. Though we do not
identify the plain honest Christian with the ironist we recognize
the essential identity or compatibility of their views.

In the fourth mode, in practice not always easy to distinguish from the others, the ironist will withdraw completely. He will neither speak in his own words, disguising his attitude or opinion, nor present himself lightly disguised as a simpleton, nor have an ingénu as a mouthpiece, but instead simply present an ironic situation or event, for example, some fool expressing his confidence in Bolingbroke's being a holy man. This is the mode of irony practised by dramatists and widely by novelists. When we need a name for it as a technique we may call it Dramatized Irony, since it is no more, ironologically speaking, than the presentation in drama or fiction of such ironic situations or events as we may find in life.

IV

THE FOUR MODES

1 · *Impersonal Irony*

This is the most common of the first three modes since it includes sarcasm, which everyone employs, and does not, like the other two, demand length or a dramatic imagination. The distinguishing quality of Impersonal Irony is the absence of the ironist as a person; we have only his words. Consequently, Impersonal Irony, when Covert, is generally, though not always, dispassionately expressed. The 'dryness' of the simple 'dry mock' is no more than the avoidance of the personal tone, the sarcastic edge, or the note of triumph in the voice of a man directly expressing his feelings. We all know those adepts in what we call dry humour: with a straight face, a steady voice, a quite ordinary tone, they will propose some absurd plan of action or defend some outrageous opinion. They do not nudge their audience or wink. Some would rather be misinterpreted than obvious. The response they most appreciate is not a laugh or even a smile but a grave reply in kind from those who have learnt to detect their barely perceptible hesitations and emphases. And there are some who like best to see their irony go unperceived.

Mark Twain is a good example of the poker-face ironist. For him, gravity of utterance was a requisite quality of the humorous story:

> The humorous story is told gravely; the teller does his best to conceal the fact that he even dimly suspects that there is anything funny about it.[1]

What Lamb says in praise of Bensley's acting of Iago can largely be applied to ironical gravity:

> His Iago was the only endurable one which I remember to have seen. No spectator from his action could divine more of his artifice

than Othello was supposed to do. His confessions in soliloquy alone put you in possession of the mystery. There were no by-intimations to make the audience fancy their own discernment so much greater than that of the Moor – who commonly stands like a great helpless mark set up for mine Ancient, and a quantity of barren spectators, to shoot their bolts at. The Iago of Bensley did not go to work so grossly. There was a triumphant tone about the character, natural to a general consciousness of power; but none of that petty vanity which chuckles and cannot contain itself upon any little successful stroke of its knavery – as is common with your small villains, and green probationers in mischief.[2]

The impersonal ironist's gravity of demeanour is part of his pretence that what he is saying is purely a matter of fact or of logic. He himself is disinterested or at least impartial; after long debate he has come to certain conclusions; he appeals to reason or justice or common sense, 'I Profess, in the Sincerity of my Heart,' writes the author of the *Modest Proposal*:

> that I have not the least personal Interest, in endeavouring to promote this necessary Work; having no other Motive than the *publick Good of my Country, by advancing our Trade, providing for Infants, relieving the Poor, and giving some Pleasure to the Rich.*

Though covertly emotional, the *Modest Proposal* is ostensibly dispassionate throughout, except, very cleverly, in those passages in which the writer is talking not of his scheme but of the present state of Ireland. Thus he can say quite calmly:

> I rather recommend buying the Children alive, and dressing them hot from the Knife, as we do *roasting Pigs* . . .

but speaks indignantly and with feeling of,

> . . . those *Voluntary Abortions*, and that horrid Practice of *Women murdering their Bastard Children*; alas! too frequent among us; sacrificing the *poor innocent Babes*, I doubt, more to avoid the Expence than the Shame; which would move Tears and Pity in the most Savage and inhuman Breast.

As long as irony takes such forms as those of direct advice, persuasion, or statements of fact, particularly when supported by evidence or reasoning, the grave, or rather the dispassionate, impersonal manner seems the most effective. But this absence of tone though it is the most representative is not the only manner employed by the Impersonal Ironist. Sometimes, to avoid the overtness of a tone congruous with his real meaning, the ironist may go beyond dispassionate gravity or neutrality of tone into an expression of feelings congruous with his ostensible meaning and pretend anxiety, enthusiasm, wonder, or modesty. His manner, whether grave or enthusiastic, is demanded of him in his role of pseudo-victim (see pp. 35 and 51), for it is part of the definition of the victim that he takes himself seriously or is full of passionate intensity.

It is not with any prospect of easy success that I approach the task of listing the forms or tactics of Impersonal Irony. For several reasons it seems perverse even to make the attempt. To begin with, being ironical is an art, and ultimately art is repugnant to minute classification; no net however finely reticulated will draw the moon from the millpond. In the second place, the law of diminishing returns means that there is a constant pressure upon Covert Ironists to avoid easily recognizable techniques and develop new ones, and this suggests that there may be something odd about listing irony according to technique when the subtlest irony is intent upon avoiding recognition through technique. In the third place, there is the familiar difficulty of telling whether one is dealing with different techniques or different forms of the same technique. And finally, such a list if it included techniques infrequently employed would be very long and, even so, incomplete since no one can be familiar with all the ironical literature ever written.

I shall none the less list, with some help from Knox, what seem to me to be the principal techniques employed in Impersonal Irony. This can only be done somewhat awkwardly for the following reasons. The point at which one technique can be defined as different from another depends upon the level of generality at which one does the defining. If (verbal) irony is defined, at the highest level of generality, as 'saying one thing and meaning another' no distinctions are possible. At a lower level of generality we can say that sometimes irony takes the form of asserting what is known to be false. This excludes some techniques but not others.

Of these others some can then be less abstractly defined and put in sub-classes of their own (while still belonging to the larger class), but some instances of irony can only be called asserting what is known to be false. Some techniques again can be distinguished on more than one principle. Parody, for example, can be regarded as a form of stylistically signalled irony or as a form of overstatement. What I am obliged to do, therefore, is to distinguish and name techniques according to what seems to be the dominant aspect in each case.

I propose merely to list these though one could work out a rough classification which would distinguish (*a*) Victim-oriented ironies; for example, pretended praise or advice, (*b*) Self-oriented ironies; for example, pretended doubt or ignorance, (*c*) Contradictions and disparities not classifiable as (*a*) or (*b*); for example, fallacious reasoning or parody, and (*d*) Ambiguities and concealed analogies. The list is as follows:

I · PRAISING IN ORDER TO BLAME

This may take several forms:

(a) *Praise for desirable qualities known to be lacking:* as when, by a reversal of facts (see XIV, Misrepresentation, p. 73) a politician is praised for the scrupulous conscience he lacks ('Praise undeserved is scandal in disguise').

(b) *Praise for having undesirable qualities or for lacking desirable qualities:* Here, by a reversal of values, the undesirable is presented as if it were desirable and vice versa, as when a great rogue, such as Jonathan Wild, is praised for his roguery under the name of greatness, or praised for being free of such a snivelling quality as modesty. Erasmus's *Praise of Folly* and Arbuthnot's *Art of Political Lying* may be cited as examples.

(c) *Inappropriate or irrelevant praise:* as when, vital principles being at stake, one praises an ecclesiastical measure for being convenient or economical or politically shrewd. The irrelevance of Chaucer's praise of the Prioress's table manners is underlined by his omission of any comment relevant to her qualities as a religious.

II · BLAMING IN ORDER TO PRAISE

This has the same forms as praising in order to blame and is simply a matter of 'reversing the signs':

(a) *Blame for undesirable qualities known to be lacking:* as when a father teases his handsome daughter, pretending to think her ugly. Or as when Cervantes writes in his Prologue to *Don Quixote*:

> I am too spiritless and lazy by nature to go about looking for authors to say for me what I can say myself without them.

(b) *Blame for having desirable qualities or for lacking undesirable qualities:* as when Pope writes of himself, 'Our other pastoral writer . . . deviates into downright poetry.'[3]

(c) *Inappropriate or irrelevant blame:* We might cite Robert Graves's '1805' in which a blimpish admiral is presented complaining of Nelson's 'unServicelike, familiar ways':

> The most bird-witted, unaccountable,
> Odd little runt that ever I did spy.
> One arm, one peeper, vain as Pretty Poll, . . .[4]

It is, of course, Graves being ironical, not the admiral.

III · PRETENDED AGREEMENT WITH THE VICTIM

A great deal of Impersonal and Self-disparaging Irony *implies* agreement with the victim. Sometimes we find explicit agreement, as when Plato, in Swift's *Battle of the Books*, says he believes the Moderns' claim to owe nothing to the Ancients.[5] What has been called in France 'l'ironie par impassibilité' might come under this heading though it is not so much agreement with the victim that is expressed as the absence of disagreement. André Hallays, speaking of Flaubert's *Bouvard et Pécuchet*, describes this technique of irony:

> Flaubert . . . does not mock his characters. He sets down quite simply their gestures and conversation and does so without turning a hair. But there is a profoundly and powerfully effective comedy in the contrast enforced at every point by the opposition of the

steadfast serenity of the author and the monstrous stupidities he
records, the poverty of thought he presents, and the vulgarity of
sentiments he reports.[6]

IV · PRETENDED ADVICE OR ENCOURAGEMENT TO THE VICTIM

Swift's *Directions to Servants*, his *Polite Conversation*, and his *Modest
Proposal* show something of the range and potential of this
technique. There are many works that employ this technique
from Defoe's *Shortest Way with the Dissenters* (1702) to Stephen
Potter's 'Lifemanship' books. And of course everyone uses it in
conversation.

V · THE RHETORICAL QUESTION

This may be used ironically since, while it can have only one
answer, its form, the form of a question, implies the possibility
of more than one:

> Canst thou draw out leviathan with an hook? or his tongue with a
> cord which thou lettest down?
> Canst thou put an hook into his nose? or bore his jaw through with
> a thorn?
> Will he make many supplications unto thee? will he speak soft
> words unto thee?

VI · PRETENDED DOUBT

A similar ironical technique is to express doubt where nothing
is doubtful:

> The Aged Duchess of Athlone
> Remarked, in her sub-acid tone,
> 'I doubt if He is what we need!'
> With which the Bishops all agreed.[7]

The irony of pretended doubt could also be regarded as a form of
understatement (see XVIII).

F

VII · PRETENDED ERROR OR IGNORANCE

As when Othello says to Desdemona:

> I cry you mercy then:
> I took you for that cunning whore of Venice
> That married with Othello.

VIII · INNUENDO AND INSINUATION

In a sense, all ways of being ironical depend upon innuendo; the ironist only intimates, and what he leaves unsaid has to be supplied by the reader's understanding. But since I am distinguishing techniques by dominant aspects I should give a separate heading to instances of irony that are more clearly innuendo than anything else. For example, Ambrose Bierce's definition of 'satiety' in his *Devil's Dictionary*: 'The feeling that one has for the plate after he has eaten its contents, madam.' Not unlike this is Dryden's way of saying in his *Defence of an Essay of Dramatic Poesy* that Sir Robert Howard's play, *The Duke of Lerma*, is undramatic and unoriginal:

> To begin with me – he gives me the compellation of *The Author of a Dramatique Essay*, which is a little discourse in dialogue, for the most part borrowed from the observations of others: therefore, that I may not be wanting to him in civility, I return him his compliment by calling him *The Author of The Duke of Lerma*.[8]

IX · IRONY BY ANALOGY

I understand that some Russian satirists unable to launch a direct attack upon abuses in their own country situate these abuses in America or Albania. (It is an additional irony if this subterfuge goes unperceived by those who award literary prizes.) Swift's history of the three churches (Peter, Martin, and Jack), Arbuthnot's *History of John Bull*, and Tibor Déry's *Niki*, not to mention much Utopian and 'Dystopian' literature, are fictionalized versions of this technique. It is not always easy to distinguish Irony by Analogy from Innuendo as may be seen from the following extract from a work attributed to Arbuthnot: *An Account of the*

Sickness and Death of Dr W—dw—rd. What is said of the state of Woodward's body is to be referred to his character and opinions, in particular his theory of 'biliose salts':

> His body pursuant to his own desire was opened by Mr Marten, in the presence of three or four foreign *virtuosos*: the complexion of the skin was parti-coloured, and had something of the tarnish and sully natural to a jaundice. We first viewed the abdomen: the musculus rectus continued fleshly to the very middle of the sternum before it began to be tendinous, as is observed in the simia; which contrivance of nature no doubt facilitates the wriggling motion of that animal . . . In the cavity of the stomach, as an ocular proof of his doctrine, presented itself an incredible quantity of bile sufficient to produce that modulation upon the brain which he gave the first hint of to the world . . . The spleen was of a triangular figure, large, tense, and in some places schirrose; abounding with a thick heavy *atra bilis* . . . The heart was very flabby, and for the most part unsound and rotten; upon the left ventricle appeared a very virulent ulcer . . . Upon opening the brain, there were evident marks of the cruel ravages and depredations of the biliose principles. The dura mater was fretted, and wholly unstrung; the circumvolutions in the cerebrum all obliterated, and the surface quite plain and even; which Doctor Willis has observed to be the case of some particular persons. The vacuities in his venter were large to an uncommon degree. The pineal gland was perfectly flaccid, so that it seemed to have been incapable for some time of giving any proper directions to the will. However, the nervous system was tense, and peculiarly adapted for vibration.[9]

We can perhaps place under the same heading Whately's *Historic Doubts relative to Napoleon Buonaparte* (1819) which shows the weakness of the rationalist attack upon the historicity of the Scriptures by demonstrating that the rationalist method can be used to cast doubt upon the existence of Napoleon.

X · AMBIGUITY

The eighteenth century had a pleasant way of ambiguously confirming pretended praise, saying, for example, that a book was written with equal learning and spirit, or afforded the reader as much improvement as entertainment, or that an action showed no less honesty than good sense. In the following passage from *The Way of the World* (Act III, Sc. i) there is an ironical *double entendre*:

> LADY WISHFORT: I won't be too coy neither. I won't give him despair – but a little disdain is not amiss; a little scorn is alluring.
> FOIBLE: A little scorn becomes your ladyship.

Since Lady Wishfort does not see the irony in Foible's remark the situation as a whole is an example of dramatic irony. It would no less be dramatic irony if Foible herself did not know what she was saying, but it would no longer be Impersonal Irony. That is to say, Foible would no longer be an ironist and we should only have Congreve's Dramatized Irony. To this example we might add the concealed *doubles entendres* of the letter, quoted on p. 37, from *Les Liaisons Dangereuses*.

XI · PRETENDED OMISSION OF CENSURE

There is an example in Junius (Letter 34, 12 December 1769):

> If any man, for example, were to accuse him of taking his stand at a gaming-table, and watching, with the soberest attention, for a fair opportunity of engaging a drunken young nobleman at piquet, he would, undoubtedly, consider it as an infamous aspersion upon his character, and resent it like a man of honour. Acquitting him, therefore, of drawing a regular and splendid subsistence from any unworthy practices, either in his own house, or elsewhere, let me ask your Grace, for what military merits you have been pleased to reward him with military government?

XII · PRETENDED ATTACK UPON THE VICTIM'S OPPONENT

An ironist could, for example, accuse of narrow-minded intolerance those who deny that Bolingbroke was a holy man but, in the course of his attack, by a reversal of values similar to that noticed in I(*b*), let it be understood that by narrow-minded intolerance he means firm principles. So Gibbon, in a familiar passage, pretends to attack sceptics and Gnostics in order to show up Orthodox acceptance of the Old Testament.[10]

XIII · PRETENDED DEFENCE OF THE VICTIM

Since defence may take the form of argument, an ironical defence may employ not only false statements (see XIV) but also fallacious reasoning (see XVI), this latter also implying an 'internal' contradiction (see XV). Knox has rescued a delightful instance of the deliberately inept defence, Francis Hare's *New Defence of the Lord Bishop of Bangor's Sermon*.[11]

XIV · MISREPRESENTATION, OR FALSE STATEMENT

As when one asserts what is known to be false or denies what is known to be true and relies upon the reader's or listener's prior knowledge for the contradiction. I(*a*) and II(*a*) may also be seen as instances of this. Flaubert's *Dictionnaire des idées reçues* misrepresents platitudes as useful knowledge. In the following passage from Swift's *Modest Proposal* there is a vciled misrepresentation (as indeed there is in the whole work):

> Some Persons of a desponding Spirit are in great Concern about that vast Number of poor People, who are Aged, Diseased, or Maimed; and I have been desired to employ my Thoughts what Course may be taken, to ease the Nation of so grievous an Incumbrance. But I am not in the least Pain upon that Matter; because it is very well known, that they are every Day *dying*, and *rotting*, by *Cold* and *Famine*, and *Filth*, and *Vermin*, as fast as can be reasonably expected. And as to the younger Labourers, they are now in almost as hopeful a Condition: They cannot get Work, and consequently pine away for Want of Nourishment, to a Degree, that if at any Time they are accidentally hired to common Labour, they have not Strength to perform it; and thus the Country, and themselves, are in a fair Way of being soon delivered from the Evils to come.

Swift has blandly treated a moral problem as an economic incumbrance, changing, 'What can we do to relieve the poor?' into 'How can we be relieved of the poor?'

XV · INTERNAL CONTRADICTION

The ironist may not always be able or willing to rely upon an external contradiction of his ostensible meaning. For example, Mrs Slipslop not being a public figure, Fielding cannot ironically call her a 'fair creature' until he has told us that she is ugly. In such cases the ironist will contradict or modify in a more or less camouflaged form what he has elsewhere asserted. The assertion and its contradiction may appear together as in a *double entendre* or may be very widely separated.

Diderot's use of cross-references in his Encyclopaedia exemplifies both covert and (comparatively) overt contradiction, though it is to be noticed that he connects only the latter with irony. Having spoken first of the connecting and reconciling function of cross-references he continues:

> Moreover, whenever the occasion demands, they will also lend themselves to a contrasting purpose – they will confront one theory with a contrary one, they will show how some principles conflict with others, they will attack, undermine and secretly overthrow certain ridiculous opinions which no one would dare to oppose openly . . .

> Finally, there is a kind of cross reference – it can refer either to words or to things – which I should like to call satirical or epigrammatic. Such, for example, is the one to be found in one of our articles where, at the end of a pompous eulogy, one reads: 'See CAPUCHON.' The comic word, 'capuchon' [monk's hood], together with what the reader will find under the heading 'CAPUCHON', can easily lead him to suspect that the pompous eulogy was meant ironically, and that it is wise to read the article with the utmost precaution and with attention to the careful weighing of every word.[12]

Flaubert simplifies cross-reference irony. Reading through his *Dictionnaire des idées reçues* one comes across:

Blondes – Plus chaudes que les brunes (Voy. Brunes).
Brunes – Plus chaudes que les blondes (Voy. Blondes).
Négresses – Plus chaudes que les blanches (Voy. Brunes et Blanches).
Rousses – (Voy. Blondes, Brunes, Blanches et Négresses).

In *Paradise Lost* Milton, more subtly, contradicts at the level of
imagery what Eve says at the literal level:

> *Adam*, well may we labour still to dress
> This Garden, still to tend Plant, Herb and Flour,
> Our pleasant task enjoyn'd, but till more hands
> Aid us, the work under our labour grows,
> Luxurious by restraint; what we by day
> Lop overgrown, or prune, or prop, or bind,
> One night or two with wanton growth derides
> Tending to wilde. Thou therefore now advise
> Or hear what to my mind first thoughts present,
> Let us divide our labours, thou where choice
> Leads thee, or where most needs, whether to wind
> The Woodbine round this Arbour, or direct
> The clasping Ivie where to climb, while I
> In yonder Spring of Roses intermixt
> With Myrtle, find what to redress till Noon.
>
> (IX, 205–19)

She is herself the garden 'tending to wilde', the *hortus inclusus* of
the Song of Solomon. She is also the wifely woodbine and the
'female ivy' (and these familiar symbols are reinforced here by
their association with the nuptial arbour). At this symbolic level,
therefore, she is unconsciously teaching husbands to 'prune, or
prop, or bind' their wives while at the literal level she is asserting
her independence. Among the roses and myrtles that both signify
love she will 'find what to redress', though blind to what most
needs redressing in her love.

XVI · FALLACIOUS REASONING

The ironist may convey to us that what he says is not what he
means by deliberate, though more or less veiled, false reasoning,
by suppressing, for example, an untenable major premise:

Cet animal est très méchant,
Quand on l'attaque il se défend.

And Voltaire makes Pangloss say:

> Private misfortunes contribute to the general good, so that the more
> private misfortunes there are, the more we find that all is well.[13]

Here we have to think of Voltaire saying this ironically and not of
Pangloss saying it seriously. In Pangloss's mouth it is uninten-
tional irony of which he himself is the unconscious victim. (See
Irony of Self-Betrayal, Chapter V, Section 4.)

XVII · STYLISTICALLY SIGNALLED IRONY

There are many ways in which an ironist may use stylistic re-
sources. Any divergence in fact from the stylistic level appropriate
to the ironist's subject or his ostensible meaning might be a warning signal, and the range of divergence is from sustained mock-
heroic to the slightly excessive frequency of a Stracheyan 'Could
it be perhaps . . .?' I can mention only some of these ways.

(a) *The Ironical Manner:* A certain kind of Impersonal Irony,
falling just short of the covert, is characterized by a recognizable
ironical style or manner the chief feature of which is a pon-
derously or excessively latinate vocabulary and a hackneyed urbanity. The following from Lecky's *History of European Morals*
is an amusing but otherwise representative example (the first
sentence is not ironical):

> Clement of Alexandria – a writer of wide sympathies, considerable
> originality, very extensive learning, but of a feeble and fantastic
> judgement – who immediately succeeded Justin Martyr, attributed
> all the wisdom of antiquity to two sources. The first source was
> tradition; for the angels, who had been fascinated by the ante-
> diluvian ladies, had endeavoured to ingratiate themselves with their
> fair companions by giving them an abstract of the metaphysical and
> other learning which was then current in heaven, and the substance of
> these conversations, being transmitted by tradition, supplied the
> Pagan philosophers with their leading notions. The angels did not

know everything, and therefore the Greek philosophy was imperfect.[14]

(b) *Stylistic 'Placing'*: By using words which are slightly out of place or which the ironist can rely upon to have certain connotations for the reader, by repeating a word or phrase until it becomes suspect and therefore ironical, by changing his whole style, or by adopting the style of his victim (as George Eliot does in the example on p. 45) an ironist can contradict himself, or, what is more frequent with these ironical devices, suggest that he is not to be taken in all seriousness and that things are not quite what they seem. One may hint a fault and hesitate dislike even by a rhythm or a cadence or by the careful insertion of the right word in exactly the right wrong place.

For example, Henry James's *Daisy Miller* begins in this way:

> At the little town of Vevey, in Switzerland, there is a particularly comfortable hotel; there are indeed many hotels; since the entertainment of tourists is the business of the place, which, as many travellers will remember, is seated upon the edge of a remarkably blue lake – a lake that it behoves every tourist to visit.

Here the slightly unusual word 'behoves' is used to hint at an irony at the expense of the tourists who do what the guide books tell them, and our recognition of this suggests to us that the phrase 'a remarkably blue lake' may be a guide-book phrase. James's use, farther on, of inverted commas – 'the "grand hotel" of the newest fashion', 'a flitting hither and thither of "stylish" young girls' – is only a more overt way of 'placing' his subject and distancing himself. The inverted commas deny any connexion between such usages and himself; they are not *his* words.

Sometimes the irony may be carried and released through the repetition of a word or phrase. Thomas Mann frequently employs a kind of *leit-motiv* irony. When in *The Magic Mountain* Hans Castorp meets the admirable Settembrini he is at a loss for the right term with which to define the Italian's impressive powers of expression. 'Plastic?' suggests Settembrini himself, and 'plastic' it is until with constant repetition and the growing perceptiveness of both Castorp and the reader the word becomes more and more destructively ironical.

An ironist may go beyond the occasional use of a word or a phrase and adopt *in toto* the style of a different cultural level or a different way of thinking or even invent a style, his purpose being not simply to 'place' what the adopted or invented style represents, not simply to indicate its distance from him, but to distance and liberate himself. Modern self-conscious man knows that a 'natural' style is the product of the writer's environment; his knowing this inhibits him from writing uncritically or spontaneously. The only way to write freely is to write 'artificially', as Joyce and Thomas Mann have done. The latter, commenting in his diary upon a public reading by Bruno Frank, writes:

> But what strikes me as odd is this: he uses the humanistic narrative style of Zeitblom [the fictional biographer of *Doktor Faustus*] with complete seriousness as his own. In matters of style I really no longer admit anything but parody. In this, close to Joyce. . . .[15]

(c) *Parody:* The word 'parody' more commonly means in English not the adoption or invention of a style but the exaggerated imitation of a style in order to satirize or ridicule either stylistic mannerisms or mannered ways of thought or both, as in *Rejected Addresses*, *A Christmas Garland*, or Frederick Crews's *The Pooh Perplex*. Here the ironist's ostensible meaning is what you would suppose him to be saying if you did not know you were reading a parody, while his real meaning is the inferable criticisms of the style he is caricaturing. Generally the parodist chooses for his ostensible subject something inappropriate or trivial as an additional device for drawing our attention to the mannerisms he is ridiculing. That parody was at least on one occasion in the early eighteenth century regarded as irony may be seen in a note to Pope's *Memoirs of P.P., Clerk of this Parish*:

> Honest Tom Corgate [sic] hath written many things in simple *earnest*, after the *vein* and *manner* of this ironical discourse.[16]

Parody, stylistic 'placing', and the ironical allusion (see p. 102) are perhaps the only techniques that can be developed to any extent in non-verbal irony. Musicians, painters, and film producers frequently parody their fellow-artists. I once saw an actor parodying in Bottom's cat-tearing scene his own gestures when acting the more violent scenes in *King Lear*. One trusts that a good deal of modern architecture is inspired by a spirit of parody. Tchaikovsky's *1812 Overture*, with its deliberate 'mis-quotation' of a few bars of 'The Marseillaise', is a well-known example of musical irony. In a more subtle manner *Don Giovanni* 'quotes' first from Martin's 'Una Casa Rara', then from Sarti's 'I Due Litiganti', and finally from Mozart's own *Nozze di Figaro* which is said to have owed a good deal to the influence of 'I Due Litiganti'.

(d) *Mock-heroic:* Satirical Mock-heroic presents a 'low' subject in language conventionally reserved for and associated with the sublime or dignified. When it would kill a calf, it does it in a high style, the incongruity of subject and style emphasizing the contemptibility of the subject. Boileau, Dryden, Swift, and Pope can provide examples. But often Mock-heroic is used with affectionate playfulness, and sometimes only pretends to make fun as when the writer is unwilling to express his real feelings. This we might call Self-protective Irony for which there are several other causes (see pp. 236 f). There is affectionate playfulness as well as satire in Pope's description of Belinda at her toilet in *The Rape of the Lock* and perhaps something of Self-protective Irony in Fielding's description of Sophia in *Tom Jones* since 'most of all she resembled one whose image never can depart from my breast'.[17]

(e) *Burlesque:* This term has been used to signify satirical Mock-heroic (High Burlesque), Parody, and Travesty. I use it here in the narrower sense of Low Burlesque to signify what is the opposite of Mock-heroic – a 'low' style (and generally a 'low' story) applied to a presumed 'high' victim (as in *Hudibras*). In such works the technique is similar to Irony by Analogy (see IX): we are made to laugh at A: we are shown or infer that A resembles B, and so we laugh at B.

(f) *Travesty:* By travesty I understand a sort of burlesque parody, a deliberately inept imitation of a high style or manner as in the tedious brief scene of *Pyramus and Thisbe*. Like burlesque, travesty is often without any satirical intention and then it is merely amusing or wantonly destructive or both. And like burlesque it is generally so overt as to be only minimally ironical.

XVIII · UNDERSTATEMENT

In terms of form there are two kinds of understatement or *litotes*, both of which I can illustrate from *Huckleberry Finn*. One, to which the term litotes is sometimes restricted, is a denial of the contrary: 'There warn't no real scarcity of snakes about the house for a considerble spell.' The other, sometimes called *meiosis*, substitutes a minimum for a maximum or superlative. Huck throws a piece of lead at a rat, misses him, and says: 'If he'd a stay'd where he was he'd a been a tolerable sick rat.' The second form seems to be far more common and to be more capable of elaboration. Expressions that are understatements in form are frequently not ironical; the ostensible and the real meaning have coalesced and so degenerated into ordinary language, for example, 'I'm not feeling the best.'

Understatement is said to be, historically speaking, one of the earliest forms of irony, and with sarcasm it makes up a large part of the eloquence of the unsophisticated. In the native tradition of English as of Germanic poetry understatement is very frequent, especially the ironic understating of a misfortune. The following is from the German epic *The Nibelungenlied*:

> Finding no treachery in the lord of Verona, she [Kriemhild] at once swore to give Bloedelin some broad march-lands formerly held by Nuodung: but Bloedelin was later slain by Dancwart, with the result that he forgot the gift.[18]

Scottish humour is particularly rich in understatement and especially in dry off-hand expressions of mock-commiseration that are grossly inadequate to the cruel or grim situations that call them forth.

Understatement tends to appear, paradoxically, in situations that call for a strong emotional response; enthusiasm is damped down and disaster made light of. There is perhaps an element of understatement in the reply made by a Guards officer when questioned about the Dunkirk evacuation: 'My dear! The people! And the noise!'

There are several writers who have cultivated and elaborated understatement. Mark Twain evidently built upon the native

American tradition. His irony is rarely subtle but it is often highly skilful:

> There is no character, howsoever good and fine, but it can be destroyed by ridicule, howsoever poor and witless. Observe the ass, for instance: his character is about perfect, he is the choicest spirit among all the humbler animals, yet see what ridicule has brought him to. Instead of feeling complimented when we are called an ass, we are left in doubt.[19]

Slow-burning fuses or delayed explosions of this kind very frequently characterize Understatement as well as other forms of Impersonal Irony.

XIX · OVERSTATEMENT

This plays a very large part in ironical writing. It is a necessary component of parody since an exact imitation of the style, even of Browning or Carlyle, would not be ironical. With other ways of being ironical, overstatement or exaggeration functions as an additional means of presenting or enhancing the ironic contradiction: if it is ironical to say, 'Bolingbroke is a holy man,' it may be more strikingly ironical to say, 'Bolingbroke was the most devout Christian of his day.' The subjective equivalent of overstatement is a pretended enthusiasm on the part of the speaker (see Self-Disparaging Irony, Chapter IV, Section 2).

Ironical overstatement or exaggeration frequently spills over into farce as in *Hudibras* and *Don Juan*. A fine example is the passage praising marriage in Chaucer's *Merchant's Tale*. But it is a complex example since Chaucer seems himself to be ironizing the merchant's ironical tirade. This long *o altitudo* of the unhappily married merchant is irresistibly, gloriously comical simply because the irony is so transparent and so overdone (it breaks down once or twice) and because it goes on and on, as if the merchant, having happily chanced upon a means of relieving his bitterness, was quite unable to stop himself.

XX · IRONY DISPLAYED

On pp. 42–43 I noted the distinction between Verbal and Situational Irony, between saying, 'He is being ironical,' and 'It is ironic that . . .' and I added that one way of being ironical is to present ironic situations. I was thinking primarily of the dramatists and novelists who present their characters as victims of Situational Irony, but we can now ask in what other circumstances we say a man is being ironical when he shows us something that is ironic. Merely to point to an ironic situation and say 'Isn't that ironic!' is only to give evidence of a sense of irony. It is going farther to take something which on the face of it is not ironic but which, being inherently self-contradictory or false or absurd, might be seen as ironic and to present it in such a way as to bring out the latent irony. This presentation may be 'dramatized' as in a play or a novel, but it may also be done 'impersonally'. There seem to be two principal ways in which Impersonal Ironists bring out the latently ironic. One way is to restate the situation cutting out all the obscuring irrelevancies so as to reveal a clear and close confrontation of incompatibles. It is what Cicero did speaking against Verres:

> I asserted my belief that, one of these days, communities from the provinces would send deputations to the people of Rome requesting that the extortion law and its court should be abolished. For if no such court existed, they suppose that each governor would only take away with him enough for himself and his children. At present, on the other hand, with the courts as they are, a governor takes enough for himself, and his protectors, and his counsel, and the president of the court, and the judges!

He then restates the position even more pointedly:

> A greedy man's lust for gain they could satisfy, but they cannot afford a guilty man's acquittal.[20]

The other way is to accept the situation or the victim's position but develop it according to the victim's premises until the absurdity of the conclusion confronts the plausibility of the begining. This is how Johnson dealt with Soame Jenyns's philosophical speculations and how Brecht neatly and effectively dealt with the East German government in his poem 'Die Lösung', translated by Martin Esslin as 'The Solution'.[21] The occasion of this poem was the memorable workers' uprising of 17 June 1953. The first six or seven lines tell us of the government-inspired leaflets, handed out in the Stalinallee after the rising, deploring the fact that the government had lost its confidence in the people. Only by working harder than ever could the people win back the government's esteem. Brecht then briefly proposes an alternative and rather simpler solution: the government could dissolve the people and elect another. The logical process is very short; but then the attitude of the East German government was scarcely a step away from palpable absurdity.

In none of these instances does the ironist add anything *of his own* to create a confrontation of incompatibilities and this is what distinguishes it from Internal Contradiction (see XV), though in practice one will certainly find borderline cases as well as combinations of this technique with others.

The reader may very properly object that this list of the tactics or techniques of Impersonal Irony is incomplete. With equal propriety he may object that it is neither always easy nor always profitable to pin one of my labels to actual passages of irony. I can only repeat my excuses, that I am not writing as a literary critic and that actual instances of irony may be enormously complex even though built upon quite simple principles. What I am doing may perhaps be compared to the work of someone listing and classifying metres and rhyme-schemes. He knows very well that his list will be incomplete since he cannot examine every poem in the language, that a poem is much more than its metrical structure, and that two poems with the same metrical structure will be very different, even rhythmically very different, from each other. He is obliged to disregard all this but he will not suppose that because his work has a limited value it has little or none.

It might perhaps be of some interest to conclude this section with an analysis of an actual piece of irony in terms of my classification. Swift's *Modest Proposal* is a work which employs more than half of the techniques I have listed and will besides be sufficiently familiar for this purpose.

If we ask what Swift's basic strategy is in this work, three or four answers seem possible. The title suggests that we should regard it as Pretended Advice (IV): Swift is advising the Irish, and the Anglo-Irish in particular, to eat the children of the poor (who are Catholics). But whereas in his *Directions to Servants* or in Copleston's *Advice to a Young Reviewer* the ironist's advice is to do what servants or reviewers already do, here Swift is advising the Irish to do in reality what so far they have done only metaphorically and in part:

> I grant this Food will be somewhat dear, and therefore very *proper for Landlords*; who, as they have already devoured most of the Parents, seem to have the best Title to the Children.

Again, it may seem to us that what Swift is doing is bringing out or displaying an irony (XX) inherent in the attitude of the English and the Anglo-Irish towards the plight of the Irish poor, the same irony as is expressed in William Hone's pamphlet *The Late John Wilkes's Catechism* – 'Thou shalt not call starving to death murder'[22] – and in Clough's poem, *The Latest Decalogue*:

> Thou shalt not kill; but need'st not strive
> Officiously to keep alive.

Like these, Swift is pointing out that there is *not* all the difference in the world between killing and allowing to die (and from the sufferer's point of view particularly) and he implies as well that those in power, who are so deficient in conscience as to allow people to die, are scarcely in a position to object to their being killed, especially since they can be killed at a profit, profit being a motive for such people where pity is none. We can, moreover, say that he accepts the position as it is, he accepts the fact that the Irish poor are completely brutalized, and simply draws the obvious conclusion with the effect of a *reductio ad absurdum*.

But we can also regard the *Modest Proposal* as being an instance of Misrepresentation (XIV). Swift presents a human problem as a purely economic one by treating children as animals. Adopting his method we can say he proposes to alleviate the burden of economic imbalance by the simple expedient of marketing a commodity which otherwise would be a mere unprofitable charge.

Swift does not, however, simply treat children as if they were animals and leave it to his readers to bear in mind that by breeders he means mothers and by carcasses the bodies of children. And though he does not use the word 'cannibalism', the horrible and unthinkable nature of cannibalism, which is the background against which the whole pamphlet is written, appears allusively or by Innuendo (VIII) in the phrases 'a very knowing *American*' and 'the famous *Salmanaazor*, a Native of the Island *Formosa*'.

The emotional impact of the *Modest Proposal* is, in fact, principally derived from the simultaneous suppression and presentation of the idea of cannibalism, so that the ironic strategy here may be regarded as Internal Contradiction (XV). Swift's dispassionate tone is violently contradicted by the emotionally abrupt transitions from the language of the farm, the butcher's shop, and the kitchen to that of family relationships and civilized life; so that the work may be said to function, on one level, by means of emotional contradiction. We read:

> Child . . . dropt from its Dam . . . Souls . . . Breeders . . . Boy or a Girl . . . saleable Commodity . . . young healthy child, well nursed . . . Stewed, Roasted . . . Fricasie, or Ragout . . . Family . . . fore or hind Quarter . . . Infants Flesh . . . Carcase of a good fat Child . . . Shambles . . . Butchers . . . Children alive . . . hot from the knife.

or in one brief paragraph:

> Those who are more thrifty (*as I must confess the Times require*) may flay the Carcase, the Skin of which, artificially dressed, will make admirable *Gloves for Ladies*, and *Summer Boots for fine Gentlemen*.

There is a further internal contradiction between the violent emotional reaction his proposal is designed to elicit and the style of the economic pamphleteer. With its careful calculations, its 'fifthly's' and 'sixthly's', its protestations of public spirit and disinterestedness, its parade of modesty and reasonableness, its transparently self-absorbed and self-congratulatory undertone, *A Modest Proposal* is an excellent imitation of the usual characteristics of a projector's pamphlet. It may be called a parody (XVII(c)) if we can say so without implying that Swift's aim, or even one of his aims, was to attack the *style* of the political projector; he is only using the parodic method for a much more important purpose.

A more detailed examination of the text shows Swift employing at least fifteen of the techniques discussed in this section and employing most of them more than once. The most frequent is Praising in order to Blame (I(*a*), I(*b*), I(*c*)).

> Sixthly, This would be a great Inducement to Marriage, which all wise Nations have either encouraged by Rewards, or enforced by Laws and Penalties. It would increase the Care and Tenderness of Mothers towards their Children, when they were sure of a Settlement for Life [Ambiguity (X)], to the poor Babes, provided in some Sort by the Publick, to their annual Profit instead of Expence. We should soon see an honest Emulation among the married Women, *which of them could bring the fattest Child to the Market.*

The next most frequent is Misrepresentation (XIV):

> For we are told by a grave Author, an eminent *French* Physician [i.e. Rabelais] . . .

This is followed by Internal Contradiction (XV):

> Supposing that one Thousand Families in this City, would be constant Customers for Infants Flesh; besides others who might have it at *merry Meetings,* particularly *Weddings* and *Christenings.*

And by Understatement (XVIII):

> And besides it is not improbable, that some scrupulous People might be apt to censure such a Practice (although indeed very unjustly) as a little bordering upon Cruelty.

And Overstatement (XIX):

> They can very seldom pick up a Livelyhood *by Stealing* until they arrive at six Years old; except where they are of towardly Parts; although, I confess, they learn the Rudiments much earlier.

The irony is occasionally only the merest flick as it is in the probable reference to Walpole in Swift's mention of the Formosan 'prime Minister of State'.

2 · Self-disparaging Irony

Into irony in this second ironic mode, which is commonly called Irony of Manner, there enters, as an additional and often as a principal factor, the character and personality of the speaker or writer. The ironist is present not simply as an impersonal voice but, in disguise, as a person with certain characteristics. And the sort of person the ironist presents himself as being is our guide to his real opinion. He understates or overstates himself, assuming such qualities as ignorance, deference, complaisance, co-operativeness, naïvety, over-enthusiasm, eagerness to learn, and inability to understand. But his disguise is meant to be penetrated, and our judgement is directed not against the ignorance or naïvety of the speaker but against the object of the irony. It is often difficult and not always profitable to draw a line between Impersonal and Self-disparaging Irony, for it may be only a short step from, say, the impersonally presented inept defence or pretended agreement to the inept defence or the pretended agreement that is intended to give us an impression of an ignorant or naïve speaker.

Socrates has given his name to one variety of Self-disparaging Irony. According to G. Lowes Dickinson, Socrates 'adopted the pose of a man who knew nothing and was asking for information; that is the famous "socratic irony" '.[23] That is perhaps misleading. Plato presents Socrates as confessing ignorance not as pretending to be ignorant. In the *Euthyphro* Socrates says, 'For what can I have to say who confess myself wholly ignorant in the matter [of stories about the Gods]?' In *The Apology* he claims his superior wisdom consists only in the knowledge of his ignorance. In the *Meno* he says, 'It isn't that, knowing the answers myself, I perplex other people. The truth is rather that I infect them also with the perplexity I feel myself.' We should rather say that what Socrates pretends, when he meets men who speak glibly about such things as virtue, justice, and holiness, is first that he is the sort of person who sits admiringly at the feet of wise men eager to learn at last the answers he has so long been vainly looking for, and secondly, that he is the sort of person who can only understand things when they are put simply. His ironic naïvety is not that he presents himself falsely as knowing nothing but

falsely as supposing he will learn something. We read in the
Euthyphro:

> SOCRATES: Then according to this definition, holiness would be the
> science of requests and offerings to the gods.
> EUTHYPHRO: You have understood my meaning perfectly.
> SOCRATES: Because I thirst for your wisdom, my friend, and I wait
> and watch, so that no word of yours falls to the ground . . . For
> unless you had known, and known perfectly, what holiness is and
> unholiness, you would never have dreamt of prosecuting your
> old father for murder on a slave's account; you would have feared
> to rouse the anger of the gods by something wrong in the deed,
> and you would have shrunk from the indignation of men. But as
> it is, I am sure you believe you understand perfectly the difference
> between holiness and wickedness: so you must tell me, dear
> Euthyphro, and not hide your opinion any more.
> EUTHYPHRO: Some other time then, Socrates; I am in a great hurry
> now, and it is time for me to be off.
> SOCRATES: Oh, my friend, my friend! You dash all my hopes to the
> ground and leave me desolate! And I had hoped to learn from you
> what holiness really was; and then I should have freed myself from
> the change Meletus has brought against me; for I could have
> shown him that I had learnt all about it at last from Euthyphro,
> and need make no more theories of my own in ignorance, nor
> coin a new religion, and, above all, that for the rest of my days
> I should lead a better life.[24]

And when Protagoras makes a long speech trying to avoid being
pinned down, Socrates, wishing to limit him to brief statements,
says, 'Protagoras, it is my misfortune to be a forgetful sort of person, and if a man makes me a long speech, I forget what it is all
about.' But as Alcibiades is made to say a little later Socrates is
only pretending to have a bad memory.

The function of Socrates' pretended admiration for and eagerness to learn from these clever men is to flatter them into thinking
they have an opportunity for displaying their knowledge. The
function of his pretended simplicity is to force them into positions
where they can only answer 'Yes' or 'No' until they discover they

have contradicted themselves. These are not Socrates' only ironical methods, but they are the basis of his irony.

Among those who have adopted similar strategies, Pascal and Chaucer should certainly be mentioned. The irony in Pascal's *Les Provinciales* derives most of its strength from the brilliant clarity and the effortless organizational power of his mind and only a part from his presentation of himself as a humble and earnest seeker after truth. But the element of self-depreciation is far from negligible especially in the earlier letters.

Chaucerian irony in this mode shows more variety than either Pascal's in *Les Provinciales* or even Socrates', as presented by Plato. Like Socrates, Chaucer makes a pretence of simplicity, and pretends naïvely to admire those whose folly or greater ignorance he very clearly sees. But the *persona* that Chaucer has developed for himself is a complex figure capable of discharging several functions and of moving in both social and moral spheres.

This *persona* no doubt derives in part from the 'modesty' formulae that Curtius has traced back to Cicero and in part from that long line of works – from Boethius's *Consolations of Philosophy* to the French dream allegories such as the *Romance of the Rose* – in which the poet presents *himself* as ignorant and eager to learn though it is the reader who is to be instructed. The first appearance of this *persona* in Chaucer is in *The Book of the Duchess*; here the poet presents himself as rather slow on the uptake and if not actually tactless at least socially rather clumsy and intellectually rather dense. In its second appearance, in *The House of Fame*, as later in *The Parliament of Fowls*, *Troilus and Criseyde*, and *The Legend of Good Women*, this self-irony is developed, and Chaucer appears as a bookworm with no real knowledge of love or life, merely turning into such English verse as he can manage what he has read but is incapable of understanding. This self-irony is, for the most part, purely comic as may easily be supposed when one pictures Chaucer reading his own poems to an audience that knows him and can therefore estimate the accuracy of his self-portraiture. Not that Chaucer is in all respects the opposite of what he presents himself as being: his self-portrait seems rather to be a caricature, partly true, partly false, partly exaggerated.

In *The Canterbury Tales* he presents himself as a pilgrim who

has set himself, all unworthy as he is, to describe his companions
and report the tales they tell. Additional body is given to this
persona by the 'murye wordes of the Hoost to Chaucer' and by
the 'drasty' tale of *Sir Thopas* that follows. But it should not be
thought that the poet has made of Chaucer the Pilgrim anything
like a fully dramatized character. It is true that there is a certain
naïve and indiscriminate admiration for the other pilgrims which
is in keeping with one whose wit is so short that he cannot 'set
folk in hir degree'. And we might say that the disjointedness of
the descriptions of some of the pilgrims is evidence of a simple
muddled mind. (I need not point out that this very disjointedness
serves functionally to present ironic juxtapositions.) On the other
hand, much of what we are told of the pilgrims comes, as John
M. Major points out, from the conventionally omniscient author.
We ought perhaps to follow Major and see Chaucer's *persona* as
'little more than a shadowy extension of the poet himself, put
forth and withdrawn to suit the poet's needs'.[25]

But this is all we need for irony in this second mode. Socrates,
Chaucer, and Pascal do not fully dramatize themselves but they
'play a part' in a much more obvious sense than, say, Gibbon does.
We might distinguish Self-disparaging irony as semi-dramatized;
it is moving away from the ordinary impersonal irony of essays,
pamphlets, and histories in the direction of plays and narrative
fiction but not reaching them since we are still aware of the ironist
behind the mask.

An interesting example of Self-disparaging Irony is to be found
in *Culture and Anarchy*. Arnold presents himself as a defective
'Philistine' in order to praise himself in order to disparage the true
Philistines. From the Philistines' point of view this is self-dispar-
agement since Arnold admits that he does not come up to their
standards. From his own point of view it is only pretended dis-
paragement, Arnold regarding the Philistines as Milton's Jesus
regarded the populace, 'Of whom to be disprais'd were no small
praise'. It is one of those cases in which one is ironical by telling
the truth:

> But with oneself one may always, without impropriety, deal quite
> freely; and, indeed, this sort of plain-dealing with oneself has in it,

as all the moralists tell us, something very wholesome. So I will venture to humbly offer myself as an illustration of defect in those forces and qualities which make our middle class what it is.[26]

There is a full-scale development of Self-disparaging Irony in Arnold's *Friendship's Garland*.

3 · *Ingénu Irony*

Although Chaucer, Pascal, and Arnold present themselves as ingénus, it is part of their intention that we should see the ironist beneath the disguise. The pilgrim who reports the Canterbury Tales and describes the other pilgrims is clearly a misrepresentation of Chaucer, but just as clearly he is not a representation of someone else; he is not an independent character. To take this further step and present a 'real' not a pretended innocent or ignoramus is to move from the mode of Self-disparaging Irony to the modes either of Ingénu Irony or of Dramatized Irony.

Ingénu Irony is almost archetypically represented by Hans Andersen's fable, *The Emperor's New Clothes*. The effectiveness of this kind of irony comes from its economy of means: mere common sense or even simple innocence or ignorance may suffice to see through the woven complexities of hypocrisy and rationalization or pierce the protective tissues of convention and *idées reçues*. The ironist does not need to put forth all his powers.

The ingénu, as an ironical device, is a frequent figure in literature. One need only mention Cervantes' Don Quixote, Shakespeare's Fool in *King Lear*, Grimmelshausen's Simplicissimus, Sterne's Uncle Toby, Diderot's Orou in the *Supplement to Bougainvilles's 'Voyage'*, Jane Austen's Catherine Morland, Twain's Huck Finn, Lewis Carroll's Bruno in *Sylvie and Bruno*, and Shaw's black girl in search of God. Some of these function only partly or intermittently as ingénus and obviously Don Quixote is much more than an ingénu. A more recent example is the hero of Salinger's *The Catcher in the Rye*. Holden Caulfield, the inarticulate, sub-literate, 'sad screwed-up' adolescent has, none the less, a clear enough perception of the phoneyness of his whole environment. But he does not have the questioning innocence of the typical ingénu.

None of these characters is an ironist pretending to be simple, foolish, childlike, or unsophisticated. Voltaire's Ingénu, though he has 'un grand fonds d'esprit', is not Voltaire in disguise. But to the extent that the ingénu and the ironist who creates him share the same ideas and ideals the former may be regarded as a mouthpiece for the latter. It is clear, however, that Ingénu Irony is much closer to being 'dramatized' or 'fictionalized' than Self-disparaging Irony, in which the ironist has not withdrawn himself so far. In some instances of Ingénu Irony it is difficult to say whether it is the innocent eye that sees the nakedness of the victim or whether it is the victim that exposes his nakedness to the innocent eye, that is to say, whether the innocent eye is primarily active or passive. And in some cases, indeed quite often, the innocent eye would be misleadingly called either active or passive. The ingénu by his questions or responses may bring about an exposure without being at all aware of having done so. Such instances represent the borderline between or, more often, a combination of Ingénu Irony and what I have called Dramatized Irony in which the ironist withdraws completely leaving the victim to expose himself directly to the reader. Moreover, in *Don Quixote* and in some eighteenth-century works the ingénu is himself sometimes a victim of irony, exposed as well as exposing.

4 · *Dramatized Irony*

The function of the ironist in Dramatized Irony is simply to present ironic situations or events to our sense of irony. (Ironic situations and events themselves I shall discuss and attempt to classify in the next chapter.) In this ironic mode the ironist does not appear either as an impersonal voice or in any disguise. He simply arranges that the characters of his play or novel, story, verse narrative, or dramatic monologue expose themselves in their ironic predicament directly to the audience or reader. He himself is the puppet-master and as such out of sight. This is the only way in which dramatists can be ironical (short of bringing themselves more or less identifiably on stage). This is the way in which such novelists as Flaubert and Joyce are ironical. Novelists, such as Thackeray, who comment on their characters may be ironical in other ways as well.

It goes without saying that an ironist gifted with verbal imagination will more often be found employing the forms of Impersonal Irony and that an ironist gifted with a dramatic imagination is more likely to employ Dramatized Irony or Dramatized Irony in combination with Self-disparaging or Ingénu Irony. It is also true that a good deal of Impersonal Irony is employed merely as a device for dealing with something else. The Impersonal Ironist is very often primarily a controversialist, orator, satirist, or moralist using irony as his weapon. On the other hand, Dramatized Irony, though it may be used as a weapon, is very often the expression of a comic or ironic vision. This distinction can only be valid by excepting the exceptions; an ironist like Gibbon who favours the technique I have called Irony Displayed (see p. 82) may have more in common with the Dramatizing Ironist than with the debating society ironist who praises in order to blame. But we are more likely to find an Impersonal Ironist using irony to satirize, say, vanity, hypocrisy, or rationalizing, and more likely to find a Dramatizing Ironist looking upon manifestations of vanity, hypocrisy, and rationalizing as being in themselves instances of irony and content simply to present them as such. Swift is an unsurpassable ironist if we think only of the variety of the techniques he practised and his skill in their use. But Shakespeare has a 'purer' sense of irony. Fielding we may take as a representative of the much larger territory in between. He has less skill and variety than Swift, and a less pure sense of irony than Shakespeare. It is clear that he delights in ironic situations but he nearly always hitches a moral or satiric purpose to the ironic situations he presents.

The deeper distinction then is between ironists; the techniques they choose are only a more or less reliable guide to their particular gifts as writers, their interests, and the degree to which their sense of irony is developed. As far as ironic detachment goes the writer who merely employs irony from time to time as it suits his purposes or who merely employs irony because he has a talent that way is to be distinguished from the man whose irony is an expression of his character. The former pretends detachment as an essential element in his ironic strategy; the latter may really be detached. The former, if he is a satirist, may be motivated by indignation, disgust, or contempt; but as an ironist he will conceal his real feelings under a show of dispassionate logic, gravity, or urbanity, or even go beyond neutrality to express the opposite of what he really feels by pretending sympathy, earnestness, or enthusiasm. The latter, being really detached, being the kind of man who looks at the whole world through irony-coloured spectacles, has no need to pretend; he simply presents the ironic for its own sake.

Although ironists of both kinds have appeared in all ages there are grounds for thinking that historical changes now favour the second kind. Until the latter half of the eighteenth century, literature was regarded as a public activity with an obligation to be morally profitable, to instruct as well as delight. Irony, until about the same time, was also, with a few exceptions, irony with a purpose. But gradually irony began to be attended to for its intrinsic interest and delight; and irony for irony's sake emerges at much the same time as, or perhaps rather earlier than the doctrine of art for art's sake. Kierkegaard pointed out that irony of this latter kind – to Kierkegaard a 'true' ironist is one who is always an ironist – operates upon the aesthetic not the ethical plane. The tendency to present irony, as distinct from employing it, is connected with several other historical developments such as the growth of relativistic thought, but so large a topic must be reserved for a later chapter.

Since a Dramatizing Ironist presents ironic situations which he sees and feels as ironic it is proper that we ask here what is meant by a sense of irony. I see it as being an imaginative faculty related to wit, and perhaps a kind of wit in its perceptive, but not its expressive, aspect. But where wit enables a man to see 'occult resemblances in things apparently unlike', to use Johnson's words, a sense of irony enables a man to see occult incompatibilities within a total situation and to see a 'victim' confidently unaware of them. For example, a man without a sense of irony would read a newspaper report of a clergyman suing an estate agent for recovery of money obtained under false pretences and pass on to the next item of news. But it might well occur to an atheist with a sense of irony that the clergy themselves subsist upon money obtained as agents for non-existent heavenly mansions. The form in which I have presented this particular example reveals an occult resemblance, but it is a resemblance that implies an incompatibility – that between the clergyman's behaviour and his situation (in the eyes of the atheist). The irony resides not in the incompatibility alone but also in the clergyman's unawareness of it.

This litigating clergyman is fictitious; but the following newspaper item is evidence that truth is as ironic as fiction:

CALL FOR DROUGHT PENANCE

Personal atonement by the people of New South Wales might break the State's drought, the Roman Catholic Bishop of Bathurst, the Most Reverend A. R. E. Thomas, said last night.

He repeated his warning that the drought was God's punishment for a misplaced love of material things.

Bishop Thomas issued his warning in a Lenten pastoral letter read in every parish of Bathurst.

He nominated the Sunday before Easter as a day of atonement throughout the diocese.

On this day the people of his diocese would be asked to give financial assistance to the building of a church school at Bathurst.

'We can't do penance in sackcloth and ashes these days,' he said.

The reader familiar with Chaucer will recall the portrait of the Friar:

> He was an esy man to yeve penaunce,
> Ther as he wiste to have a good pitaunce.
> For unto a povre ordre for to yive
> Is signe that a man is wel yshrive;
> For if he yaf, he dorste make avaunt,
> He wiste that a man was repentaunt;
> For many a man so hard is of his herte,
> He may nat wepe, althogh hym sore smerte.
> Therfore in stede of wepynge and preyeres
> Men moot yeve silver to the povre freres.

A highly developed sense of irony would be one capable of discovering ironic incompatibles as readily as Sir Thomas Browne
could discover quincunxes. What this implies is not only that
quickness in discerning which I have likened to wit but also a
well-stored memory, a widely and freely ranging mind, and
above all a high degree of sapience in matters relating to life and
conduct. A man with a developed sense of irony will be able to
confront anything whatever with something with which it is
incompatible. When he reads in Browning's *Prospice*:

> I was ever a fighter, so – one fight more,
>> The best and the last!
> I would hate that death bandaged my eyes, and forbore,
>> And bade me creep past.
> No! let me taste the whole of it, fare like my peers
>> The heroes of old,
> Bear the brunt, in a minute pay glad life's arrears
>> Of pain, darkness and cold.

he will mentally confront it with a similar though very much
earlier composition of Browning's:

> Good people all who want to see
> A boy take physic, look at me!

When he reads the following blandly reasonable argument from
the *Summa Theologica* he will have in his mind the lovely, soul-
caressing, deeply satisfying screams of burning men:

*Whether Those Who Return from Heresy Are to Be Taken Back by the
Church.*
   . . . *I reply that* the Church, agreeably with the Lord's institution,
extends her charity to all, not only to friends but also to foes who
persecute her (Matt. v. 44). Now an essential part of charity is to
will the good of one's neighbour and to work for that end. But good
is twofold: there is the spiritual good, the soul's salvation, which is the
principal object of charity; for this is what a man ought, out of
charity, to will for another. Hence, as far as this good is concerned,
heretics who return, however often they have relapsed, are received
by the Church to Penance by means of which the way of salvation
is opened to them.

Now the other good is that which is a secondary object of charity, namely, temporal good: such as the life of the body, worldly property, a good reputation, ecclesiastical or secular position. This good we are not bound out of charity to will for others, except in order to the eternal salvation both of them and of others. Hence if the existence of any of such goods in an individual might be able to hinder eternal salvation in many, we are not bound in charity to will that good for that individual; rather should we wish him to be without it; for eternal salvation is to be preferred to temporal good; and, besides, the good of many is to be preferred to the good of one. Now if heretics who return were always taken back, so that they were kept in possession of life and other temporal goods, this might possibly be prejudicial to the salvation of others; for they would infect others, if they relapsed, and also if they escaped punishment others would feel more secure in lapsing into heresy . . . Therefore, in the case of those who return for the first time, the Church not only receives them to Penance, but preserves their lives, and sometimes by dispensation restores them to their former ecclesiastical position, if they seem to be genuinely converted . . . But when, after being taken back, they again relapse . . . they are admitted to Penance, if they return, but not so as to be delivered from sentence of death . . .[27]

This doctrine of a twofold charity had not been forgotten even as late as the eighteenth century as we may see in Fielding's *Grub Street Opera*:

LADY APSHINKEN: Servants are continually jealous of the least thrift of a master or mistress; they are never easy but when they observe extravagance . . . I wish you would give us a sermon on charity, that my servants might know that it is no charity to indulge [our guests in] a voluptuous appetite.

PARSON PUZZLETEXT: There is, Madam, as your ladyship very well knows, a religious charity and an irreligious charity. – Now the religious charity teaches us rather to starve the belly of our friend, than feed it. Verily, starving is voluptuous food for a sinful constitution.[28]

One is naturally a little suspicious of the perpetually ironical man who is unable ever to be wholly serious, as Max Beerbohm's cartoon presents Matthew Arnold. It would in fact be ironic to be imprisoned by one's sense of irony within the one unchanging complacently ironical mood. Nor is this an ironic situation that can be wholly evaded by self-irony. But life generally sees to it that there are things one cannot be ironical about.

Much more might be said of the ironical man (both for and against), and something more will be said in the last chapter. Our next business, however, is to distinguish the several kinds of ironic situations. And here we begin gradually to turn away from a consideration of the techniques and strategies of irony and to pay more and more attention to irony as a way of looking at the world. The emphasis, but only the emphasis, will shift from form to content, from the 'internal' structure of irony – its essential characteristics and its distinguishable classes, grades, modes, and strategies – to the preoccupations of the ironist and to the 'external' relationships of irony – the ways in which irony has developed in response to changes in the way men have thought and felt about the world, the growing self-consciousness of the ironist, the nature of ironic detachment and mobility, the ironist's own vulnerability to irony, and the moral status of irony. The next two chapters attempt to distinguish the several kinds of situations that tend to be seen as ironic.

V

IRONIC SITUATIONS

Men practised irony (in some of the ways I have been discussing) and ironic situations were appreciated long before either kind was called irony. But as I mentioned earlier, the ironies of ironic situations are, lexicologically speaking, very recent arrivals: it was not until the later eighteenth and the nineteenth century that they were recognized, accepted, and named. Of the names they were then and subsequently given – Sophoclean Irony, Tragic Irony, Dramatic Irony, Irony of Things, Irony of Fate, Irony of Chance, Irony of Life, Irony of Circumstances, Cosmic Irony, Irony of Events, Irony of Character – some retain their usefulness and appear in my classification.

In discussing and classifying ironic situations I shall cite indifferently examples from life or from literature. The provenance of an ironic situation does not determine or affect its nature. We are now, of course, looking at irony from the observer's not the ironist's point of view, and from this point of view it does not matter whether the ironic situation be actual or imagined. Nor, in discussing ironic situations presented by ironists, do we need to take it into account that the ironist might be simultaneously employing more than one mode of irony. I propose, as a beginning, to distinguish five simple 'kinds' of ironic situations asking the reader to remember that what I distinguish as different kinds may only be different aspects. The same situation could be presented in different ways and with different emphases, and the label we put upon it will depend upon the way it is presented, or the way we look at it.

For there to be an ironic situation four things are required. The first three are the 'formal' qualities, the duality, the opposition of its terms, and the element of alazony (the necessary complement to irony), the victim's confident imperception or ignorance of there being anything in the situation beyond what he sees. The victim does not have to be thought blameworthy in a strictly moral sense; nor does he have to be specified or even identifiable. It is simply that we cannot see a situation as ironic unless we believe there are those who do not. (When we recognize that we ourselves are in an ironic situation what I say here will need qualification – see Irony of Dilemma, pp. 113–14.) The fourth thing required is, since irony is in the eye of the beholder, an observer with a sense of irony. But in the discussion that follows I shall take this for granted.

1 · *Irony of Simple Incongruity*

Since there is incongruity in all ironic situations, the kind of ironic situation that, for want of any other distinguishing characteristic, appears under this unsatisfactory heading must be regarded as, formally speaking, a sort of minimal irony. It is irony in its barest and simplest terms uncomplicated by the *presentation* of action or character or the victim's imperception (though, of course, there is an imperception to be inferred).

One of the stock examples of irony in French encyclopaedias is Gautier's statement, 'Quelle ironie sanglante qu'un palais en face d'une cabane!' Here we have a striking incongruity which we feel to be ironic if we feel that the palace is an oblique social comment on the hovel or vice versa or that their juxtaposition is a comment upon a society which, since it permits the juxtaposition, is evidently unaware of the ironic incongruity. When Heine saw a neo-Gothic church set among the eighteenth- and early nineteenth-century buildings of Berlin he found the juxtaposition ironic though in saying so he pretends that the irony was intentional:

> I am not at all scoffing at the new Werder Church, that Gothic cathedral in miniature, which could have been put there among the modern buildings only from a sense of irony, to show in allegorical fashion, how silly and ridiculous it would be if we were to re-establish the ancient, long-defunct institutions of the Middle Ages in the very midst of the new creations of a new age.[1]

In *Madame Bovary* Flaubert presents simultaneously the agricultural fair at Yonville with its speeches and prizes and Rodolphe's well-worn line of love-talk, the one as banal as the other. In the following passage from Musil's *Man without Qualities*, the opposition is that of points of view:

> It happened once when they were driving through the countryside, the car bowling past delightful valleys where hill-sides covered with dark pine-woods sloped down to the road, that Diotima pointed at them, quoting the lines:
>
> 'Who was it, lovely woods, did plant you there on high?'
>
> (She quoted these lines as part of a poem, it goes without saying, and without even the faintest suggestion of the tune to which the song goes, for that she would have thought threadbare and trite.)
>
> And Ulrich replied: 'The Lower-Austrian Land Bank. Don't you know, cousin, that all the forests around here belong to the Land Bank? And the creator you are intent on praising is a forester in its employ. Nature in these parts is a planned product of the forest industry, a store-house – rank upon rank – of cellulose manufacture, which is, indeed, what it looks like.'
>
> The answers he gave were very often of this kind. When she spoke of beauty, he spoke of the fat-tissues supporting the skin. When she spoke of love, he spoke of the annual curve showing the automatic rise and fall in the birth-rate. When she spoke of great men in art, he began talking about the chain of borrowings that links these great men to each other. What it really came to always was that Diotima began talking as though God had on the seventh day put man, like a pearl, into the shell of the world, and Ulrich then reminded her that mankind was a heap of little dots on the outermost crust of a midget globe.[2]

Life often presents ready-made ironic juxtapositions to our sense of irony as when in a bookshelf we find, for example, *Lolita* accidentally alongside *Alice in Wonderland*. The ironical man is he whose more developed sense of irony can see what juxtapositions would be ironical. He becomes an ironist (I think the distinction may sometimes be useful) when he presents or displays the ironies he sees. Sir Willoughby Patterne in *The Egoist* was an ironical observer in his travels, an ironist in his letters home:

H

[Willoughby] carried his English Standard over that Continent [America], and by simply jotting down facts, he left an idea of the results of the measurement of his family and friends at home. He was an adept in the irony of incongruously grouping. The nature of Equality under the stars and stripes was presented in this manner.[3]

Eliot in *The Waste Land* jots down not facts but values and leaves an idea of what western civilization measures up to:

> The nymphs are departed.
> And their friends, the loitering heirs of city directors;
> Departed, have left no addresses.
> By the waters of Leman I sat down and wept . . .
> Sweet Thames, run softly till I end my song,
> Sweet Thames, run softly, for I speak not loud or long.
> But at my back in a cold blast I hear
> The rattle of the bones, and chuckle spread from ear to ear.

2 · *Irony of Events*

Here the ironic incongruity is between the expectation and the event. We say it is ironic when, after we have more or less explicitly or confidently expressed reliance in the way things go, some subsequent unforeseen turn of events reverses and frustrates our expectations or designs. It is ironic when we meet what we set out to avoid, especially when the means we take to avoid something turn out to be the very means of bringing about what we sought to avoid. It is ironic when we get at last what we no longer desire.

For these kinds of irony I have chosen to use the term Irony of Events as being either less narrow or more neutral than other available terms. If we wished we could apply the term Irony of Chance to those ironic reversals which come about through coincidence or some other statistical improbability. But these are not the only ironies of events. The terms Irony of Fate, Irony of Life, and Irony of Things seem all to be metaphysically loaded terms, and consequently ought to be employed only by those who hold the peculiar beliefs which the terms imply. For example, Irony of Fate, if we take the term seriously, implies a belief, not necessarily formulated with any philosophical precision, in a relentless, unavoidable series of events or 'final' event. A man is a victim of the Irony of Fate when the steps he takes to avoid his fate are either simply in vain or precisely the steps which lead him to his fate. In so far as Fate is thought of as a supernatural or quasi-divine agency he is a victim not of an ironic situation or event but of an ironist employing what Thirlwall calls Practical Irony. The term Irony of Life seems also to imply a belief in a semi-personified life force that takes a delight in designing ironic reversals.

The term Irony of Things seems also to suggest that 'things' have their own purposes and that these more or less designedly frustrate or at least completely ignore the purposes of men. Fr. Th. Vischer's novel *Auch Einer* (1879) was the first German treatment of the *Tücke des Objekts*, the malice of things: a sneezy cold, for example, intervenes at a critical moment to change the subsequent course of events, but the cold is a manifestation of the power of a malicious spirit. Here, of course, we are in touch with the mythology of brownies, pucks, and gremlins.

An example of the irony of meeting what one sets out to avoid is provided by one of Eric Gill's engravings for the Temple Shakespeare:

The victim, his nakedness signifying his vulnerability, is so intent
upon escaping what he takes to be his present predicament that
he has no eyes for what is before him. The naked figure might be
Oedipus thinking to escape his fate by leaving Corinth but really
leaving Corinth that the prophecy might be fulfilled concerning
him. A nice story illustrating this form of the Irony of Fate is to
be found in the Masnavi of Jalal al-Din Rumi:

Solomon and the Angel of Death

One day in mid-morning a nobleman ran into Solomon's judgment-
hall, his face pale with anguish, his two lips blue. Solomon said to
him, 'Sir, what has happened?'

'Azrael, the angel of death,' said the man, 'has looked upon me so
angry and baleful.'

'Well, what is your wish?' asked Solomon. 'Declare it.'

Said the man, 'Command the wind, O lord-protector, to transport
me hence unto Hindustan; it may be that coming there, your slave
will save his soul alive.'

Solomon ordered the wind to bear him swiftly over the waters to
the depths of India.

The following day, when his court was in session, Solomon spoke
to Azrael thus: 'Did you look on that true believer so balefully to
drive him a wanderer far from home?'

Said Azrael, 'When did I look on him balefully? I beheld him with
astonishment as I passed by, for God had commanded me, saying,
"This very day seize you his spirit in Hindustan!" I said to myself in
wonder, "Even though he had a hundred wings, for him to be in
India this day is a far journey." '[4]

3 · Dramatic Irony

Generally speaking the irony is more striking when an observer
already knows what the victim has yet to find out. To the
examiner who has already failed the student whom he hears
expressing a confident expectation of passing, the situation is
already ironic; to others there is no irony until the results come
out. On these grounds we distinguish between Irony of Events,

which needs to be completed by the discomfiture of the victim, and Dramatic Irony, which is immediately ironical and not dependent upon any subsequent 'reading of the results'. The difference between the effect of Dramatic Irony and the effect of Irony of Events resembles the difference between suspense and surprise. The Eric Gill illustration is, pictorially, Dramatic Irony, since we see what is going to happen. But the story it illustrates could be presented as Irony of Events by concealing until later the waiting arm of the robed figure.

Dramatic Irony is pre-eminently the irony of the theatre, being implicit in the very nature of a play, 'the spectacle of a life in which . . . we [the audience] do not interfere but over which we exercise the control of knowledge', as Sedgewick says in his *Of Irony, Especially in Drama*. But Dramatic Irony is also to be found outside the theatre, as when Joseph, unknown to his brothers, entertains them in Egypt. It would, of course, be no less Dramatic Irony if Joseph did not recognize his brothers provided the reader does.

Dramatic Irony becomes even more effective when accompanied by *double entendre*, the victim saying quite innocently or accepting in all innocence something which is true in another sense than he imagines. In Sophocles' *Electra* Aegisthus has returned to the palace to hear that strangers have arrived bringing proof of the death of Orestes. He says to Electra:

AEGISTHUS: This is good news – the best you have given me yet.
ELECTRA: I wish you joy of it – if you find it so.
AEGISTHUS: Enough then. Open the doors! Let all my people
See this sight. And fools who fixed their hopes
On this poor creature, when they see his corpse,
May now accept my yoke, and not require
My whip to humble them.
ELECTRA: I need no teaching.
I have learned my lesson at last, learned how to serve
The will of those who have the upper hand.

The Palace doors are opened, disclosing ORESTES *and* PYLADES *standing beside the body of* CLYTEMNESTRA. *The body is covered.* AEGISTHUS *goes up and looks at it for a moment in silence.*

AEGISTHUS: Surely, O God, there is example here
   Of righteous retribution. If it be so,
   In the presence of Nemesis, let me say no more.
   Uncover the face, for I must mourn my kindred.
ORESTES: You, sir, not I, should lift this veil, and look
   On what lies here, and make your kind farewell.
AEGISTHUS: True. So I will. (*To* ELECTRA) Call Clytemnestra here,
   If she is in the house.
ORESTES: She is near you now,
   Not far to seek.
AEGISTHUS *uncovers the body.*[5]

Some writers restrict the term Dramatic Irony to such instances as these in which words have a double meaning. *The Shorter Oxford English Dictionary*, for example, treats 'dramatic or tragic irony' as a form of verbal irony, defining it as, 'use of language having an inner meaning for a privileged audience, an outer for those immediately concerned'. There is certainly a distinction to be made between a situation in which a man does not fully understand the meaning of the words he uses or hears and one in which he does not fully understand the situation he is in, but both are forms of Dramatic Irony.

There is a subtler kind of Dramatic Irony which may be found in Shakespeare and which has recently been noticed in Racine as well. Here the characters unknowingly employ images and allusions that will be actualized in some subsequent scene.

In a recent article Dr Ivan Barko sees an early speech of Theseus's in *Phèdre* as a tissue of anticipatory and allegorical ironies:

> Here Theseus announces, without realizing it, the events in which he is soon to be involved. The irony of the situation is the more subtle in that Theseus himself is not alone in being unaware of the prophetic meaning of his words; the spectator himself sees at first only the surface meaning.

Later, having quoted the lines:

> J'ai vu Pirithoüs, triste objet de mes larmes,
> Livré par ce barbare à des monstres cruels
> Qu'il nourissait du sang des malheureux mortels.

Dr Barko writes:

> Pirithoüs-Hippolyte [the 'identification' of these two has been
> established earlier in the article] is delivered over to cruel monsters.
> The reader familiar with this symbol will have recognized the two
> monsters that bring about the death of Hippolyte: the sea-monster
> sent by Neptune in answer to Theseus's prayer and the allegorical
> monster, Phèdre herself. This 'barbare' [Aidoneus, tyrant of Epirus]
> that the narrator refers to with so much contempt and detestation
> is paradoxically Theseus himself. Theseus's speech reaches here its
> highest point; this involuntary and unconscious prediction of the
> truth by a Theseus full of indignation for the barbarousness of the
> king is an irony both profound and dramatic.[6]

4 · *Irony of Self-betrayal*

Under this heading I place a very familiar kind of ironic situation
which, none the less, ironologists have often ignored or failed to
distinguish from Dramatic Irony. It is exemplified whenever
someone, by what he says or does (not by what happens to him),
exposes unawares his own ignorance, weaknesses, errors, or follies:
' 'Tis not the first time I have constrained one to call me knave,'
says Sir Andrew Aguecheek proudly. And the Pharisee: 'God, I
thank thee, that I am not as other men are.' This kind of irony, or
ironic situation, is found in Greek drama, in Plato's dialogues, and
in Lucian. It is found everywhere in Shakespeare and Molière,
and since Fielding it has been a favourite irony of the novel. The
dramatist or novelist who is interested in people will be aware
that, in spite of much unexceptionable advice, mankind's progress
in self-knowledge has been indifferent; he hath ever but slenderly
known himself, and consequently can scarcely open his mouth
without betraying himself. I take the following example from
Carson McCullers' *The Heart is a Lonely Hunter*:

> 'What'll they do to those prison guards?' Mick asked.
> 'Honey, I just don't know,' Portia said. 'I just don't know.'

'They ought to be treated just like they did Willie and them. Worse. I wish I could round up some people and kill those men myself.'

'That ain't no Christian way to talk,' Portia said. 'Us can just rest back and know they going to be chopped up with pitch-forks and fried everlasting by Satan.'[7]

So far as I know, the earliest sustained presentation of this kind of irony is the *Epistolae Obscurorum Virorum*, that series of one hundred and eighteen letters pretendedly written by the anti-humanist enemies of John Reuchlin and by some people accepted as authentic. The writers, who are bachelors and masters of theology, are made to reveal themselves as comprehensively ignorant, intolerant, sycophantic, and withal complacent, but at the same time so openly and self-consciously foolish, graceless, vain, and childish that they suffer the indignity of being treated as beneath indignation. The writer of the following letter attends a dinner to meet Erasmus whom he ingenuously confesses never to have heard of before:

Our host . . . who is a humanist of parts, fell to some discourse on Poetry, and greatly belauded *Julius Caesar*, as touching both his writings and his valorous deeds. So soon as I heard this, I perceived my opportunity, for I had studied much, and learned much under you in the matter of Poetry, when I was at *Cologne*, and I said, 'Forasmuch as you have begun to speak concerning Poetry, I can therefore no longer hide my light under a bushel, and I roundly aver that I believe not that *Caesar* wrote those *Commentaries*, and I will prove my position with argument following, which runneth thus: Whosoever hath business with arms and is occupied in labour unceasing cannot learn Latin; but *Caesar* was ever at War and in labours manifold; therefore he could not become lettered and get Latin. In truth, therefore, I believe that it was none other than *Suetonius* who wrote those *Commentaries*, for I have met with none who hath a style liker to *Caesar's* than *Suetonius*.' After I had thus spoken, and much else which here, for brevity's sake, I set not down – since, as you know from the ancient saw, 'The moderns delight in brevity' – *Erasmus* laughed, but said nothing, for I had overthrown him by the subtility of my argument.[8]

There is no lack of other examples. Of those that come immediately to mind I mention *Holy Willie's Prayer*, *The Diary of a Nobody*, the earlier parts of *Barry Lyndon*, Mrs Norris and Mrs Elton, Mr Chadband and Mr Pecksniff, Jean Giono's *Le Moulin de Pologne*. The following passage is from *Tom Sawyer Abroad*. Huck Finn is arguing that the balloon they are in cannot have crossed the border between Illinois and Indiana because the country is still green and Indiana is pink. Tom is disgusted by this ignorance:

'Indiana *pink*? Why, what a lie!'

'It ain't no lie; I've seen it on the map, and it's pink . . . what's a map for? Ain't it to learn you facts?'

'Of course.'

'Well, then, how's it going to do that if it tells lies? That's what I want to know . . . You git around *that*, if you can, Tom Sawyer.' He see I had him, and Jim see it too; and I tell you, I felt pretty good, for Tom Sawyer was always a hard person to git ahead of. Jim slapped his leg and says:

'I tell *you!* dat's smart, dat's right down smart. Ain't no use, Mars Tom; he got you *dis* time, sho'!' He slapped his leg again, and says, 'My *lan'*, but it was a smart one!'

I never felt so good in my life; and yet *I* didn't know I was saying anything much till it was out. I was just mooning along, perfectly careless, and not expecting anything was going to happen, and never *thinking* of such a thing at all, when, all of a sudden, out it came . . . I don't claim no great things – I don't reckon I could 'a' done it again – but I done it that time; that's all I claim.[9]

Shakespeare's comic characters from Jack Cade onwards frequently reveal their ignorance in their very claims to knowledge. But it is not only his comic characters who condemn themselves out of their own mouths. The noble Brutus's wife, the noble Portia, in claiming to be more than a mere woman reveals the conventional feminine frailties, vanity, inquisitiveness, illogicality, and a readiness to apply moral coercion:

PORTIA: No, my Brutus;
    You have some sick offence within your mind,
    Which by the right and virtue of my place

I ought to know of: and, upon my knees,
I charm you, by my once commended beauty,
By all your vows of love and that great vow
Which did incorporate and make us one,
That you unfold to me, yourself, your half,
Why you are heavy, and what men tonight
Have had resort to you; for here have been
Some six or seven, who did hide their faces
Even from darkness.

BRUTUS: Kneel not, gentle Portia.

PORTIA: I should not need, if you were gentle Brutus.
    Within the bond of marriage, tell me, Brutus,
    Is it excepted I should know no secrets
    That appertain to you? Am I yourself
    But, as it were, in sort or limitation,
    To keep with you at meals, comfort your bed,
    And talk to you sometimes? Dwell I but in the suburbs
    Of your good pleasure? If it be no more,
    Portia is Brutus' harlot, not his wife.

BRUTUS: You are my true and honourable wife,
    As dear to me as are the ruddy drops
    That visit my sad heart.

PORTIA: If this were true, then should I know this secret.
    I grant I am a woman, but withal
    A woman that Lord Brutus took to wife:
    I grant I am a woman, but withal
    A woman well reputed, Cato's daughter.
    Think you I am no stronger than my sex,
    Being so father'd and so husbanded?
    Tell me your counsels, I will not disclose 'em:
    I have made strong proof of my constancy,
    Giving myself a voluntary wound
    Here in the thigh: can I bear that with patience
    And not my husband's secrets?

BRUTUS: O ye gods,
    Render me worthy of this noble wife!

It is not long before she has to withdraw from the street to prevent herself from telling Brutus's secret to the next chance-comer.

> I have a man's mind, but a woman's might:
> How hard it is for women to keep counsel!

Another lady who deceived herself, but on a really magnificent scale, was Samuel Butler's mother, if indeed she was the model for Christina Pontifex in *The Way of All Flesh* and for the mother of the supposed author of *The Fair Haven*, from which the following is taken:

> Several times she expressed to us her conviction that my brother and myself were to be the two witnesses mentioned in the eleventh chapter of the Book of Revelation, and dilated upon the gratification she should experience upon finding that we had indeed been reserved for a position of such distinction.

> She was not herself indeed to share either our martyrdom or our glorification, but was to survive us many years on earth, living in an odour of great sanctity and reflected splendour, as the central and most august figure in a select society. She would perhaps be able indirectly, through her sons' influence with the Almighty, to have a voice in most of the arrangements both of this world and the next. If all this were to come true (and things seemed very like it), those friends who had neglected us in our adversity would not find it too easy to be restored to favour, however greatly they might desire it – that is to say, they would not have found it too easy in the case of one less magnanimous and spiritually-minded than herself.

> In eighteen hundred and sixty-six, should it please God to spare her, her eyes would be gladdened by the visible descent of the Son of Man with a shout, and with the voice of the Archangel, with the trump of God; and the dead in Christ should rise first; then she, as one of them that were alive, would be caught up with other saints into the air, and would possibly receive while rising some distinguishing token of confidence and approbation which should fall with due impressiveness upon the surrounding multitude.[10]

In this last example, as in the passage from *Middlemarch* quoted on p. 45, the victim's thoughts are presented not directly but by a sort of *oratio obliqua*, the result being a similar combination of Impersonal Irony (Ironical Manner) and Irony of Self-betrayal. In both we find that distinctive ironic style in which the high proportion of latinate words enables the ironist to maintain an impersonal air and at the same time adds a touch of formality and pomposity to enhance a ridiculous situation.

These examples of the Irony of Self-betrayal have all been taken from imaginative literature. But life provides examples in plenty for everyone to see; the example from Butler is itself perhaps not far from life. An instance of irony that will be familiar to all those who read books about Shakespeare is to be found in the way Shakespeare seems to resemble so closely, in his preoccupations and ways of thinking, so many of those who write about him. Even those who write about irony are not exempt from the Irony of Self-betrayal. We read in an East German publication, Georgina Baum's *Humor und Satire in der bürgerlichen Ästhetik*,[11] a condemnation of the ahistorical and unpolitical theories of comedy in the nineteenth century, theories which reflect a society afraid of change. For example, the view that 'basic' human frailties like laziness and stupidity may be corrected by laughing at them is in effect a defence or exoneration of existing social conditions. But when the author turns her attention to humour and satire in communist societies we discover that since there is no scope for satire against social conditions laughter can be properly employed only in correcting individual frailties which may, she admits, be found even in positive characters. In other words, communist humour must be ahistorical and unpolitical and so, by the same process of reasoning, reflects a society afraid of change.

But the discovery of the Irony of Self-betrayal in others we ought to take as a warning of the 'dexterity of self-love' to deceive ourselves. As La Rochefoucauld says, 'Quelque découverte que l'on ait faite dans le pays de l'amour-propre, il y reste encore bien des terres inconnues.'

5 · *Irony of Dilemma*

I have already had occasion to say something of this kind of irony when I was distinguishing (see p. 20 and pp. 24 f.) between Simple Irony in which the lower level of the ironic duality, the level of the victim, was opposed and corrected by the upper level, and Double Irony in which this opposition was obscured, the dominant feature being an opposition of equally valid or invalid terms at the lower level. Ironies of the second kind usually take the form of logical contradictions, paradoxes, dilemmas, or what we are pleased to call 'impossible situations'.

The victim of a dilemma or some other 'impossible situation' may be a victim of an ironic situation in several different ways. He may, for example, be confidently unaware of being so situated. In this position would be the judge who accepts without question the 'legal doctrine that no person can be allowed to give evidence in a court of justice who does not profess belief in a God . . . and in a future state', since, as John Stuart Mill explains:

> the rule . . . is suicidal, and cuts away its own foundation. Under pretence that Atheists must be liars, it admits the testimony of all Atheists who are willing to lie, and rejects only those who brave the obloquy of publicly confessing a detested creed rather than affirm a falsehood.[12]

In such cases a man is a victim of an ironic situation precisely because of his confident assumption that he is not in an absurd one. In this he resembles the victims of other ironic situations. If Oedipus knew who he was and if Mrs Malaprop were really a mistress of orthodoxy and reprehended the true meaning of what she said they would not have been the victims of their ironic predicaments.

On the other hand, a man may believe that he is in an 'impossible position'. He may be in a position like that of Buridan's ass between two bundles of hay, unable to act because the alternative courses of action are equally attractive. Or he may find, like the victims of Morton's Fork, that the alternatives are equally disadvantageous. We would think these situations ironic if we

ourselves could see the solution and at the same time see that
the victim assumed that no solution was possible.

There is a third case to be considered, that in which the ironist
or the ironical observer is himself convinced of the dilemma or
feels the impossibility of the situation no less than the victim, and
is therefore himself a victim. Thirlwall drew attention to the irony
inherent in situations in which

> good and evil are so inextricably blended on each side, that we are
> compelled to give an equal share of our sympathy to each, while we
> perceive that no earthly power can reconcile them; that the strife
> must last until it is extinguished with at least one of the parties, and
> yet that this cannot happen without the sacrifice of something which
> we should wish to preserve.[13]

In reading Trollope we find a pleasure in watching him elaborate situations in which whole armies of convincing arguments,
sound motives, weighty considerations, and unavoidable external
pressures are mustered on both sides, neither side being allowed to
surpass or fall short of the other. In reading Musil we find a
similar pleasure in watching him confront one convincing point
of view with a second which is its contrary, and as often as not the
second is logically derived from the first. We are in much the
same situation of being both observers and victims when we see
ourselves involved in the inescapable ironies of current history as
so ably presented by Niebuhr in his *Irony of American History*.

If we are victims of such impossible situations, dilemmas, or
paradoxes, it is because we are trapped or puzzled. But if we are
to be victims of *irony* it must be because we still manage to believe we live in a world in which one ought not to be trapped or
puzzled in these peculiar ways, a world in which impossible
situations ought to stay impossible. As victims we cannot escape
the irony for as long as we believe or assume that we inhabit a
rational or moral universe. We can escape only by finding and
adopting a detached position from which we can regard the co-
existence of contraries with equanimity, that is to say by abandoning the concept of a rational or moral world, but abandoning
despair as well as hope.

Now that these five kinds of ironic situations have been illustrated we are in a better position to see that the name we give an ironic situation will depend upon how we look at it or how it is presented to us. Let us take as an example the recognized ironic situation of a democracy which, in order effectively to defend its ideals of individual liberty against a hostile totalitarian state, finds itself not only allied with other totalitarian states (for purely military considerations) but also obliged to abandon its ideals and become a totalitarian state itself. If we look at this as something happening contrary to our expectations and intentions we call it an Irony of Events. If we see others confidently unaware that this has happened we call it Dramatic Irony. If we hear one of our leaders defending totalitarian measures as a bulwark against totalitarianism we might see it as Irony of Self-betrayal. If we see the situation as a dilemma we call it Irony of Dilemma. We could even isolate and juxtapose exactly parallel incidents from the opposed camps and speak of Irony of Simple Incongruity.

Part Two

Mit der Ironie ist durchaus nicht zu scherzen.
FRIEDRICH SCHLEGEL,
Über die Unverständlichkeit.

VI

GENERAL IRONY

1 · *Introduction to General Irony*

The distinction made in Chapter II, Section 2, and again in the last section, between simple corrective ironies and the ironies of paradoxes, dilemmas, and other impossible situations can now be used as the basis of a more important distinction, that between ironies which may be called specific or particular and ironies which may be called general or universal.

So far, most of the instances of irony I have concentrated upon have been specific or particular: by this I mean that they have involved single victims or victimizations, single exposures of aberrancy in a world otherwise safely moving on the right track, or at least in a world whose own possible aberrancy was, for the purposes of the irony, not in question. Such irony is corrective or normative irony, the kind employed in the service of satire or controversy or, though not exclusively, presented in comedy or tragedy: an engineer is hoist with his own petard to the great diversion of the spectators upon whose heads he will *not* fall; a foolish opinion, a narrow doctrine, a rigid institution, an ignoramus, a hypocrite, a fop, a pharisee, a politician, a blind, presumptuous generation, or simply a thoughtless, unlucky fellow is made or becomes a spectacle to be looked down upon from the unassailable battlements of universal reason, honesty, prudence, commonsense, good fortune, unassumingness, or insignificance. When the victim is dealt with the incident is closed, the irony is over. In these instances of irony the victim is isolated; he is 'in the wrong' and over against him are the rest of society or mankind who are 'in the right' and safe. The position of the ironist, *vis-à-vis* the victim, is only a tactical and temporary stance. The superior position of the observers is only that of chance bystanders or invited witnesses.

This is what I call Specific Irony. It is characteristic of, though by no means confined to, a society with a more or less 'closed ideology', that is a society whose values are more or less established, whose members, as a body, are 'assured of certain certainties'. But what I call General Irony is life itself or any general aspect of life seen as fundamentally and inescapably an ironic state of affairs. No longer is it a case of isolated victims; we are all victims of impossible situations, of universal Ironies of Dilemma, of Amiel's Law of Irony, and of Kierkegaard's World Irony. One has to remember, of course, that in literature and especially in tragedy the victim, though a single character, may in fact be playing the role of Everyman, and his predicament, though a particular one in the story, may be universalized as a symbol or allegory of the predicament of all men. In such a case the irony may be General though it has the appearance of being Specific. On the other hand, if the protagonist, even in his role of Everyman, is presented as being 'in the wrong' *vis-à-vis* the gods with the implication that he would have been safe had he been less hubristic or more circumspect, the irony is still only Specific. For General Irony, the gods would need to be shown as utterly implacable or utterly indifferent or as capable of being moved only by such abject piety as would seem to be worse than any punishment they might inflict.

General Irony has been described by Kierkegaard:

> Irony in the eminent sense directs itself not against this or that particular existence but against the whole given actuality of a certain time and situation . . . It is not this or that phenomenon but the totality of existence which it considers *sub specie ironiae*.[1]

Or, as a French critic, Georges Palante, says:

> The metaphysical principle of irony . . . resides in the contradictions within the universe or God. The ironic attitude implies that there is in things a basic contradiction, that is to say, from the point of view of our reason, a fundamental and irremediable absurdity.[2]

The province of General Irony is not so much the manners of men as 'the morals of the Universe' to adopt an excellent phrase of Morton Gurewitch's. Consequently, General Irony is not

primarily corrective or normative; we are all in the same hole and
there is no way of getting out of it. None the less, there is more
than one way of responding to such a predicament, and in so far
as irony is a better way there may be a corrective, or at least a
heuristic element in the ironical presentation of a General Irony
situation.

'Objectively', General Irony lies in those contradictions,
apparently fundamental and irremediable, that confront men
when they speculate upon such topics as the origin and purpose of
the universe, free will and determinism, reason and instinct, the
scientific and the imaginative, ends and means, society and the
individual, art and life, knowing and being, self-consciousness
(what is conscious of what?), the meaning of meaning, and the
value of value. Most of these, it may be said, are reducible to one
great incongruity, the appearance of free and self-valued but
temporally finite egos in a universe that seems to be utterly alien,
utterly purposeless, completely deterministic, and incompre-
hensibly vast. I had better hasten to add that our concern here is
with the world as men see or have seen it and not with the world
as it is or may be. Philosophers who find no fundamental contradictions in the world are entitled to be ironical at the expense
of those who do, but that is another matter. We have to live in
the world as it is, and the philosopher is committed to the task of
seeing it as it is. But the ironist is not a philosopher. As, or like
an artist, he sees the world 'aesthetically', that is, from the proper
aesthetic distance but not outside the human context. He sees
what the scientist or philosopher shows him but he sees it in
relation to the beliefs and assumptions, fears and desires of men.
Science and philosophy themselves he sees also in their human
context.

Such inescapable contradictions and incongruities as emerge
from a consideration of the human condition are not ironic in
themselves. They can become so only by the addition of the element of 'innocent unawareness'. We may see, for example, a
romantic lover complacently unaware that it is an animal drive
that has made him a sonneteer. We may see him aware of this yet
assuming that something must be wrong with the world for there
to be such an incongruity. In a moment of enlightenment we

may see ourselves as only too ready to expect the universe to be a good universe and take itself and us seriously. Alternatively an ironist may present a General Irony situation *as if* he were unaware of the contradiction or as if he innocently thought the world should not be contradictory.

Subjectively, General Irony lies in our response to what we see, truly or falsely, as fundamental contradictions and paradoxes in life, contradictions that strike us not simply as puzzles – this would result only in trivial ironies – but as *predicaments* many of which have forced men into a realization of their essential and terrifying loneliness in relation to others or to the universe at large. Since these contradictions persist, responses to them frequently take the more permanent form of attitudes which naturally are as various as the men who hold them. The ironic attitude of a 'General Ironist' is complicated by his own equivocal position. On the one hand his sense of irony implies detachment, and since the irony he perceives is General Irony, as I have defined it, he will be detached from life itself or at least from that general aspect of life in which he perceives a fundamental contradiction. On the other hand, the picture he sees of an ironic world must show himself as a victim. So he is at the same time involved and detached, both within and without the ironic situation (as in the Specific Ironies of Dilemma), and his response therefore will not be a simple one. If he feels equally involved and detached, this may find expression in self-mockery, in ambivalent fictional characters, such as the hero-villain, or even in *doppelgänger* motifs. But perhaps it is more common to find either the feeling of involvement or the feeling of detachment predominant. And these feelings may be either welcomed or resisted, so that the expression of an ironic attitude may be coloured by feelings of sentimentality, resignation or despair, compassion or bitterness, scepticism, nihilism, melancholy, or serenity. As we shall see, when speaking of Cosmic Irony (pp. 147–51), a good many writers particularly in the nineteenth century were disposed to arraign the ways of God. Others with more resilient minds, and of these Heine is a good example, found a way of escape and consequently a sense of freedom through the very ability of the mind to recognize the inescapable predicaments they were in.

Historically, General Irony characterizes (though it is not confined to) the modern period and more particularly the last two hundred years. It emerges, as I have said, from an awareness of life as being fundamentally and inescapably at odds with itself or with the world at large. Such an awareness must be as old as reflective thought itself. Opposed to man's natural desires there stood the certainty of his death, the 'impenetrability' of the future in other respects, the limitations of his powers, the strength of his biological drives, the will of others, and the obstinacy or ineluctability of natural forces. Everywhere the infinite insatiability of desire is met by the finite possibilities of satisfaction. As Musil puts it, 'It is only the unimaginative resistance put up by reality that introduces into the poem Man the awareness of the contradictions there are.' Desire is poetry; reality is science; their confrontation makes for irony.

Religion, one might say, partly evolved as a way of solving such contradictions by denying the ultimate reality of this world; the heavens remain when earth shall pass away and desires unsatisfied on earth will be fulfilled in heaven. The earth may be finite and fallen, changeable, illusory, and wretched, but heaven for which man is designed is infinite, immutable, real, and blessed. Much the same could be said of Platonic philosophy, and has been said by Ortega y Gasset:

> Socrates was the first to realise that reason is a new universe, more perfect than and superior to that which we find, spontaneously, in our environment . . . Neither our environment nor our inner self affords a safe and solid refuge for the mind. On the other hand, pure ideas, or *logoi*, constitute a set of immutable beings, which are perfect and precise.[3]

But since man, though belonging to heaven, still had to live on earth, the effect of religion and philosophy was, in the long run, both to exacerbate and multiply the contradictions. The belief in a world beyond the world, a world free of contradictions, heightened man's awareness of the contradictions there are. His commitment to heaven burdened him with the added obligations to behave as if he were there so that he could get there. His commitment to the realm of mind made him an altogether grander poem but by no means lessened the resistance put up by the irrational forces within him. Centuries of transcendental Christian theology produced many such complaints as the following in Chapman:

> Oh of what contraries consists a man!
> Of what impossible mixtures! Vice and virtue,
> Corruption, and eternnesse, at one time,
> And in one subject, let together loose![4]

or in Fulke Greville:

> Oh wearisome Condition of Humanity!
> Borne under one Law, to another bound:
> Vainely begot, and yet forbidden vanity;
> Created sicke, commanded to be sound:
> What meaneth Nature by these diverse Lawes?
> Passion and Reason, selfe-division cause.[5]

The consolations of religion and philosophy were not altogether efficacious. What is more to the purpose is that even though, in the event, it was the heavens themselves that passed away, even though man began to lose his sense of the reality of the other world and to abandon Platonic idealism, the ideals of reason and conduct which philosophy and religion had so strongly sanctioned still survived, preserving the old contradictions and forming new ones with the multiplicity of ideas which the last two or three centuries have produced. It is of course generally true that old ways of thinking do not immediately disappear upon the arrival of new ones, but co-exist with them, even when, as frequently in the modern period, the new ideas are the reverse of the old.

From the sixteenth century onwards, at first slowly and then with ever-increasing speed, men became more and more aware of fundamental contradictions in life. Many of these can be seen as falling into two closely related groups. The first of these is the group of contradictions that arose between the older 'closed ideology' which began to break up in the sixteenth century and its opposite, the new 'open ideology' (if a term so nearly self-contradictory may be allowed me) which has gradually been replacing it. The second is simply the old fundamental contradiction between the ego, with all its values and desires, and objective reality, but a contradiction now writ large as the post-Renaissance reciprocal and hypertrophic development of subjectivity and objectivity, the humane and the scientific, the emotional and the rational.

What is to be understood here by a 'closed ideology' is a way of thinking governed by the (Christian) concept of a world that is (i) temporally and spatially limited, the terms 'eternity' and 'infinity' being applicable only to the translunary or 'heavenly', and (ii) hierarchically and statically ordered – at least in principle – change being either cyclic (the alternation of seasons, growth and decay), and therefore not really change, or deplored as aberration or degeneration. There was little sense of historical change, development, or progress. Such a world was regarded as being made for men and therefore meaningful only in relation to this purpose; but man was made for heaven, oriented towards a future beyond the world. Culturally, there was an orientation towards the past, men looking back either to the simplicity of the Golden Age or to the greater civilizations of classical antiquity. As late as 1711 Addison, following Boileau, is saying:

> Wit and fine Writing doth not consist so much in advancing Things that are new, as in giving things that are known an agreeable Turn. It is impossible, for us who live in the later Ages of the World, to make Observations in Criticism, Morality, or in any Art or Science, which have not been touched upon by others. We have little else left us, but to represent the common Sense of Mankind in more strong, more beautiful, or more uncommon Lights.[6]

Goethe, more surprisingly, said something similar even later (1828):

> Besides, the world is now so old, so many eminent men have lived and thought for thousands of years, that there is little new to be discovered or expressed.[7]

In an 'open ideology' all this changes. Eternity and infinity, which before were exclusively transcendental qualities, are now seen as immanent. All the implications of being in a cosmos infinite in duration and extent could not at first have been recognized except by men of the calibre of Pascal, and perhaps the concept of 'cosmological' infinity was in itself relatively unimportant though it probably contributed to the sentiment of human alienation, as well as to the sense of infinite possibility expressed by Newton shortly before his death in 1727 in words which sharply contrast with those of Addison:

> I don't know what I may seem to the world, but as to myself, I seem to have been only like a boy playing on the sea-shore and diverting myself in now and then finding a smoother pebble or a prettier shell than ordinary, whilst the great ocean of truth lay all undiscovered before me.[8]

Wordsworth, in his lines on Newton, fused the ideas of infinite possibility with infinite duration:

> I could behold
> The antechapel where the statue stood
> Of Newton with his prism and silent face,
> The marble index of a mind for ever
> Voyaging through strange seas of Thought, alone.[9]

An orientation towards the future was not, of course, restricted to science.

The world also came to be regarded as basically dynamic. Spenser's 'hardy Titanesse', Mutability, is now cast as the heroine, Progress, and the new villains are the obstacles to free growth and development: customs, laws, institutions, and to some extent, even civilization, systematic thinking, and art. As soon as one begins to think of life as dynamic, anything that stabilizes life will be deplored. Any kind of system, for example, will appear as a solidification of something essentially fluid and hence as a falsification and an obstruction. The rules of art and the concept of genres will seem to restrict the free play of natural genius. The regularity of metres and stanza forms will seem an external ordering arbitrarily imposed upon the free movement of thought; the institution of marriage will seem to shackle the free spirit of love. Civilization will seem a monstrous grid clamped down upon the living spirit. Even thought itself, in so far as it is an essentially abstracting process giving semi-permanent conceptual form to the flow of sensations and feelings, will become suspect. And if one thinks art should represent life, then art too becomes suspect, since a work of art is a static representation of what is essentially dynamic. In the words of Friedrich Schlegel:

> While art is bounded on every side, nature, on the contrary, is everywhere vast, illimitable and inexhaustible.[10]

When man deserted the 'closed world', that legitimate wife created for him by God, and found himself married to the infinite universe, he experienced at first the enormous bliss of liberation. But the honeymoon was not over before the thought struck him, as it was to do more and more frequently as time went on, that he was not so much married as unable to get a divorce. And the more he reflected upon the incomprehensible vastness of a bride who showed no signs at all of loving, honouring, or obeying him, the more he was likely to feel trapped in a despairingly meaningless and absurd situation. It was, moreover, a situation in which he was obliged, having discovered that there was no God, to find his own meanings and values and shoulder alone the immense responsibility for his own existence. Two supports he might find to rely on: understanding and fortitude, and if he could steel them with irony so much the better.

Apart from its being a crucial chapter in the history of European thought, the change-over from a 'closed' to an 'open ideology' is of central importance in the history of irony. This is partly because of the oppositions between the two 'ideologies' but principally because General Irony, in its subjective aspect, is itself an 'open ideology' phenomenon. The 'openness' of General Irony, the General Ironist's distrust of systems, his acceptance of impermanence as normal, his ability to see 'that it might just as well have happened the other way round', can all be very amply illustrated in Musil. His *Man Without Qualities* (1930–2) is in itself as complete a textbook for General Irony as Swift is for Impersonal Irony and Thomas Mann for Romantic Irony. In fact the General Ironist *is* the 'man without qualities', the man of whom nothing can be predicated except everything, the man who has knocked off being anything particular because being only something is a limitation and because 'realization attracts him less than non-realization', the man who, accepting 'the fact that the unity of Nature is based upon opposites', confronts every idea of the modern world with its equally valid (or invalid) counter-idea, and continually ironizes people who cannot tolerate a plurality:

> Diotima made some strange discoveries about the nature of great ideas.
>
> It became apparent that she was living in a great time, for the time was full of great ideas. Yet it is extraordinary how difficult it is to put into reality what is greatest and most important among great ideas, as soon as all the pre-conditions are fulfilled except one – namely, knowing what *is* greatest and most important. Every time when Diotima had almost decided in favour of one such idea, she could not help noticing that it would also be a great thing to give reality to the opposite of it. Well, that's the way it is, and she wasn't to blame. Ideals have remarkable qualities, among them that of suddenly turning into their opposite the moment one tries really to live up to them.
>
> Diotima could never have imagined a life without eternal verities, but to her amazement she discovered that each eternal verity exists twice over and even in a multiplicity of forms. That is why rational man – and in this case this was Permanent Secretary Tuzzi, whose honour was, as a result, to some extent vindicated – has a deeply rooted mistrust of eternal verities; although he will never deny that they are indispensable, he is convinced that people who take them literally are mad. According to Tuzzi's way of thinking – which he helpfully put at his wife's disposal – ideals make excessive demands on human nature, such as must lead to ruin if one does not from the very beginning avoid taking it all entirely seriously.[11]

With the decline of the 'closed ideology', and almost as if the fading out of God as the supreme authority left a vacuum which had to be filled, we have the simultaneous and reciprocal development of two rival principles, objectivity and subjectivity, each claiming to be the ultimate reality. The progress of science is achieved, on the one hand, by getting rid of all subjective factors in the observer, and on the other hand, by regarding any subjective factors in what is being observed as an unnecessary hypothesis. Science deals in facts and numbers and looks for a unity in laws. From the subjective point of view, however, it is that which cannot be reduced to facts, numbers, and laws which matters; dealing in affections, values, and purposes, subjectivity looks for a unity in love and imagination.

This opposition between objectivity and subjectivity should not blind us to the fact that the scientific and the romantic attitude, though in different ways, are both 'open'. One can see, therefore, that General Irony, as the irony of the 'open ideology', is the characteristic irony both of an age of science and of romanticism. Like the scientist, the General Ironist has a need and a capacity for endless revision and self-correction, for questioning and suspending judgment, for living 'hypothetically and subjunctively' as Kierkegaard says, and keeping alive a sense of an infinity of possibilities. According to Goethe one must have a sense of irony to be a good scientist, since any results one arrives at may be superseded. According to Eugenio d'Ors:

> Science is irony: science is in a sense aesthetic like art. At every point of its progress, science accepts implicitly, notes in its own margin, the possibility of contradiction, the progress to come. It defines, it cannot dogmatize.[12]

Science is, of course, much more than this and much more complex an affair, as one may see in Musil's *Chapter Seventy-two*. Relative to irony it is also less. For although the dialectic of science accepts the possibility of contradiction, its eye is fixed more firmly on that other possibility, the possibility of reunification. It continually looks beyond the possible antithesis to the possible synthesis; its ideals are simplicity and unity. Irony, on the other hand, needs and looks for contradictions and dualities. And though the scientist would do well to have a sense of irony if that would prevent him from mistaking hypotheses for truths, he would be in a bad way if his sense of irony persuaded him of the essential futility of an endless series of theses and antitheses.

Moreover, the outlook of the General Ironist differs from that of the scientist in that, unlike the scientist, he cannot be outside what he observes since what he observes is the predicament he and all men are in, caught between objectivity and subjectivity, the scientific and the humane, thinking and feeling, the true and the valuable, 'it is' and 'one ought', 'as a result of' and 'so that'. The scientist (and the positivist thinker generally) is concerned with certainty alone, in the sense of getting things right and straight, freed from subjective distortion: so justice be done it is no matter if the heavens fall. The General Ironist is, on the whole, the sort of person who, while accepting or seeing no way of rejecting the positivist view, likewise sees no way of rejecting the opposite view and consequently is very much aware of the pathos of heaven's falling; he 'cannot but remember such things were that were most precious' to him. He dwells, historically, in the densely populated no-man's land between the old and the new differing from his fellow countrymen in that he knows where he is, knows, that is to say, that there are two sides and that he cannot take either side or bring them into accord. What he *can* do is to recognize them and, by presenting them ironically, transcend them – though not absolutely.

Having before him this objective–subjective polarity, with man stretched along its axis as 'the glory and the scrapings of the universe', to quote Pascal, the General Ironist can be ironical in both directions. Musil again can provide all the examples one would need:

> One can begin at once with scientific thinking's curious preference for mechanical, statistical, material explanations that have, as it were, the heart cut out of them. Regarding goodness as only a particular form of egoism; relating emotions to internal secretions; asserting that man is eight- or nine-tenths water; explaining the character's celebrated moral freedom as an automatically evolved philosophical appendix of free trade; reducing beauty to a matter of good digestion and well-developed fat-tissue; reducing procreation and suicide to annual curves, showing what seems to be the result of absolute free will as a matter of compulsion; feeling that ecstasy and mental derangement are akin; putting anus and mouth on one level, as the rectal and oral ends of one and the same thing – such ideas, which, in a manner of speaking, lay bare the sleight of hand in the conjuring-trick of human illusion, always meet with something like a prejudice in their favour,

which allows them to pass as particularly scientific. Admittedly, it is truth that one so loves here. But all round this shining love is a partiality for disillusion, compulsion, inexorability, cold intimidation and dry reproof, a malicious partiality or at least an involuntary emotional radiation of this kind.

In short, the voice of truth has a suspicious undertone of 'interference', but those most closely concerned pretend they don't hear it.[13]

And elsewhere:

There it is. Knowledge is an attitude, a passion. Actually an illicit attitude. For the compulsion to *know* is just like dipsomania, erotomania, and homicidal mania, in producing a character that is out of balance. It is not at all true that the scientist goes out after truth. It is out after him. It is something he suffers from. The truth is true and the fact is real without taking any notice of him. All he has is the passion for it. He is a dipsomaniac whose tipple is facts, and that leaves its mark on his character. And he doesn't care a damn whether what comes of his discoveries is something whole, human, perfect – or indeed, *what* comes of them! It's all full of contradictions and passive suffering and at the same time enormously active and energetic.[14]

The opposition between science and the humanities can be paralleled on the political level. Just as Musil can ironize science from the point of view of the humanities and vice-versa, so a man with political interests may find himself with ambivalent attitudes towards both the old world and the new.

Heine's *Deutschland, ein Wintermärchen* (1844) shows at the same time not only his cheerful irreverence towards superstitious piety and his hatred of political and religious reactionaries but also his horror at the destructiveness of the coming revolution. In this poem he wanders through Cologne in a dream followed by a shadowy hooded *doppelgänger* figure carrying an executioner's axe. This figure is the deed that follows Heine's thoughts, the revolution that springs from liberal propaganda.

> On we went! And in my breast
> My heart was torn and bruised.

And from the deep wound of my heart
The drops of scarlet oozed.

Sometimes I plunged my fingers in,
And sometimes I would spread
Over the doorposts, as I passed,
A smear of bloody red.

And every time I marked a house
In such a way, there fell
Moaning sadly and softly afar
The sound of a tolling-bell.

They enter the Cathedral, symbol, for Heine, of futile catholic
obscurantism still lingering on:

At last we came to a dazzling room
And saw a bright display
Of silver, gold, and precious stones;
Here the Three Kings lay.

But wonders of wonders! the Three Holy Kings
Who'd been content to lie
So still, were sitting upright now
On their sarcophagi.

Three skeletons, in fantastic dress,
With sceptres in their hands;
Atop their wretched, yellowed skulls
Were crowns of the eastern lands.

Like jumping-jacks they moved their bones,
That had slept for ages there;
A smell of incense and of mould
Arose and fouled the air.

One of the monarchs moved his mouth
And delivered a long oration,
Explaining why he'd a right to demand
My awe and admiration.

First, because he was a corpse,
Second, because a king,

And third, because he was a saint –
But it didn't mean a thing.

Laughing aloud, I answered him:
Your speech was very clever,
But I can see that you belong
To a time that is gone forever.

Out! out of here! You should have crawled
Down to your graves before.
Life is now coming to confiscate
This chapel's treasure-store.

The future's joyous cavalry
Shall here at last be housed.
And if you're not willing, I'll turn to force:
I'll club you till you're deloused!

So I spoke, and wheeled around;
I saw the terrible glint
Of my silent lictor's terrible axe –
He understood the hint.

He came up close and savagely
Smashed them, sceptre and crown;
And with one blow those bones of false
Belief came tumbling down.

Horribly boomed through all the vaults
The echo of that stroke.
Streams of blood shot from my breast,
And suddenly I awoke.[15]

Perhaps the most convenient way to deal with General Irony
in its objective aspect will be to present a number of the more
common topics of this kind of irony. Some of these may be seen
as falling into groups that parallel the different kinds of 'specific'
ironic situations I have already described; there is, for example, a
General Irony of Events as well as a Specific Irony of Events, the
former being a generalization of the latter or the latter seen in its
philosophical aspect. But it must again be stressed that the classification is not a system of separate compartments.

K

2 · *General Irony of Events, or Vanity of Human Wishes*

We say it is ironic when Arcite in the *Knight's Tale*, having won the battle for Emily, is accidentally killed, thus enabling Palamon to win in spite of losing. Such isolated instances of the Irony of Events may be seen as manifestations of a general principle, namely that the future is essentially unknowable or inescapable and therefore that there can be no confident anticipations. Life presents a continual contrast, Thirlwall says 'between man with his hopes, fears, wishes, and undertakings and a dark inflexible fate'. But if by fate we understand some mysterious supernatural entity consciously acting in opposition to the aspirations and undertakings of those men only who have been insufficiently circumspect as to the future, we have made of Fate a mere moral agent, and can be said to have moved only in the direction of the concept of General Irony. On the other hand, if we put the emphasis on the absolute impenetrability or on the absolute inflexibility of fate against which no degree of caution or width of experience, against which not even the gods can prevail, then we have a real foundation for General Irony.

We can see as ironic under this heading Hegel's 'List der Vernunft' or 'Ruse of Reason':

> Reason is as cunning as it is powerful. Its cunning, to speak generally, lies in the mediative action which, while it permits the Objects to follow their own (sc. finite or apparent) nature, and to act upon one another until they waste away, and does not itself directly interfere in the process, is yet only working out its own aims. With this explanation, divine Providence may be said to stand to the world and its process in the relation of absolute cunning. God lets men do as they please with their particular passions and interests; but the result is the accomplishment of – not their plans but his, and these differ decidedly from the ends primarily sought by those whom he employs.[16]

We know what crosses and afflictions wait upon those who too confidently think to arrange the contents of the future, erecting probabilities into certainties and looking upon intentions as achievements. Yet as soon as we try to say what degree of confidence in the future is permissible, we are forced to recognize that everything we do is based on assumptions for which we have no absolute warrant. We cannot be quite certain of not being struck by a meteorite. Even the man who has realized this, who knows how often our hopes are frustrated and how often even our fears are in vain, even he may be the victim of irony. This was Jacob's predicament in Mann's *Joseph and his Brothers*: 'How shall a man live if he can no longer rely upon things turning out differently from what he thought?' Anything less than the complete awareness God alone possesses puts man in an ironic position for as long as he retains the notion or feeling that somehow he ought to have an absolute warrant for at least some of his assumptions.

This is not all. Not only can we *not* trust the future: we *must* trust it. Life cannot be lived unless we take no thought for the morrow. The point is illustrated by Kafka's story, *The Burrow*. Here we are shown, by a fable of a mole-like creature endeavouring in vain to guard himself against attack, that foresight and prudence are not virtues but vices: foresight can always foresee additional dangers and prudence drives one to take additional precautions; but the multiplication of precautions results in a multiplication of risks and hence in the need to take further precautions. Peace of mind is to be achieved not by foresight and prudence but by blindness and recklessness. This too may be seen as a General Irony.

There is a General as well as a Specific Irony of Events in our knowing that we must die but not when. Yet the deeper irony of death is not that it may come when least expected but that life can be lived only by not expecting it, even though we do know and should know that it will come, and may at any moment. I find the following in the *Talmud*:

R. Eliezer said: Repent one day before your death. His disciples asked him, Does then one know on what day he will die? Then all the more reason that he repent today, he replied, lest he die tomorrow, and thus his whole life is spent in repentance. And Solomon too said in his wisdom, *Let thy garments be always white; and let not thy head lack ointment.* R. Johanan b. Zakkai said: This may be compared to a king who summoned his servants to a banquet without appointing a time. The wise ones adorned themselves and sat at the door of the

palace, ['for',] said they, 'is anything lacking in a royal palace?' The
fools went about their work, saying, 'can there be a banquet without
preparations?' Suddenly the king desired [the presence of] his servants:
the wise entered adorned, while the fools entered soiled. The king
rejoiced at the wise but was angry with the fools. 'Those who
adorned themselves for the banquet,' ordered he, 'let them sit, eat
and drink. But those who did not adorn themselves for the banquet,
let them stand and watch.'[17]

One can imagine the sort of comment we might have had from
Samuel Butler, how he would have dwelt on the heat and the
glare from the hard marble steps, the fretfulness of the children,
the mounting boredom, the heavy, ridiculous, and all too soon
crumpled and dirty clothes, and finally the murmuring against
the king and his inconsiderateness.

There is a General Irony again in the whole concept of progress.
In one obvious sense – that of technological advance – progress is
a fact; it would be hard to persuade an astronomer with access to a
computer or the health authorities in a country which has elimi-
nated smallpox or malaria that progress has not been made.
They might, however, be open to the view that solving one
problem is the surest means of discovering further unsuspected
problems. Looking back, we can see how far we have come; but
looking forward

> behold with strong Surprise
> New distant Scenes of *endless* Science rise.

Is an endless multiplication of problems really progress? Like the
sorcerer's apprentice, knowing the magic spell but not the counter-
spell, we have brought about a state of affairs that we can now do
nothing about. Progress has got out of hand; having chosen to
begin we cannot choose to stop and so chase our own tail at ever-
increasing speed. It is also ironic that progress has been and
perhaps can only be on one plane. It is as if a man's hands, his
manipulative organs, had become several times larger than the rest
of his body and in growing had developed a mind and a will of
their own. It is now the hands that, with a reversal of the usual em-
barrassing situation, do not know what to do with the man that
is so awkwardly attached to them.

3 · *General Dramatic Irony*

We call it Dramatic Irony when we see a man acting in complacent ignorance of the real state of affairs, especially when the situation as he sees it is the contrary of the real situation. To see man as always and necessarily ignorant of the real state of affairs or obliged to act as if he were ignorant is to see him as a victim of a General Dramatic Irony. The perennial question whether we have free will or not provides an example. Tolstoy in *War and Peace* saw Napoleon as a victim of what we would call Dramatic Irony: Napoleon thought he made history, but in Tolstoy's view it was history that made Napoleon; Napoleon believed he was a free agent in ordering his armies to invade Russia, but Tolstoy saw him as history's slave:

> Though Napoleon at that time, in 1812, was more convinced than ever that it depended on him, *verser (ou ne pas verser) le sang de ses peuples* – as Alexander expressed it in the last letter he wrote him – he had never been so much in the grip of inevitable laws, which compelled him, while thinking that he was acting on his own volition, to perform for the swarm-life – that is to say for history – whatever had to be performed.[18]

There is no reason to suppose that Napoleon's ironic predicament is not in essence a universal one. We all feel ourselves to be free agents; we all behave as if we were free agents, accepting responsibility, apportioning praise and blame, and feeling guilty from time to time. But it is not easy to argue against the proposition that what we are, all that we think, and all that we 'choose' to do has been determined by an unbroken chain of cause and effect. When we try to demonstrate our freedom of will, we find, as Tolstoy did, that we are reduced to utterly trivial and morally insignificant acts such as moving our finger to the left or the right.

It is not difficult to see Napoleon and other people (including our own past selves) as victims of this irony – historically determined but believing themselves to be free agents – because we can only see them from outside and cannot experience *their* feeling of being free. But it is difficult to be convinced of the irony of our

own theoretically identical positions. However irrefutably reason
tells us that we are wholly conditioned by physical, biological,
social, and psychological pressures, self-awareness *makes* us feel
free; we *cannot* feel ourselves not to be fundamentally free; 'We
know our will is free, and *there*'s an end on't.' These emphases indicate an involvement almost too strong for self-irony on this
point.

The irony implicit in this problem of free will and determinism
was presented by Musil in the form of a dilemma:

> If man is morally free, he must in practice be subjected, by means of
> penalties, to a compulsion in which, theoretically, no one believes;
> if, on the contrary, he is regarded as not being free, but as the
> meeting-place for irrevocably linked natural processes, then, though
> one may cause him effective discomfort by means of penalties, one
> cannot consider him morally accountable for what he does.[19]

There are further ironies encountered in this matter of free
will. We protest and struggle against those who tell us that we are
simply what chemistry, evolution, climate, national boundaries,
and so on have made us and that what we most firmly and
passionately believe are not so much beliefs that we hold as
beliefs by which we are held; but would we protest so loudly if
we considered that the alternative to determinism would be a
state of affairs in which we should act without cause, motive, or
reason in a completely lawless and arbitrary way? Submission to
necessity feels like freedom when compared with subjection to
mere chance and hazard; as Engels said, 'Freedom is the recognition of necessity.' Many people, perhaps most, find that free will
with its attendant responsibilities and feelings of guilt is too
heavy a burden; and feel that real freedom is to be found only in
obedience to some mother-country or Mother Church, some
Führer or Father in whose service is perfect freedom. The
classical exposition of this irony is the Grand Inquisitor episode in
The Brothers Karamazov.

A belief in predestination, as distinct from necessitarianism, can
equally well form the basis of irony. Diderot's *Jacques le fataliste*
is a good example of the fictional treatment of the irony of predestination. Jacques believes that, 'everything that happens here

below, good or bad, is written on high', and with this thought he sometimes consoles himself; but as often as not he behaves as if he did not believe his theory:

> . . . and I had in reserve five louis which my elder brother Jean had made me a present of when he left on his unhappy Lisbon voyage . . . (here Jacques began to weep and his master to point out to him that it was written on high). It is true, sir, I tell myself so a hundred times; yet for all that I cannot stop myself weeping . . .[20]

The clashes between a purely determined objective world and our subjectively felt freedom seem more fruitful of irony when it is a question of a man's being necessarily at odds with 'irrational' forces *within* him. There is irony in the spectacle of a man's being inevitably, being by nature, imprisoned in a world to which he feels he does not really belong; it is more strikingly ironical to recognize one's self as one's own prison:

> O who shall, from this Dungeon, raise
> A Soul inslav'd so many wayes?
> With bolts of Bones, that fetter'd stands
> In Feet; and manacled in Hands.
> Here blinded with an Eye; and there
> Deaf with the drumming of an Ear.
> A Soul hung up, as 'twere, in Chains
> Of Nerves, and Arteries, and Veins.
> Tortur'd, besides each other part,
> In a vain Head, and double Heart.[21]

It is not only that the body imprisons the soul; the instincts lead the mind a dance, the emotions deceive the reason, and the unconscious plays tricks upon the conscious. What makes the irony general is the fundamental and inevitable incompatibility felt between soul and body. This is part of the meaning Heine found in *Don Quixote*:

> May not the deep-browed Spaniard have meant to deride mankind in an even profounder way? Did he, perhaps, in the figure of Don Quixote, intend an allegory of the soul, and in Sancho Panza that of the body? May not the entire poem be a great mystery, in which the

problem of matter and spirit is treated with a most terrifying reality? This much I understand by the poem; that poor material Sancho must suffer greatly for spiritual Don Quixote; that the noblest intentions of his master bring him but so many drubbings; that he is always more sensible than his prancing master. He knows that the cudgels are not to his taste; while the small sausages in an olla-podrida are. For in truth, the body often has greater insight than the spirit. And man more often thinks rightly with his back and his belly than with his head.[22]

There is a very simple ironic situation in Don Quixote's transformation of the farm-girl Aldonza Lorenzo into the peerless Dulcinea del Toboso and again in the spectacle of 'a blemished and unsightly woman basking in a lover's adoration', as Lucretius says. But Lucretius went beyond this specific irony:

> One man scoffs at another and urges him to propitiate Venus because he is the victim of such a degrading passion; yet as like as not the poor devil is in the same unhappy plight himself, all unaware.[23]

Notice that Lucretius's awareness of a common predicament transforms an object of scorn and derision into an object of something like pity, a 'poor devil' in an 'unhappy plight'. One step farther and we see the blindness of love not as a corrigible fault but as something inevitable in human nature, as an instance of General Irony. The beauty of a beloved is then an illusion of biological origin. One may go even farther and see the sentiment of love itself with all its refinements and accompaniments of fidelity, chastity, chivalry, devotion, even virginity, as biological mechanisms that in the long run more efficiently promote the preservation of the species than uncontrolled lust and promiscuity. But to see sentiment as biology does not involve for the general ironist the rejection of sentiment as being less real than biology. He will rather, while recognizing illusions as illusions, insist that the illusions are as real as the biology. He would think it no less ironic to reject the sentiment than to be blind to its nature.

But an abstract, sterilized word like 'biology' fails to reveal the full range of ironic disparity inherent in the phenomenon of love. Against Blake's:

> Love seeketh not itself to please,
> Nor for itself hath any care,
> But for another gives its ease,
> And builds a Heaven in Hell's despair.

we set, not only, as he does,

> Love seeketh only Self to please,
> To bind another to its delight,
> Joys in another's loss of ease,
> And builds a Hell in Heaven's despite.

but also the whole sado-masochist complex. And against the paradisal garden of love:

> Fair is my Love that feeds among the lilies,
> The lilies growing in that pleasant garden
> Where Cupid's Mount that well beloved hill is,
> And where that little god himself is warden.
> See where my Love sits in the beds of spices,
> Beset all round with camphor, myrrh, and roses,
> And interlaced with curious devices
> Which her apart from all the world incloses![24]

we set its dark hell:

> Behold yond simpering dame,
> Whose face between her forks presages snow,
> That minces virtue and does shake the head
> To hear of pleasure's name;
> The fitchew, nor the soiled horse, goes to't
> With a more riotous appetite.
> Down from the waist they are Centaurs,
> Though women all above:
> But to the girdle do the gods inherit,
> Beneath is all the fiends';
> There's hell, there's darkness, there's the sulphurous pit,
> Burning, scalding, stench, consumption; fie, fie, fie! pah,
> pah! Give me an ounce of civet, good apothecary, to sweeten
> my imagination.

Yeats brings the two together:

> 'Fair and foul are near of kin,
> And fair needs foul,' I cried.
>
> 'A woman can be proud and stiff
> When on love intent;
> But Love has pitched his mansion in
> The place of excrement.'

There is a vast potential for General Irony in the psychoanalyst's discovery of the unconscious processes of the mind. We are told of radical oppositions within the psyche, of self-submissive and self-assertive instincts, of the masculine Persona and the feminine Anima, of the death-wish, of the Super-ego and the Id. Our conscious life it seems is a façade behind which a very different 'real' life goes on in secret; our hidden fears and desires evade the Censor and emerge disguised in symbolic form to betray us. The operations of the unconscious are described in much the same terms as we use when talking of irony: a man intends to say one thing but by a Freudian slip he says something quite different and so reveals his real preoccupation; artists through their unconscious 'choice' of subjects, symbols, or motifs, reveal meanings they did not intend; the concept of 'compensating' enables us to reverse the ostensible meaning of everything men say or do (the psychoanalysts, being aware of this, are obliged to psychoanalyse themselves and this resembles the obligation upon ironists to practise self-irony).

In our conscious life we have all the 'innocent unawareness' of the typical victim of irony who assumes that things are what they appear. This makes us all unconscious hypocrites living a 'life of continuous and uninterrupted self-deception', as the Satanic angel in Mark Twain's *Mysterious Stranger* puts it. The things which we would say happen to us against our will may really be things which secretly we will to happen. We may have our reasons for accidentally breaking our leg, getting hopelessly in debt, falling sick, or, as a nation, getting involved in a war; even the thought of universal nuclear suicide is undeniably attractive.

Again, we can look upon the Ego as being in an ironic predicament, caught between the amoral, irresponsible, nonconforming Id and the moral, responsible conforming Super-ego, much like Prince Hal between Falstaff and the Lord Chief Justice, the former life-giving and dynamic, the latter life-denying and orderly. The words of the Id are, 'Let us take any man's horses, the laws of England are at my commandment'; but the function of the Super-ego is to 'rate, rebuke, and roughly send to prison'. The irony lies in the contradictory opposition of values; we feel we must be for and against both sides. The attractively dynamic, libertarian irresponsibility of the Id may also be seen as conservative, stuck in the mud of unreflective life and therefore as life-denying in the fully humane sense of the word 'life', while the conforming and repressive activities of the Super-ego may be seen as the element of control that makes higher achievements possible: 'He that findeth his life shall lose it; and he that loseth his life for my sake shall find it.'

The fact that manifestations of both the Id and the Super-ego may be seen either as good or as bad may explain the wide divergence of opinion among the critics of the Henry IV plays, some calling Prince Hal a prig and others seeing his rejection of Falstaff as necessary and proper. It seems to me that to take sides here is to ignore Shakespeare's fondness for the *mise en question*; one must take both sides and neither side, and see both loss and gain in the Prince's choice. It might be going too far to suggest (or deny) that Shakespeare saw the Falstaff–Kingship choice in general terms or as a universal predicament. But there is no difficulty in seeing this for ourselves. Falstaff represents the immediacy of life in all its vitality and irresponsibility. But anyone who wants to do something in life, besides living, will find that he cannot advance on so broad a front, that he must sacrifice to the future something of the present. On the other hand, to become a king (and a politician) one would have to sacrifice too much, as perhaps Hal did.

That Shakespeare had in some sense thought along these lines seems at least probable when we find the hero of *Antony and Cleopatra* faced with a not dissimilar choice. Antony is in an impossible position; to beat Caesar on Caesar's terms he would have to deny all the qualities we admire in him and become as shrewd a politician as Caesar; to live with Cleopatra (that Falstaff of the muddy Nile) he would have to deny all his nobler Roman qualities. In spite of all that makes *Antony and Cleopatra* so different from *Henry IV* there is still the same impossible choice between irresponsibility and politics, the present and the future, living and making something of life, and (the colloquial terms are most appropriate) getting with it and getting on.

Frisch says somewhere that life and morality are incompatible and this seems to be true in several senses of the word 'life' and 'morality'. There seems, for example, to be a fundamental opposition between the self-assertive and the self-submissive instincts: man is held to be both an essentially solitary and selfish animal and an essentially gregarious animal, loving and needing to be loved. We can see the opposition in Hesse's *Steppenwolf*: when Harry was a wolf his human consciousness spoilt his animal pleasures, and when he was a man his wolfishness scorned his fine and noble emotions. Amiel saw much of life as being governed by a 'law of irony' by which our altruistic aspirations are opposed by a fundamental egoism:

> The heart yearns for a way of life in which everyone would think first of others, a life of brotherly love and spreading sympathy in which the good of all would result from a universal disregard of self. But the world is built upon a different plan; it rests upon personal interest and self-love . . . The unconscious sophism, the not disinterested contradiction is found everywhere among so-called Christian peoples, as in the clergy itself. Law of irony: the more refined the maxims, the more gross what lies beneath.[25]

It is not only our instinctive life that runs counter to morality. Life, as socially organized, is in fundamental opposition to morality. Machiavelli saw clearly enough that a man cannot be both a successful ruler and a Christian; Swift saw that real Christianity was 'utterly inconsistent with all our present schemes of Wealth and Power'; Mandeville went farther and denied the existence and possibility of real Christianity, that is, of *disinterested* virtue, as well as arguing that 'our present schemes of Wealth and Power', society as we desire to have it, depends upon the practice of what Christians are obliged to regard as vices:

> Fools only strive
> To make a Great an Honest Hive.
> T'enjoy the World's Conveniences
> Be fam'd in War, yet live in Ease,
> Without great Vices, is a vain
> EUTOPIA seated in the Brain.
> Fraud, Luxury and Pride must live,
> While we the Benefits receive.[26]

There is no doubt that Mandeville appreciated the irony of his paradox: Christianity obliges man to transcend his animal nature and live rationally and selflessly; but if this could be done civilization would collapse and man would be reduced to the level of a defenceless, if noble, savage. Kierkegaard adds what is now a commonplace that if a single man should attempt to imitate Christ he would find, the world being what it always has been, that his imitation would not stop short of Calvary. Brecht too, in *The Good Woman of Setzuan*, shows the impossibility of following the injunction of the Gods 'to be good and yet to live':

> When we extend our hand to a beggar, he tears it off for us
> When we help the lost, we are lost ourselves
> And so
> Since not to eat is to die
> Who can long refuse to be bad?
>
> It was when I was unjust that I ate good meat[27]

It is more strikingly ironic when the failure to be good is presented as being implicit in the very attempt. In Pascal we read:

> L'homme n'est ni ange ni bête, et le malheur veut que qui fait l'ange fait la bête.[28]

There are other ways in which man deceives himself by confidently assuming obligations which his very nature prevents him from fulfilling. Jules de Gaultier in his *Le Bovarysme* (1902) sees this self-deception as both a universal and an inevitable predicament. He begins, however, by speaking of *bovarysme* as a *défaillance de la personnalité*:

> A dissolution of personality, such is the initial factor which makes all Flaubert's characters imagine themselves other than they are. Given a specific character they assume a different one at the dictate of an enthusiasm, an admiration, an interest, a vital necessity. But this breakdown in their personality is always accompanied by a power-lessness, and though they imagine themselves other than they are they never manage to match the model they have set themselves to imitate. Self-love, however, prevents them from admitting to them-selves their inability, and, clouding their judgment, it puts them in a position to pull the wool over their own eyes and identify them-selves, in their own view, with the image they have substituted for themselves. In order to assist this deception they imitate, as far as it is possible to imitate, all the exteriority, all the appearance, of the character they have resolved to be: . . . this imitation is, in fact, a parody.[29]

Gaultier then goes on to demonstrate the presence of *bovarysme* in other spheres; there is a *bovarysme* in our illusions of free will, in the misdirected aspirations towards classicism in the Renais-sance and again in the eighteenth century (which necessarily led only to parodies of true classicism), in the contradiction of love and the sexual drive, in the mirage of progress, and even in the most scrupulous self-examination:

> The ego cannot arrive at a complete knowledge of itself. In order to know itself, it divides itself, and it is only one part taking cognizance of the other.[30]

And any attempt to know the knowing part leads to a further and still less satisfactory division, and so on. There is in fact 'an irreducible antagonism between these two: being and knowing'. I shall return later to this irreducible antagonism, but I should say here that though Gaultier is right about the elusiveness of the ego it does not follow that our inability to apprehend it deprives us of any useful knowledge of ourselves.

What is particularly interesting about this work is that in the later sections the author drops his concepts of *bovarysme* as a

regrettable 'défaillance de personnalité' and an inevitable predicament of human existence and sees it instead as a fundamental 'loi de
l'évolution' quite as if he had come across Bergson for the first
time when his book was half written. To-see-oneself-as-one-is-not
is now a necessary pre-condition of evolutionary progress. But
whether regrettable or necessary, inevitable self-ignorance is a
topic for General Irony.

4 · Cosmic Irony

General Irony becomes possible with the raising of doubts about
the purpose of life, and about the existence and nature of God and
of the world beyond the world. Ironists in the last two hundred
years especially have again and again realized this potential.

In *King Lear*, to take an earlier example, Shakespeare raises
several times the question of the justness of the gods, a question
that the play only partly answers. Sometimes what is said about
the gods is clearly to be ascribed to the state of mind of the
speaker, but so much is said that it is difficult to avoid thinking
that Shakespeare intended both to ask and, as a part of the tragic
effect, to leave unanswered this fundamental question.

A more specifically anti-Christian line is much commoner.
Philo, for example, in Hume's *Dialogue concerning Natural
Religion* perverts the argument from design which Cleanthes has
employed as a proof of the existence of a single intelligent
Creator:

> In a word, Cleanthes, a man who follows your hypothesis is able,
> perhaps, to assert or conjecture that the universe sometime arose from
> something like design; but beyond that position he cannot ascertain
> one single circumstance, and is left afterwards to fix every point of
> his theology by the utmost license of fancy and hypothesis. This
> world, for aught he knows, is very faulty and imperfect, compared
> to a superior standard, and was only the first rude essay of some infant
> deity who afterwards abandoned it, ashamed of his lame performance;
> it is the work only of some dependent, inferior deity, and is the
> object of derision to his superiors; it is the production of old age and

dotage in some superannuated deity, and ever since his death has run on at adventures, from the first impulse and active force which it received from him.

> Look round this universe. What an immense profusion of beings, animated and organized, sensible and active! You admire this prodigious variety and fecundity. But inspect a little more narrowly these living existences, the only beings worth regarding. How hostile and destructive to each other! How insufficient all of them for their own happiness! How contemptible or odious to the spectator! The whole presents nothing but the idea of a blind nature, impregnated by a great vivifying principle, and pouring forth from her lap, without discernment or parental care, her maimed and abortive children![31]

Views similar to these of Philo's have been embodied in one of Laurence Housman's *Ironical Tales*.[32] Two gods, called respectively Law and Order, both make a world. Law's world is an autonomous system of cause and effect and Law's purpose in making it was to observe its natural growth. Order, on the other hand, made his world so as to have something to order about. In the course of time and evolution Law's world came to be inhabited by creatures who believed that such natural phenomena as earthquakes and pestilences were sent by an angry god whom they tried to propitiate by sacrifices, while in Order's world, which he had wantonly tormented with earthquakes and pestilences, the inhabitants had worked out a scientific explanation of all their sufferings, so that for them god was an unnecessary hypothesis.

The angel called Satan in Mark Twain's *Mysterious Stranger* is used to present a bitter parody of God's dealings with men:

> While he talked he made a crowd of little men and women the size of your finger, and they went diligently to work and cleared and leveled off a space a couple of yards square in the grass and began to build a cunning little castle in it, the women mixing the mortar and carrying it up the scaffoldings in pails on their heads, just as our work-women have always done, and the men laying the courses of masonry – five hundred of these toy people swarming briskly about

and working diligently and wiping the sweat off their faces as natural as life.

We angels, Satan was saying, are ignorant of sin:

'. . . we are not able to commit it; we are without blemish, and shall abide in that estate always. We —' Two of the little workmen were quarreling, and in buzzing little bumblebee voices they were cursing and swearing at each other; now came blows and blood; then they locked themselves together in a life-and-death struggle. Satan reached out his hand and crushed the life out of them with his fingers, threw them away, wiped the red from his fingers on his handkerchief, and went on talking where he had left off; 'We cannot do wrong; neither have we any disposition to do it, for we do not know what it is.'

He went right on talking, just as if nothing had happened, telling about his travels, and the interesting things he had seen in the big worlds of our solar system and of other solar systems far away in the remotenesses of space, and about the customs of the immortals that inhabit them, somehow fascinating us, enchanting us, charming us in spite of the pitiful scene that was now under our eyes, for the wives of the little dead men had found the crushed and shapeless bodies and were crying over them, and sobbing and lamenting, and a priest was kneeling there with his hands crossed upon his breast praying; and crowds and crowds of pitying friends were massed about them, reverently uncovered, with their bare heads bowed, and many with the tears running down – a scene which Satan paid no attention to until the small noise of the weeping and praying began to annoy him, then he reached out and took the heavy board seat of our swing and brought it down and mashed all those people into the earth just as if they had been flies, and went on talking just the same.

An angel, and kill a priest! An angel who did not know how to do wrong, and yet destroys in cold blood hundreds of helpless poor men and women who had never done him any harm! It made us sick to see that awful deed, and to think that none of those poor creatures was prepared except the priest, for none of them had ever heard a mass or seen a church. And we were witnesses; we had seen

L

these murders done and it was our duty to tell, and let the law take
its course.

But he went on talking right along, and worked his enchantments
upon us again with that fatal music of his voice.[33]

In short, God and the devil are indistinguishable.

Others writers specifically call the Author of our being an
ironist and the world an ironical show. Adrian Harley in Meredith's *Ordeal of Richard Feverel* 'accepts humanity as . . . a supreme
ironic procession with laughter of the Gods in the background'.[34]
When he first read *Don Quixote*, Heine tells us, he 'was a child and
did not know the irony with which the Lord has permeated the
world, and which the great poets have reflected in their published
microcosms',[35] Later he could say:

> Alas, the irony of God weighs heavily upon me. The great Author
> of the universe, the Aristophanes of heaven, wished to show me –
> the little, earthly, so-called German Aristophanes – as glaringly as
> possible what feeble little jests my most bitter sarcasms were in
> comparison with His own, and how inferior I was to Him in humour
> and in giant wit.[36]

Hardy's works postulated sometimes ironical deities sporting
with mortals and sometimes a blind indifferent It mechanically
turning 'the handle of this idle show' we figure in. In the *Dynasts*,
writing of George III's madness, he says:

> The tears that lie about this plightful scene
> Of heavy travail in a suffering soul,
> Mocked with the forms and feints of royalty
> While scarified by briery Circumstance,
> Might drive Compassion past her patiency
> To hold that some mean, monstrous ironist
> Had built this mistimed fabric of the Spheres
> To watch the throbbings of its captive lives,
> (The which may Truth forfend), and not thy said
> Unmaliced, unimpassioned, nescient will![37]

We do not need to imagine either a malignant or an indifferent
deity in order to see the world as in an ironic predicament. It is
only a matter of confronting our life and all its rational and pur-

poseful actions with some statement of ultimate purposelessness. We might for example, as in *The Magic Mountain*, equate life and death by seeing them only in terms of organic chemistry.[38] Or we might see the organic as a disease of the inorganic, or self-conscious life as a disease of life at the instinctive level, or confront the whole of biological existence with the inconceivably vaster extent, in both time and space, of the inorganic, so that the former appears as a freakish short-lived eruption, a tiny flash, so to speak, in the cosmic dark, or as Lucky says:

> in the great cold the great dark the air and the earth abode of stones in the great cold alas alas in the year of their Lord six hundred and something the air the earth the sea the earth abode of stones in the great deeps the great cold on sea on land and in the air I resume for reasons unknown in spite of the tennis the facts are there but time will tell . . .[39]

5 · Ironies of Inevitable Ignorance

In the field of human knowledge there is wide scope for general irony since there is an opposition, not always recognized, between the obstacles to knowledge and the impulse, desire, and self-imposed obligation to know. I am not saying that our limited knowledge and understanding, whether of ourselves or of the world at large, is ironic in itself any more than the limited understanding of a bird is ironic. It becomes ironic, however, when we recognize in what various ways our knowledge and understanding is necessarily limited and at the same time feel that it ought not to be limited, that we ought to know everything.

To Bacon and even to Marlowe's Faustus knowledge was for use, 'a rich storehouse, for the glory of the Creator, and the relief of man's estate' (*Advancement of Learning*). And yet both Marlowe and Bacon were strongly attracted by the concept of knowledge as a good in itself, the one speaking of our souls as

Still climbing after knowledge infinite,

and the other saying that 'all knowledge and wonder (which is the seed of knowledge) is an impression of pleasure in itself', and that the inquiry, knowledge, and belief of truth 'is the sovereign good of human nature'. In this century the sentiment that, irrespective of use, everything should be known and nothing forgotten may be regarded as generally established. But we do not stop there for we think it in some way reprehensible that everything should not be known. And thinking this we are in an ironic predicament since everything cannot be known.

The science of astronomy, for example, is limited in its observations by the velocity of light: and it is in fact the very success of astronomical research that has brought its limiting factors into such clear relief. The layman, whose interests are more practical than theoretical, can scarcely fail to see an irony in the fact that our knowledge of many heavenly systems can never be less than millions of years out of date, especially if, as he is told is statistically probable, some of these systems contain planets inhabited by rational beings, for the rationality implies a possibility of communication but the time-factor an impossibility.

Again, having in mind our modern dedication to the discovery of objective and certain truth, it would be ironic if our brains after all were not adapted to such a purpose but instead constitutionally and unalterably oriented towards knowledge for action. This is what I understand Bronowski to be saying in his article 'The Machinery of Nature':

> It is not possible for the brain to arrive at *certain* knowledge. All those formal systems, in mathematics and physics and the philosophy of science, which claim to give foundations for certain truth are surely mistaken . . . No knowledge can be certain that continues to expand with us as we live inside the growing flesh of our experience . . . In this nexus, we cannot reach certainty because it is not there to be reached . . . and the certain answers ironically are the wrong answers. Certainty is a demand that is made by philosophers who contemplate the world from outside; and scientific knowledge is knowledge for action, not contemplation.[40]

There would be little point in dwelling upon some of the necessary limitations to human omniscience, those which the ironists themselves have not thought striking enough to exploit. There are, I suppose, very few who see Heisenberg's Principle of

Indeterminacy as ironic though there is surely irony in the fact that the action of observing renders the object to be observed unobservable. Yet it is precisely this impasse that confronts the mole-like creature of Kafka's *The Burrow*. From time to time the owner and maker of the burrow is driven to emerge from his stronghold into the open air. On these occasions one of his activities is to watch over the concealed entrance to see if any potential enemies come sniffing about. None do. But is this precisely because he is *not* in his burrow? Is it because his enemies know they are being watched? In short, though he can watch the outside of the entrance only from the outside, he cannot effectively watch the outside because he is outside watching it.

There is another field which, like Heisenberg's, involves probability theory, namely the field of social statistics, and here the ironic *has* been directly perceived. One young man of eighteen gets married because he wants to, another because his future wife wants to, and a third because his future father-in-law insists. But ninety young men of eighteen in every ten thousand get married each year because that is what the law of statistical averages demands. In other words, a reliable impersonal law is derived from, yet seems to govern, personal and chance events. Musil's hero points out the irony of this:

> 'It would be very important to me personally to know whether what is behind this is laws of collectivity or whether it is simply that by some irony of nature particularity arises out of the fact that nothing in particular happens and the highest meaning turns out to be something that can be got at by taking the average of what is most profoundly senseless.'

He then applies it very strikingly to morality:

> 'Let us therefore assume too that a certain quantity of ideas is swirling about in the present time. It produces some most probable average value. This shifts very slowly and automatically, and that is what we call progress or the historical situation. But what is most important is that our personal, individual motion doesn't matter in the least in all this. We may think and act to the right or to the left, high or low, in a new way or an old way, wildly or with circum-

spection: it is of no consequence at all to the average value. And to
God and the universe *that's* all that matters – *we* don't count!'[41]

More familiar ground for ironists is the belief that we can never
have complete authentic knowledge of other selves. This was a
favourite theme of Pirandello's and later was to be one of the
themes of *The Cocktail Party*:

> No . . . it isn't that I *want* to be alone,
> But that everyone's alone – or so it seems to me.
> They make noises, and think they are talking to each other;
> They make faces, and think they understand each other.
>
> And then I found we were only strangers
> And that there had been neither giving nor taking
> But that we had merely made use of each other
> Each for his purpose. That's horrible. Can we only love
> Something created by our own imagination?
> Are we all in fact unloving and unlovable?
> Then one *is* alone, . . .
>
>   You were saying just now
> That you never knew Celia. We none of us did.
> What you've been living on is an image of Celia
> Which you made for yourself, to meet your own needs.[42]

The play says clearly enough that this is the inevitable predicament of all but saints. The position is related to *bovarysme*, as I have
discussed it, in which the victim superimposes a fiction created by
his needs not upon others but upon himself. 'Know thyself' may
be, as Carlyle thought, an impossible precept; Forster's 'only
connect' may be another. Either, in combination with the
modern commandment 'Thou shalt not be ignorant', becomes
potentially ironic.

Since I have used the phrase 'authentic knowledge' I should say
something of the irony implicit in the variety of opposed views
as to which kind of knowledge is authentic. These oppositions are
familiar enough; we may begin with that expressed by Mark
Rampion in *Point Counter Point*:

After all, the only truth that can be of any interest to us, or that we can know, is a human truth. And to discover that, you must look for it with the whole being, not with a specialized part of it. What the scientists are trying to get at is non-human truth . . . By torturing their brains they can get a faint notion of the universe as it would seem if looked at through non-human eyes . . . it's utterly irrelevant to ordinary human living. Our truth, the relevant human truth, is something you discover by living – living completely, with the whole man.[43]

The opposition Musil presents is a similar one but not the same:

So there are in reality two outlooks, which not only conflict with each other but – what is worse – usually exist side by side, without exchanging a word except to assure each other that they are both desirable, each in its place. The one contents itself with being precise, and sticks to facts; the other does not content itself with that, but always looks at the Whole and draws its knowledge from what are called great and eternal verities. Thereby the one gains in success, and the other in scope and dignity. It is clear that a pessimist might also say the results of the one are worthless and those of the other not true. For where will it get one, on the Day of Judgment, when mankind's works are weighed in the balance, to come forward with three treatises on formic acid – or thirty, for that matter? On the other hand, what can one know about the Day of Judgment if one does not even know what may have come of formic acid by then?

It was between the two poles of this Neither–Nor that evolution was swinging to and fro when it was a bit more than eighteen and not yet twenty centuries since humanity was first informed that such a spiritual court would be held at the end of the world.[44]

Musil's dates are quite accurate; it was in the Romantic period that Goethe said:

> Grau, teurer Freund, ist alle Theorie
> Und grün des Lebens goldner Baum.

and Keats, 'I have never been able to perceive how anything can be known for truth by consecutive reasoning.' Since then, along-side the spectacular successes of objective scientific thinking, there has been a strong and persistent belief that the only knowledge that is authentic is that immediately derived from personal experience, and even that personal experience itself is the only authentic knowledge. Such beliefs have as their particular enemy all abstract thinking and theoretical knowledge, all systems of thought, for a system implies abstracting and selecting, making a simplified, generalized, and static picture of a world which is complex, dynamic, and differentiated. In so far as knowledge is a kind of translation of the world into words, the old saying holds true, *traduttori traditori*. In so far as knowledge is a kind of map of the world, it shares the defects of all maps; it is there to 'learn you facts' but in order to do so it is obliged to show Indiana as pink. 'Philosophers,' Musil says, 'are violent and aggressive persons who, having no army at their disposal, bring the world into subjection to themselves by means of locking it up in a system.' And Kierkegaard:

> The humorist can never really be a systematiser because he looks upon every philosophical system as a renewed attempt to explode the world with a syllogism . . . Whereas he himself has eyes for the incommensurable, which the philosopher can never weigh and consequently despises. He lives a complete life, and so feels how much is always lost even when he has expressed himself most happily (hence his dislike of writing). The systematiser believes that he can say everything, and that anything that cannot be expressed is false and unimportant.[45]

So that to form systems, to think in abstracts, is to take a one-sided view and so to put oneself in an ironic position.

On the other hand, it is no less one-sided or ironic not to form systems. We should attend to both parts of Friedrich Schlegel's statement that it is 'as fatal for the mind to have a system as not to have one'. What might be gained in immediacy and authenticity by not having a system would be offset by incoherence. In any case it is questionable whether one can get rid of organized thinking without getting rid of thought, whether the mind, at least in its verbal processes and perhaps even in its sense-perception is capable of not selecting and abstracting and thereby turning experience into meaning.

In the arts, however, attempts have been made to get rid of consecutive and relational thinking and even of the mind alto-gether – 'No thoughts but in things' was William Carlos Williams' slogan – and utterly meaningless works of art have perhaps emerged from time to time. Action-painting, 'happenings', computer poetry, and random composition all by-pass the con-scious mind of the artist almost as if it were a mistake on nature's part to have gone in for conscious minds. According to John Cage, 'Those involved with the composition of experimental music find ways and means to remove themselves from the activities of the sounds they make.'[46] But this concern on the part of the artist with the spontaneous, the immediate, the con-crete, the individual, and the unique is not, as has been assumed, a return to a less sophisticated, less intellectual, and therefore, from a romantic viewpoint, a more authentic way of life but is rather the product of a greater degree of sophistication, based on what it reacts against. One cannot value the individual, or have a taste for *objets trouvés*, or praise 'the sanctity of the unique object' unless one has already grown weary of the typical, the work of art, and the relational.

The feeling that nothing must remain unknown or be for-gotten has several other ironic implications. One very noticeable effect of the rapid accumulation of knowledge since the seven-teenth century is the widening gap between what is known col-lectively and what any one person knows. Today Western man may pride himself, by way of the *Readers' Digest*, on all that is known but he cannot say that anyone knows it; the more that is known the less in proportion any individual knows and the less any two people know in common. The larger the number of books published the smaller the number read and remembered by the same people, so that increasing knowledge is offset by decreasing communication; in the expanding universe of know-ledge scholars recede and diverge at ever increasing speeds; and what it all comes to is that collective knowledge entails collective ignorance.

The world has done its best to cope with such a predicament by giving a certain compensatory status to specialists and making it a breach of taste to expect them to be informed outside their specialism. But nothing has yet been done to relieve the plight of the non-specialist.

The concepts of knowledge as a good in itself and of ignorance as an evil in itself have led to an egalitarianism of facts and consequently to an inability to say that any piece of information is useless or irrelevant. Given adequate facilities, and this should be no problem in the coming electronic age, the librarian can indulge himself in the principle of universal holdings, making available to the sociologist in Winnipeg the annual reports, since its inception, of the Salisbury (Rhodesia) Madrigal Society. Archivists will be able to fulfil their obligation to preserve all the documents that the future historian will want, which is to say a complete record of the past, which is to say more than he and all his colleagues could handle. I do not suppose anyone to be unaware of such states of affairs. The Library of Congress probably has a whole shelf of material deploring the superfluity of documentation.

General Irony, as I have presented it, must be regarded as an altogether wider concept than the ironies we know as Cosmic Irony and World Irony though these are among its sub-species and deserve a certain pre-eminence on account of their emotional power. What can be more ironic than the situation of man with his high moral ideas of love and justice confronted by his maker, whether world or God, who is not conspicuous for either? Things might be worse of course, but then they would be less ironic. This situation man is in *vis-à-vis* God or the universe is not, however, his only general predicament. The incompatibilities between present proposals and future disposals, between the individual and society, between reason and instinct, contemplation and action, the conscious and the unconscious, between the desire for omniscience and the impossibility of attaining it, these and others like them are equally material for General Irony.

VII

ROMANTIC IRONY

I · *The Ironies of Art*

The ironies of art as I shall present them, the fundamental and irremediable contradictions that emerge from a consideration of the place and nature of art, could have formed an additional section in the previous chapter. But since they form part of the raw material, so to speak, of Romantic Irony, it is better that they should appear in this chapter.

The ironies of art are General Irony situations. Romantic Irony is a way of dealing ironically with General Irony situations, but principally with the ironic contradictions of art; more precisely, Romantic Irony is the expression of an ironical attitude adopted as a means of recognizing and transcending, but still preserving these contradictions. The theory of Romantic Irony is the theory that this is the only course open to the modern artist. For Schlegel, René Wellek says, irony is the 'recognition of the fact that the world in its essence is paradoxical and that an ambivalent attitude alone can grasp its contradictory totality'.[1] Schlegel himself says, 'Paradox is the *conditio sine qua non* of irony, its soul, its source, and its principle,' and 'Ironie ist Pflicht'[2] – one must be ironical. Since Romantic Irony involves ironical attitudes what I say about it here will perforce anticipate in part and in part need to be supplemented by the following chapter on Irony and the Ironist.

Art, like everything else, can be seen as ironic if it can be seen as involving a juxtaposition of incompatible elements. We are not likely so to see it if we take it for granted and do not reflect upon its nature, or if we see it only as a means to some further end, that is, if we simply decorate pots and walls with flowers and legendary figures, make songs to sing, carve deities for a temple, or tell stories of heroes and lovers. But when the work of art, and I have in mind only representative art, when the painted flower, the carved figure, the passionate utterance, or the related action is thought of, rightly or wrongly, as having some kind of ontological status, not simply as pigment, stone, or words but as flower, man, passion, or event, then we have set up a duality of life and art, a 'real world' and a looking-glass world. And having done this, contradictions, paradoxes, and ambiguities can begin to appear.

To begin with, the work of art itself now exists at two levels. Within the 'real world' Constable's Hay Wain is a painting, a flat coloured object hanging on a wall. At the imaginative level, however, it is not a picture but rather in some sense what it represents. 'Est-elle en marbre, ou non, la Vénus de Milo?' is not so easy a question as Verlaine seems to have thought. A lyric poem, if we take it at the level of 'reality' is a 'verbal contraption' as Auden puts it. It is a work designed with careful attention to form, rhythm, and diction, and it could perhaps not have been written at all without certain precedents in rhyme-scheme, rhetoric, and *topos*. It may be a translation, or the manuscript may reveal extensive and radical revision. But within the imaginative world the poem takes us to we hear a spontaneous and passionate outburst of feeling:

> O never say that I was false of heart
>   Though absence seem'd my flame to qualify!
> As easy might I from myself depart,
>   As from my soul, which in thy breast doth lie.

This double existence of a work of art can be seen as ironic when one recognizes that the mood or attitude of the artist as maker may be incompatible with the mood of the work he has made, particularly if one has been influenced by theories of art as self-expression. The well-known passage from *Tonio Kröger* is relevant here:

> Nobody but a beginner imagines that he who creates must feel. Every real and genuine artist smiles at such naïve blunders as that. A melancholy enough smile, perhaps, but still a smile. For what an artist talks about is never the main point; it is the raw material, in and for itself indifferent, out of which, with bland and serene mastery, he creates the work of art. If you care too much about what you have to say, if your heart is too much in it, you can be pretty sure of making

a mess. You get pathetic, you wax sentimental; something dull and doddering, without roots or outlines, with no sense of humour – something tiresome and banal grows under your hand, and you get nothing out of it but apathy in your audience and disappointment and misery in yourself. For so it is, Lisabeta; feeling, warm, heartfelt feeling, is always banal and futile; only the irritations and icy ecstasies of the artist's corrupted nervous system are artistic. The artist must be unhuman, extra-human; he must stand in a queer aloof relationship to our humanity; only so is he in a position, I ought to say only so would he be tempted, to represent it, to present it, to portray it to good effect. The very gift of style of form and expression, is nothing else than this cool and fastidious attitude towards humanity; you might say there has to be this impoverishment and devastation as a preliminary condition. For sound natural feeling, say what you like, has no taste. It is all up with the artist as soon as he becomes a man and begins to feel.[3]

With this we might compare Goethe's view as presented by Mme de Staël:

> Goethe now maintains that an author must be calm even when he is creating an impassioned work, and that an artist should retain his composure in order to affect his readers' imagination the more vigorously.[4]

There is a passage in E. T. A. Hoffmann's *The Sandman* which is also relevant. In this story the author of an autobiographical poem alternates between the serenity of the poet as composer and the horror induced by the poem itself:

> Eventually he [Nathanael] made a poem out of his dark foreboding that Coppelius would destroy his happiness in love. He portrayed himself and Klara as bound in true love but plagued by a black hand that thrust itself between them and snatched away their joy. In the end, when they were already at the altar, the abominable Coppelius appeared and touched Klara's lovely eyes, which sprang into Nathanael's breast, searing him like blood-red sparks. Coppelius seized hold of him and flung him into a circle of flames that spun round and round with the speed and noise of a whirlwind and dragged him away. There was a roaring sound like a hurricane

whipping up the waves of the sea so that they reared up in revolt like black giants with heads of white foam. But through this fierce roaring he heard Klara's voice: 'Can't you see me? Coppelius has tricked you. Those weren't my eyes that burnt into your breast, they were red-hot drops of your own heart's blood. I still have my eyes – just look at me!' Nathanael thought: 'That is Klara, I am hers for ever.' Then it was as though this thought had taken a grip upon the circle of flame, which came to a stop, while the roaring sound died away in the black abyss. Nathanael gazed into Klara's eyes; but it was death that looked at him with Klara's friendly eyes.

While Nathanael was composing this poem he was very calm and serene; he worked and polished each line, and since he had assumed the yoke of metre he did not rest until the whole poem was flawless and euphonious. But when at last he had finished and read it aloud to himself, he was seized with horror and cried out: 'Whose hideous voice is that?' Soon, however, the whole thing once more seemed nothing but a very successful poem, and he felt convinced that Klara's cold temperament would be set afire by it; though he had no very clear idea why Klara should be set afire or what purpose would be served by frightening her with these horrifying visions which predicted a terrible fate and the destruction of their love.[5]

But in fact when Nathanael reads the work to Klara, it is he who is carried away by his own poem while she is more moved by his distress than by what she sees as only a 'senseless insane fairy tale'. The story itself, of which Nathanael's poem is a condensed version, alternates in a similar way between the objective and subjective, and seems to pose the question whether the objective and critical is more real or less real than the subjective and creative. It does this by constantly seeing objective critical and sensible attitudes as in essence spiritual death, and subjective and creative attitudes as in essence demonic possession or insanity. A possible interpretation of this story as a whole is that it presents an Irony of Dilemma. One is faced with the 'impossible' alternatives of being either unimaginative, which means being spiritually dead, or imaginative, which means being insane. One can also read this story, and *Tonio Kröger* too, in the light of one of Schlegel's Notebook fragments which I paraphrase thus: 'Complete submergence in either feeling [*Sentimentalität*] or inventiveness [*Fantasie*] may lead to Romanticism of a sort, but only with the highest degree of both will there be created that tension of opposites which is absolute Romanticism or Romantic Irony.'6 But this is to digress.

The fact that a work of art has a double existence, both inside and outside the ordinary world is not the only potential irony of art, though it is perhaps the most important. There is also irony in the fact that art, like any other attempt to verbalize reality, must always fall short of its aim. One can say, in words or any other medium, only what things are *like*, and that only up to a point; one cannot do more. This is the theme, as I understand it, of the following poem of Elder Olson's:

> *Prologue to His Book*
> – To say
> In words the way
> The wave, the cloud –
> To read aloud
> The last wings in the late air,
> Interpret the faint character
> Of the still flower;
> Tell
> What mute leaves spell;
> Pronounce the dew,
> The hushed scent, the silent hue;
> To speak, to say
> With speech, This way,
> See, See, It was this way
> The hills, the wind –
> To say, Grief was as if . . .
> To say, And love . . . love . . . To say,
> Yes, Yes, It was like this,
> This way –7

There is potential for irony in the very nature of art if we regard it as aiming both at the particular and the general, as both an activity and the result of an activity, as the product both of conscious planning and of unconscious spontaneous invention, or as both a communication and the thing communicated, that is, as meaningful in its relation to the ordinary world and also as pure meaningless existence in itself:

> A poem should not mean
> But be.

There is also room enough for irony in the relationships between the artist and his work, and between the artist and society. Of these ironies, Thomas Mann's *Tonio Kröger* and *Doctor Faustus* give us more than a glimpse. There we find, for example, the idea that the artist must be a spiritual cripple, dehumanized, an *âme damnée*, even satanic, so that his art shall be healthy and human or at least so that it can celebrate the life the artist has to forgo. But conversely, the artist can maintain or restore his own healthy attitudes by writing a 'sick' book. This was so with Goethe's *Werther*. By presenting a romantic hero's suicide, Goethe freed himself from suicide and madness: 'I felt as one feels after a general confession, happy and free and justified in entering upon a new life.' But the wave of suicides inspired in would-be romantic heroes by *Werther* moved Goethe to preface the second edition with a short poem containing the line:

> Be a man; don't follow the track I took.

2 · *Proto-Romantic Irony*

The sophisticated or self-conscious artist who is aware of the contradictions implicit in the double nature of art will sometimes bring into his work at the imaginative level some aspects of its existence at the 'ordinary world' level as a work that is being composed, and composed to be seen, performed, or read. That is to say he will break into the artistic illusion with a reminder to his public (not necessarily an explicit one) that what they have before them is only a painting, a play, or a novel and not the reality it purports to be. This sort of thing has been called Romantic Irony, but it is only one aspect of it and it might be useful to distinguish it by a different name. The term 'proto-Romantic Irony' is intended also to suggest an historical development. The so-called destruction of artistic illusion or the entrance of an author into his work even when it is done ironically is only a step in the direction of Romantic Irony, but the artistic attitude and awareness that makes such a step possible is also a prerequisite of Romantic Irony.

The ways in which this step has been taken range from slight and temporary conflations of the two levels to such elaborate involvements of the author and the reader in the work which the one is writing and the other reading that the result is a book about a book, a fictional conducted tour through a work of fiction. A surprisingly large number of notable authors may be found in the ranks of those who have made play with the double level of art: they include Aristophanes, Chaucer, Shakespeare, Cervantes, Calderon, Corneille, Molière, Scarron, Gay, Marivaux, Fielding, Sterne, Sheridan, Diderot, Tieck, Brentano, Jane Austen, Byron, Heine, Thackeray, Machado da Assis, Mark Twain, Pirandello, Unamuno, Gide, Aldous Huxley, Mann, Waugh, Musil, Beckett, Anouilh.

In *The Frogs* Aristophanes presents Dionysus and Xanthias as being aware of their roles and of the conventional beginning of a comedy. The play opens (Gilbert Murray's translation):

In the background are two houses, that of HERACLES *and that of* PLUTO. *Enter* DIONYSUS, *disguised as* HERACLES, *with lion-skin and club, but with the high boots of tragedy and a tunic of saffron silk. He is followed by* XANTHIAS, *seated on a donkey and carrying an immense bale of luggage on a porter's pole. They advance for a while in silence.*

XANTHIAS (*looking round at his burden with a groan*):
  Sir, shall I say one of the regular things
  That people in a theatre always laugh at?
DIONYSUS: Say what you like, except 'I'm overloaded.'
  But mind, not that. That's simply wormwood to me.
XANTHIAS (*disappointed*): Not anything funny?
DIONYSUS: Not 'Oh, my poor blisters!'
XANTHIAS: Suppose I made the great joke?
DIONYSUS: Why, by all means.
  Don't be afraid. Only, for mercy's sake,
  Don't . . .

M

XANTHIAS: Don't do what?
DIONYSUS: Don't shift your luggage pole
  Across, and say, 'I want to blow my nose.'
XANTHIAS (*greatly disappointed*):
  Nor that I've got such a weight upon my back
  That unless some one helps me quickly I shall sneeze?
DIONYSUS: Oh, please, no. Keep it till I need emetics.
XANTHIAS: Then what's the good of carrying all this lumber
  If I mayn't make one single good old wheeze
  Like Phrynichus, Amipsias, and Lycis?
DIONYSUS: Ah no; don't make them – When I sit down there
  (*Pointing to the auditorium.*)
  And hear some of those choice products, I go home
  A twelvemonth older.
XANTHIAS (*to himself*):
  Oh, my poor old neck:
  Blistered all round, and mustn't say it's blistered,
  Because that's funny![8]

Though they have temporarily stepped out of the play on one level of illusion they only *seem* to have stepped out of the play into real life. Stepping out of the play is still an action in the play; the characters are still speaking lines written for them. What Aristophanes has done is to superimpose one level of illusion upon another. Something similar happens when a painter paints a life-sized fly on a three-quarter-size portrait. At first we may be deceived into thinking that a fly has settled on the painting: what has really happened is that the action of painting the fly has turned a portrait into the painting of a portrait. Once an artist has made a breakthrough of this kind it becomes possible to extend the series. In an Hanover gallery there is a seventeenth-century painting of a studio wall on which is stuck with sealing-wax an engraving of a painter in a studio painting a picture. The literary equivalent is the story in which a man tells a story in which a man tells a story, and so on *ad infinitum*. In *Point Counter Point*, Chapter XXII has the title, 'From Philip Quarles's Notebook'. Quarles, one of Huxley's characters, breaks into the novel to talk in the first person about his projected novel in which the characters and the technique will resemble those of *Point Counter Point*. Quarles too will:

> put a novelist into the novel. He justifies aesthetic generalizations, which may be interesting – at least to me. He also justifies experiment. Specimens of his work may illustrate other possible or impossible ways of telling a story. And if you have him telling parts of the same story as you are, you can make a variation on the theme. But why draw the line at one novelist inside your novel? Why not a second inside his? And a third inside the novel of the second? And so on to infinity, like those advertisements of Quaker Oats where there's a quaker holding a box of oats, on which is a picture of another quaker holding another box of oats, on which, etc., etc. At about the tenth remove you might have a novelist telling your story in algebraic symbols or in terms of variations in blood-pressure, pulse, secretion of ductless glands and reaction times.[9]

The caricaturist Steinberg has made several drawings of men in the process of drawing themselves or each other, or rather not just drawing each other but creating each other, for each has drawn the pen and the arm that is engaged in bringing him into existence as a man and as a drawing of a man (see overleaf).

The Steinberg reproduced here exemplifies several ironies. To begin with, there is an irony similar to that in *Frankenstein*; the smaller figure is dismayed, it seems, at the larger baleful figure he has himself, both deliberately and accidentally, brought into existence. Beyond this are the ironies resulting from the incompatibilities between the level of art as art and the level of art as what it represents. Normally we accept without question a necessarily static picture of something in action – a galloping horse in a picture does not seem to be suspended motionless in the air, it seems to be galloping – and at the representational level Steinberg's drawing has a temporal aspect; we are invited to see the pen as moving. But as soon as we try to imagine this more precisely a set of absurdities immediately confronts us. A man may draw a picture of a man drawing himself, but it is not the picture of an action for if we imagine the pen moving we have to imagine the picture moving and changing. Nor can we imagine how such a picture could have begun. A man may draw a picture of himself

(from *The New World* by Saul Steinberg)

but he cannot draw himself. Moreover, the plane on which the drawing exists is also, absurdly, the space in which the man exists. Again, the two figures in this illustration are both separate and continuous.

On the other hand, Steinberg's drawing, in some respects, merely brings into the open the general irony of the twofold existence of all representational art. For as long as the artist's imagination and skill persuade us that his work is, in some sense, what it represents this irony is latently there. But a moment's reflection tells us that art is full of absurdities disguised, for the most part, as conventions: the motionless galloping horse, the absurdly well-made 'well-made' play, the 'happenings' that by an altogether too unconvincing coincidence happen to happen in a theatre. Because art is mimesis and not a reproduction of life it has possibilities denied to life and these include, as not only Steinberg shows us, the representation of the impossible. The artist who forces us to see that his drawings are only drawings forces us, by the same token, to see that a drawing of the irrational is a drawing and not an irrationality, that art is more powerful than logical absurdity. To move from the rational to the irrational within art is a small step compared to the leap already taken from life to art. It is therefore misleading to say of such things as Beckett's reference to the audience in *Waiting for Godot*, that the dramatic illusion is thereby destroyed. What happens is that one level of the play's illusion is taken over by another but all within the play. The fact that we are in the theatre and not in the world outside, that we are looking at pictures and not at men, is what makes it all but impossible to destroy illusion.

There are countless examples in literature of the world of actuality being made to break into the imaginative world. Chaucer makes the Man of Law disparage Chaucer's poetic skill. Shakespeare makes the legendary Theseus say, 'I never may believe these antique fables', or makes his actors refer to acting: 'O Jesu,' says Mrs Quickly of Falstaff's acting the King, 'he doth it as like one of these harlotry players as ever I see!' Scarron, and many subsequent authors, conflate the time-scheme of their novels with the time-scheme of composition: 'The carter accepted her offer, and while his beasts were feeding, the author rested for a while and began to wonder what he would say in the second chapter.'[10] Machado da Assis, and many earlier authors, introduce the reader into the work: 'The last chapter left me so sad that I had half a mind not to write this one, but to rest a while, to purge my spirit of the melancholy that had saturated it, and to continue a little later. But no, perhaps you are pressed for time.'[11] Molière, and many subsequent dramatists, make a play out of an interrupted rehearsal of a play as in the *Impromptu de Versailles*.

Cervantes was perhaps the first writer of prose fiction who exhibited a strong critical consciousness of himself as an author and of his story as a story. There are several instances of this. Don Quixote's library contains one of Cervantes' works which the curate praises – with moderation; in Chapter IX the story breaks off and cannot continue until Cervantes has found the rest of the story in an arabic manuscript. In the beginning of Part II Don Quixote himself is told that the author is diligently looking for the manuscript of Part II. Later in Part II we meet a duke and duchess who have read Part I (Thomas Mann discusses this aspect of *Don Quixote* in his essay *Voyage with Don Quixote*). Such things ought not to be regarded as mere tricks, literary equivalents of the *trompe-l'oeil*. They have an entirely appropriate place in a work whose irony is directed against naïve romances and those who swallow them whole. Since Don Quixote suffers from the delusion that he is in a romance world and since he collides over and over again with the 'real world', it is proper that the reader whom Cervantes draws into the world of his novel should likewise be shocked out of it into the realization that this 'real world' is itself only fiction.

It is no coincidence that in the following two hundred years many novelists and dramatists followed Cervantes in writing works that shift amusingly or disconcertingly from one imaginative level to another, seemingly more realistic, one. In the age of reason and scepticism writers tended to be embarrassed and even confused by the idea of imaginative creation. Diderot could say, 'Il y a dans la poésie toujours un peu de mensonge. L'esprit philosophique nous habitue à le discerner: et adieu l'illusion et l'effet.'[12] Dr Johnson could say of *Lycidas*, 'Where there is leisure for fiction there is little grief.' The extravagances of the romances gave way to the verisimilitude of novels, which frequently claimed to be true stories or to be copied from manuscripts. And frequently the self-conscious novelist entered his novel to comment upon his characters or justify his way of writing. (An article by Wayne Booth[13] presents some very entertaining examples of intrusive authors up to the time of *Tristram Shandy*.) One explanation of this may be that the world of men and books, the social contact between the writer and the reader of a work, had come to be felt as more 'authentic' than the imaginative world created by the work. The Romantic period brought about a change, but not a reversal in favour of the work. What tended to impress the pre-Romantics and the Romantics was the superior reality and power of the creative mind over anything it might create. We find Shelley saying:

> The mind in creation is as a fading coal, which some invisible influence, like an inconstant wind, awakens to transitory brightness . . . but when composition begins, inspiration is already on the decline, and the most glorious poetry that has ever been communicated to the world is probably a feeble shadow of the original conceptions of the poet.[14]

There is obviously matter for irony in the idea that what is permanent, the created work, is necessarily less authentic or valuable than the transitory moments of creation. Shelley, however, seems rather more gratified than otherwise with this state of affairs. His sense of the ironic, fitful at best, did not reveal to him the potential irony in this predicament the poets were in. More alert were his contemporaries in Germany, as we shall see. Maurice Denhof, in an essay on Romantic Irony, draws attention to the consequences for literature of the decomposition of the artistic ego:

> One part of this ego regards not only life but also art itself as a game. Questioning all aesthetic concepts hitherto recognized, imbued with a profound scepticism as to the true nature of art, the romantic author concerned himself much less with the creation of lasting works of art than with the pursuit of speculative possibilities, ephemeral or not, which this new way of looking at art could give rise to. Curiosity carried him away; the conception of the work of art not as an end

but as a means resulted in a contempt for form such that the creation of harmonious works found itself inevitably thwarted.[15]

The tradition of self-conscious literature that received its impetus in *Don Quixote* culminated in two eighteenth-century pieces of fiction, the anti-autobiography *Tristram Shandy* (1760-7) and the anti-novel *Jacques le fataliste* (1773), and in three plays by Ludwig Tieck (1797-9) of which there is a not very sympathetic account in Thompson's *Dry Mock*. All of them in many different ways use their ostensible matter very largely as a pretext for bringing into their work both author and reader (or spectators) and for discussing the progress, the merits and even the nature of their novel or play. After these works there was no further progress in this direction until the more radical anti-literature of the twentieth century.

I do not propose to say much about *Tristram Shandy*. It is sufficiently familiar to English readers and Sterne's manner has been frequently discussed by the critics. Sterne does the most surprising things by way of giving his book an authorial or compositional dimension: Tristram Shandy tells us, for example, that the events he has been relating continue outside the book while he is digressing; that he was unable to write his preface before Chapter XX of Book III (where it appears) and managed to write it then only because all his characters were busy elsewhere or asleep; that his autobiography can never be finished because he is living 364 times faster than he can write; and that he wrote Chapter XXIV of Book IV but tore it out because it would have put the rest of the book to shame. At one point he sends a reader back to re-read a passage she read too carelessly; at another he calls in the assistance of a critic to manage a difficult bit of narration while he himself goes on with something easier. He takes account of the time it takes to read the book, the time for the action read about to transpire, the time taken by incidents mentioned in digressions within this action, and of the difference between clock-time and psychological duration. The *life* of Tristram Shandy, apart from half a dozen incidents and a brief account of his travels is not told at all. The book consists almost entirely of digressions and digressions from digressions. Chronological sequence almost disappears, to be replaced by psychological simultaneity; that is to say, every-thing of the past is simultaneously 'present' in the mind and is re-called not in chronological sequence but by association.

Diderot, as becomes a *philosophe*, has more of an eye for the contradictions that arise when one is aware of a story on its two levels. *Jacques le fataliste et son maître* begins very oddly:

> How had they met? By chance, as everyone does. What were their names? What business is it of yours? Where did they come from? From the place nearest them. Where were they going? Does one know where one is going? What were they saying?[16]

The story begins, in short, before it begins. An inquisitive reader and an uninformative author bandy question and answer on a situation that is so far presented only through their conversation, and the title of the work. Moreover, the answers made by the author involve further contradictions. It is the business of a novel-ist to excite the curiosity of his reader not to rebuke him for it. This author evidently does not know his business. But he does, for in rebuking the fictitious reader he excites the real reader's curios-ity. It is also assumed to be the business of an author ultimately to satisfy the reader's curiosity. But none of these questions except the last is answered; on these points Diderot is as uninformative over three hundred pages as he, or if you insist, his 'author' is in the first four lines. And the reason is that the wrong questions have been asked; it is not going to be that kind of story. Again, in real life, people may be said to meet by chance and it may be none of our business who they are and where they come from; and chance meetings and inquisitive strangers may be represented in fiction. But an author, if he must talk to his reader about his char-acters, ought to talk to him as a reader not as a stranger and about his characters as characters whose meetings and journeys he has planned. To this one can say that perhaps Diderot had not planned his novel and even if he had planned it he had no guarantee that it would stay planned. When the reader again asks, Where were they going? Diderot tells an anecdote of Aesop who, on his way to the baths, was stopped by the patrol:

> 'Where are you going?' 'Where am I going?' replied Aesop. 'I have no idea.' 'You've no idea? Off to prison!' 'Well?' said Aesop. 'Was

I not right to say I did not know? I wanted to go to the baths and here I am going to prison.'[17]

To return to the beginning:

> *What were they saying?* The master was not saying anything, and Jacques was saying that his Captain used to say that everything that happens to us here on earth, good or bad, was written on high.

Here the story begins with Jacques' theory of fatalism which contradicts the author's statement six lines earlier that Jacques met his master 'by chance, as everyone does'. And in making God an author who writes on one level what happens on another Diderot invites us to reflect upon a popular analogy: as the world is to God, so the novel is to the novelist. Two pages later (and elsewhere) Diderot boasts of his omnipotence and freedom of action:

> What is to prevent me from marrying off the master and making him a cuckold? from shipping Jacques to the islands? from taking his master there? from bringing them both back to France in the same ship? How easy it is to make up stories![18]

But shortly afterwards he tells the reader that though he could make the story go in the direction the reader thinks it is going, to do so would be a falsification of the facts:

> You imagine [he says to the reader] that this little armed troop will fall upon Jacques and his master, that there will be a bloody engagement, blows given, pistols fired – and it rests entirely with me to bring all this to pass; but goodbye then to the truth of the story.[19]

The story, it appears, is a true story, an account of something that really happened, having been written on high and only retold by Diderot, or, as he tells us towards the end of the work, only copied by him from a manuscript.[20] And when the story ends, in mid-sentence, Diderot, as editor, continues, and suggests three ways in which it may be concluded: if the reader takes it as a novel he too can become a novelist and finish it to suit himself; if he takes it as a true story he can hunt up Jacques who has been carried off to prison and will be glad to relieve his boredom by telling the reader what happened; if he takes it as a story edited from a manuscript, well, the manuscript breaks off but there are some rather suspect memoirs which offer three alternative endings, one excessively sentimental, one excessively romantic, and one,

> copied from the life of *Tristram Shandy*, unless these conversations between Jacques the fatalist and his master be earlier than that work and Parson Sterne be the plagiarist, which I do not believe.[21]

As well as these contradictions as to the existential status of the work – fiction, true relation, edited manuscript – there is further interplay between author and 'reader'. Sometimes when the reader expresses his curiosity Diderot will say:

> Where? Reader, your curiosity is very disagreeable! What the devil is it to you? If I should say to Pontoise, Saint-Germain, Our Lady of Loretto, or St James of Compostella, would you be any better off? If you insist, I shall tell you that they made their way towards . . . yes; why not? . . . towards an immense castle [an allegory of the world] . . . You are going to say that I am playing myself, and that not knowing what to do with my travellers I launch into allegory, the common resource of barren spirits . . . I will agree with any thing you like provided you do not pester me.[22]

Sometimes Diderot will say he knows no more than the reader and is just as curious. Sometimes he will offer two versions of what happened:

> Some maintain that Jacques [who is going to bed drunk] groped along the walls without being able to find his bed, and that he said, 'Bless me if it's there any more, or if it is, it is written on high that I shan't find it; in either case I must do without,' and that he decided to stretch himself out on the chairs. Others maintain that it was written on high that he caught his feet in the chairs, fell on the floor and stayed there. Of these two versions, you shall choose, tomorrow or the day after, when your mind is refreshed, that which suits you best.[23]

When Jacques and his master separate he offers the reader the choice of going with the one or staying with the other. If you go

with Jacques, goodness knows how long it will be before he returns; if you stay with his master, that will be civil of you, but
how boring it will be! 'You don't yet know that sort of chap.'
After less than a page of staying with the master, Diderot says,
'Well? Have you had enough of him?'[24] In another place Diderot
allows the reader to have his own way; he (Diderot) has interrupted his presentation of Jacques' account of his love-affair and
mentions a certain poet whom he once sent to Pondicherry. The
reader pricks up his ears:

> *Who is this poet?* This poet . . . But you interrupt me, reader, and if
> I interrupt myself at every step what will become of Jacques' love-
> affair? Believe me, let's leave the poet where he is . . . Jacques' host
> and hostess went off . . . *No, no, the story of the poet of Pondicherry.*
> The surgeon approached Jacques' bed . . . *The story of the poet of
> Pondicherry, the story of the poet.* One day a young poet approached me,
> as they do every day . . . But reader, what has this to do with the
> journey of Jacques the fatalist and his master? . . . *The story of the poet
> of Pondicherry.*[25]

The reader wins, and the story is told. When Jacques goes to look
for his master's watch, he finds it in the possession of the first man
he meets. When the master's horse is stolen very shortly afterwards and a man is met leading a horse, the reader is abused for
supposing this will be the stolen horse. This would only happen in
a novel, says Diderot; sooner or later in a novel the horse would
turn up, but this is not a novel. Nevertheless, the stolen horse does
turn up towards the end of this true story. Similarly, though
Diderot, at one point, forgoes describing a surgical operation because the reader thinks it would be in bad taste, at another point a
surgical operation is described without comment.

Diderot also conflates the narrative time-scheme and the time
of composition, saying, for instance, that while Jacques and his
master are resting he will tell the story he has promised us, and
later making Jacques aware that they are near the end of the book.
More interesting is Diderot's deliberate confusion of the narrative
time-scheme of the travels of Jacques and his master with the narrative time-scheme of Jacques' love-affair. Jacques begins to tell
the story of his falling in love (twenty years ago) on page three of

the story of their travels. His account is constantly interrupted by
the author's and the 'reader's' comments, by Jacques' own comments and digressions, by his master's comments and digressions,
by adventures which lead to further digressions, comments, and
stories which are themselves interrupted, so that in the end the
travel-narrative is broken off with Jacques' own love-story incomplete and Jacques himself in prison. The third alternative
ending releases him from prison and brings him and his eighteen-
year-old sweetheart together again, whereupon he marries her.
Presumably this is the conclusion of his love-story as well as of his
travels, but we began with the one taking place twenty years
earlier than the other.

In spite of his authorial intrusions, Diderot does not establish
himself as a presence in his own work nearly as much as Sterne
or even as much as Fielding. He is perhaps too much the enthusi-
ast of ideas, and though critical he is not highly self-conscious. But
he does succeed in exploiting most of the ironic potential of self-
conscious art in his presentation of a series of 'triangular' collisions
between the freely inventing author, the story he invents (which
at the imaginative level is of course presented as reality and completely independent of its maker), and the reader who eagerly
accepts his inventions as reality, 'written on high' and unalterable.
Diderot also established and brought to notice, though perhaps
unintentionally, the sheer power fiction has to hold the reader's
interests against all reminders that stories are only stories: 'de-
stroying the illusion' is not so easy to do as we might have supposed.

3 · Romantic Irony

On 29 April 1964 a Berlin audience, most of whom had lived
through the Hitler régime, saw the first night of Peter Weiss's
play *The Persecution and Assassination of Marat as Performed by the
Inmates of the Asylum of Charenton under the Direction of the Marquis
de Sade*. They found themselves confronted, in this very sensa-
tional play, by a number of theatrical devices and peculiarities
which, though not wholly typical of contemporary theatre, could

not have been entirely unfamiliar: the play within the play, the absence of a conventional resolution, the conflation or confusion of different levels of dramatic illusion, the obscuring of the dividing line between audience and performance, the deliberate ambiguity. Weiss's play exists on at least four levels: the persecution and assassination of Marat in 1793, Sade's play which presents this, the 1808 performance of this play (which includes the actors' impromptu and uncontrolled additions and the 1808 audience's reactions), and Weiss's 1964 play which presents all this together with a number of obvious topical allusions. We could perhaps add a fifth level, the performance of Weiss's play, since in at least one production the actors applauded the audience thus drawing them into the performance.

The most obvious features of the play's formal construction are the deliberate ambiguities and, bound up with this, the deliberate conflations and confusions of the play's several levels. The 1964 audience, for example, are addressed as, and therefore double as the 1808 audience. The play is both historical and topical for both the 1808 audience and the 1964 audience. When the chorus cries out 'Freedom!' is it freedom for 1793, 1808, or 1964? Or for all three, and for every other year in recorded history? The asylum director, Coulmier, who 'likes to adopt a Napoleonic pose' is given a special seat on the stage from which he reacts to the 1793 situation as if the play cast aspersions on the France of Napoleon (as no doubt it does though the 'Herald' denies it and it could not be proved). Politically sensitive conservatives among the 1964 audience were very possibly meant to react to topical allusion in the same spirit as Coulmier does.

The cast of Sade's play, as well as some of the assistants, the musicians, the 'Herald', and the dramatist-producer himself are all either mentally deranged or (cf. *Ward* 7) political prisoners conveniently classed as insane. This being so, their behaviour is to a greater or less degree beyond their own or the producer's control. The audience therefore can never be certain whether they are keeping to their script or not or whether Sade cares if they don't. Certain cuts in the text, insisted upon by Coulmier, are restored and one cannot be certain whether it was Sade or his actors who restored them. For example:

14. A REGRETTABLE INTERVENTION

A PATIENT, *a clergyman's collar round his neck, detaches himself from the group and hops forward on his knees.*

PATIENT (*stammering incoherently*):
Pray pray
O pray to him
Our Satan which art in hell
thy kingdom come
thy will be done
on earth as it is in hell
forgive us our good deeds
and deliver us from holiness
Lead us
Lead us into temptation
over and over
          Amen

COULMIER *has sprung to his feet.* MALE NURSES *throw themselves on the* PATIENT, *overpower him, put him under a shower, then bind him and drag him to the back.*

HERALD (*swinging his rattle*):
The regrettable incident you've just seen
was unavoidable indeed foreseen
by our playwright who managed to compose
some extra lines in case the need arose
Please understand this man was once the very
well-thought-of abbot of a monastery
It should remind us all that as they say
God moves like man in a mysterious way.[26]

Sade himself intervenes in his play to dispute with Marat and, in his excitement, insists upon getting whipped by Charlotte Corday. When the cast cheers Napoleon, was this in Sade's script or not? And in either case are the cheers ironical? If unscripted and ironically intended, what weight do we give the irony of lunatics? If unscripted and unironical, it is still ironic to be cheered by lunatics. If Sade's script called for cheers, there is still the question of the playwright's sanity. But after all, who were the more insane, the inmates of Charenton in 1808, or the inmates of Paris in 1793? Or the inmates of Europe in 1964? Who was the more unbalanced, Marat or the paranoic who acted his part? Charlotte Corday or the melancholic actress? Sade, Marat, Napoleon, Hitler? Is Sade's play as performed more hopelessly confused and irrational than political situations normally are? Who is right, Weiss's hero, Sade, for whom 'the only reality is imagination' (and Weiss as a dramatist presents reality through imagination) or the 'Herald', who more than any other seems to speak for Weiss in this Marxist play and for whom the only reality is what unalterably has happened?

To what I have said of this play I should like to add a paragraph from Peter Brook's introduction to the English translation:

> Weiss not only uses total theatre, that time-honoured notion of getting all the elements of the stage to serve the play. His force is not only in the quantity of instruments he uses; it is above all in the jangle produced by the clash of styles. Everything is put in its place by its neighbour – the serious by the comic, the noble by the popular, the literary by the crude, the intellectual by the physical: the abstraction is vivified by the stage image, the violence illuminated by the cool flow of thought. The strands of meaning of the play pass to and fro through its structure and the result is a very complex form: like in Genet it is a hall of mirrors or a corridor of echoes – and one must keep looking front and back all the time to reach the author's sense.[27]

The previous sections of this chapter suggest that *Marat/Sade*, along with all the less complex works of a similar kind that this century has seen, is continuing a tradition as old as Aristophanes. In England, between 1671 and 1738, there were sixty-five plays in which the setting was a theatre for a play or rehearsal. As early as Molière's *Impromptu de Versailles* the audience is made to feel something of the ambiguity of personal identity in the dispute whether 'le marquis' *is* the actor playing the part of the marquis or the person the marquis is supposed to represent. We did not have to wait for Pirandello. But if we ask where and when this way of writing, with its halls of mirrors and its unresolved ambiguities and contradictions, attained full stature and became conscious of itself, the answer is that it was in Germany at the close of the eighteenth century and in the theory of Romantic Irony.

To trace the ironies of art beyond Diderot, and even perhaps as far as Diderot if we think of his *Neveu de Rameau*, is to become involved in the complexities of Romantic Irony. To this pheno-menon, therefore, I now turn. Gabriel Bounoure's *Marelles sur le parvis* (1958) provides me with an opening:

> One day, curious to learn what Romantic Irony was, a chance reading having revealed the name and given us a glimpse of the play of lofty genius, we asked one of our teachers, and deeply wounded, heard him reply that we could not yet understand this superior invention and that we should have to confine ourselves to the rudiments.[28]

The first discovery one makes about Romantic Irony, if one starts out with a concept of Romanticism derived from a reading of the French or English Romantics and a concept of irony derived from the corrective ironies of La Rochefoucauld and Swift, Vol-taire and Fielding, is that it has nothing to do with any simple con-ventional concept of Romanticism or with ordinary satiric or comic irony. More particularly, it is not to be understood simply as irony against Romanticism, though what Jean Paul Richter says of his novels – 'Hot baths of sentiment are followed by cold douches of irony' – has more than once been misleadingly quoted as indicating its nature. Romantic Irony is a fusion of Romantic-ism and irony, in which what is Romantic cannot be understood without a new concept of irony and what is ironic cannot be understood without a much deeper and more complex under-standing of Romanticism.

The theory of Romantic Irony was developed in Germany in the last decade of the eighteenth century and the first decade of the nineteenth. As a theory it has close affinities with post-Kantian German philosophy, particularly that of Fichte, and with cer-tain other German theories of art and literature, for example, Schiller's concept of art as play and his distinction between 'naïve' and 'reflective' (*sentimentalisch*) literature, Jean Paul Richter's concept of humour, and Schelling's concept of the imagination. More distantly it is related to several basic assumptions of Roman-tic and pre-Romantic literary theorizing both in Germany and in

N

the rest of Europe, and, in particular, to theories of genius, of art for art's sake, and of art as self-expression. It would be no gross exaggeration to say that the theory of Romantic Irony was a rallying point for many of the leading ideas of Romanticism, particularly those that were to have an active career in the twentieth century. To study Romantic Irony is to discover how modern Romanticism could be, or, if you like, how Romantic Modernism is.

The principal theorists were Friedrich Schlegel (1772–1829) Adam Müller (1779–1829) and Karl Solger (1780–1819). Of these I shall pay most attention to Schlegel. The young author of what are now known as the *Lyceumsfragmente* (1797), the *Athenäumsfragmente* (1798), and the *Ideen* (1800), and of other works contemporary with these had begun brilliantly. His mind, still in its formative stage, threw off penetrating, provocative, and sometimes provokingly impenetrable aphorisms, fragments, and brief essays with the éclat and rapidity of a Catherine-wheel. His terminology, quite apart from its being too metaphysical for English empirical tastes, was shifting and unsettled; sometimes 'Witz', sometimes 'Arabeske', sometimes 'Ironie' do duty for the concept, never definitively elaborated, which only rarely and only in his Notebooks he calls 'romantische Ironie'. But sometimes 'Witz' and 'Arabeske' have other significances and are distinguished from, even contrasted with 'Ironie'. How much of his early fertility and his awareness of irony in its new sense is indirectly owing to Talmudist ways of thinking might be worth investigating. In 1797 Schlegel met Dorothea Veit, one of the very gifted daughters of Moses Mendelssohn, and lived with her for some years before their marriage. She was seven years older than he, old enough and certainly intelligent enough to have profited from her part in the philosophical colloquiums held in the family circle in the last years of Mendelssohn's life (see M. Kayserling *Moses Mendelssohn*, Leipzig, 1888). In 1808 Schlegel became a Catholic. None of his later work shows the brilliance and imaginative penetration of the Fragments and the early essays.

Besides Schlegel, Müller, and Solger there were many other Germans (most of them belonging to or connected with the Jena circle) who were using the word 'irony' in senses then unknown in France or England: Goethe, Schelling, Schleiermacher, Novalis, A. W. Schlegel, Krause, Tieck, Richter (his *Humor* is close to Schlegel's *Ironie*), G. H. Schubert, E. T. A. Hoffmann, and Hegel (to these we may add the Danish Kierkegaard). Many of these make a point of sharply distinguishing their concept of irony from the verbal irony characteristic of polemic and satire. Friedrich Schlegel, for example, says, 'No things are more unlike than satire, polemic, and irony. Irony in the new sense is self-criticism [*Selbstpolemik*] surmounted; it is never-ending satire.'[29]

Against this impressive array of names must be set, however, the fact that the theory of Romantic Irony, as found in Friedrich Schlegel, Müller, and Solger, did not make much headway. Adam Müller was comparatively a minor figure, Solger's concept of irony, even to Tieck his contemporary and, in a sense, disciple, seemed rather vague, and Friedrich Schlegel, though a more imaginative thinker than his brother August Wilhelm, did not expound his views systematically or, in his *Fragments*, always choose the happiest formulations (his definition of irony as *transzendentale Buffonerie* has been an easy mark for American critics who fail to give the adjective even as much emphasis as the noun). August Wilhelm Schlegel's much more limited and simplified concept of irony was more successfully publicized and it was in *his* sense of the term that Hegel (and, following him, Kierkegaard) understood and attacked Romantic Irony. So that even in Germany, Romantic Irony in Friedrich Schlegel's sense was imperfectly understood. In France and England it had almost no chance of becoming established. Not only was the new meaning given to 'irony' far removed from the verbal irony that alone was familiar as 'irony' in France and England, but the new meanings were dressed up in the language of German metaphysics against which there has been from its beginnings a strong and not entirely baseless prejudice. Moreover, a point I shall return to, the imaginative literature fully and clearly exemplifying German Romantic Irony was by no means rich and by no means always to the taste of non-Germans. Carlyle, of course, was one writer who appreciated German Romantic literature but his imitation of Jean Paul's *Humor* seems rather to have put him among the Germans than to have naturalized Jean Paul in England.

In this century, from about the 1930s so far as I can discover, the French began to take an interest in Romantic Irony, recognizing it as one of the seminal concepts at least of *German* Romanticism. There is a number of books and articles in French from which one may form an adequate picture of Romantic Irony (see the Bibliography for Béguin, Bertrand, Boucher, Brombert, Denhof, Jankélévitch, Léon, Rouche, Schlagdenhauffen, Camille Schuwer). In America Romantic Irony has had a bad press, too many critics having taken their cue from Babbitt's *Rousseau and Romanticism* (1919) which was unsympathetic towards even Romanticism. Moreover, American critical emphasis has been on Tieck rather than Friedrich Schlegel. These remarks do not apply to American Germanists such as Raymond Immerwahr[30] or to René Wellek[30] with his Central European background. In England, excepting always the Germanists, Romantic Irony is almost unknown. Not counting Kierkegaard, the first writer outside Germany to have shown any real understanding of Romantic Irony, or even an interest in it, seems to have been the Australian poet, Christopher Brennan, who wrote in 1910 or thereabouts 'a progressive definition' of German Romanticism.[31] This was published in 1920 but had no perceptible influence even in Australia. Brennan was not himself an ironist, romantic, or otherwise. German studies of Romantic Irony, of which, naturally, there have been a great number, have culminated in Ingrid Strohschneider-Kohrs' *Die romantische Ironie in Theorie und Gestaltung* (1960).

Romantic Irony in Germany was a matter of literary and philosophical theory, a programme for literature, rather than literature itself. Given the German situation at the time it was easier to write the programme than the literature. Not that they were entirely separate; Friedrich Schlegel's deliberate choice of the fragment as being an open, 'dynamic' form exemplifies one aspect of Romantic Irony. The programme, moreover, as presented by the theorists, has to be regarded as a 'maximum programme' and we should not expect to find it immediately and always carried out in full. On the other hand, it was far from being something thought up as a theoretical speculation. It is rather a synthesis of parallel, tenuously related movements in both literature and theory. There came a point at which the direction certain contemporary theorists and imaginative writers were moving or might move was more or less intuitively grasped by Schlegel in a way that could also throw light on certain qualities in earlier writers.

One is, all the same, slightly embarrassed when asked what there is in German Romantic literature that *fully* exemplifies and justifies Schlegel's concept of irony. The German theorists refer us to Socrates, Boccaccio, Chaucer, Shakespeare, Cervantes, and even Petrarch; 'Auch Petrarcha hat romantische Ironie,' wrote Schlegel in one of his notebooks. What he did *not* mean by this another entry informs us: 'Some people suppose it to be irony when they come to know how many children Laura had.' What he did mean we can gather from a third entry ('Even Petrarch smiles at his sentimentality')[32] and from his essay on Boccaccio in which he implies a mutually enriching interaction of subjective and objective which is certainly part of the definition of Romantic Irony:

> The sonnets of Petrarch, if examined with the eye of taste, strike us most vividly from the super-excellent and wondrous objective art employed in the treatment of themes so entirely and remarkably subjective. The beauty and harmony of both arrangement and material appear to depend on the objective and subjective tendency being combined in due proportions: together with that exquisite skill in mechanism and imagery which each Italian poet so earnestly strove to attain. In Petrarch, both are harmoniously blended.[33]

But neither Petrarch nor any of the other writers mentioned above can do more than illustrate *some* of the elements of Romantic Irony. Again Schlegel speaks of *Wilhelm Meister* as exemplifying Romantic Irony, but I doubt if that work is quite as subtle and complex as Schlegel's enthusiasm led him to believe. Of Schlegel's own *Lucinde*, written to exemplify his theory, not even Professor Strohschneider-Kohrs's 435 pages say anything much (it *is* discussed but very unfavourably by Kierkegaard). Nor can Novalis, Brentano, or Jean Paul be put forward as Romantic Ironists in the fullest sense. We are left then with Tieck, E. T. A. Hoffmann, and Heine whose work in different ways, exemplifies Romantic Irony. But the best examples of all, the most thoroughgoing, almost programmatic examples, are the novels of Thomas

Mann. Their appearance, a hundred years and more after the theory, turns our embarrassment at the paucity of earlier examples into a recognition of Schlegel's astonishing ability to see in Romanticism the seeds of modernism.

Perhaps, in any case, one should not be disturbed by the small number of authors whose works *fully* exemplify Romantic Irony, but point instead to the way in which Romantic Irony in one or another of its various aspects has entered into and coloured the works of a great many authors, before and after as well as in the Romantic period. The names of Socrates, Boccaccio, Petrarch, Chaucer, Shakespeare, and Cervantes have just been mentioned, and to these names we may add those mentioned in the section on proto-Romantic Irony and many others that might have been mentioned there. German literature of the Romantic period is full of works in which one or another aspect of Romantic Irony is exemplified. The following authors may be cited: Friedrich Schlegel himself, Goethe, Tieck, Hoffmann, Richter, Novalis, Brentano, Grabbe, Chamisso, von Arnim, and La Motte-Fouqué. Morton Gurewitch, in his thesis, *European Romantic Irony*, distinguishes the Romantic Irony of the theorists from the simpler variety of it as sometimes practised by 'Byron, Carlyle, Leopardi, Musset, Gautier, Stendhal, Büchner, Heine, Baudelaire, and Flaubert', and which is identified by the ironist's 'simultaneous commitment to exalted visions and to a renegade impulse which mockingly dissolves them'.[34] Though I cannot agree with Gurewitch's contention that *European* Romantic Irony is 'spiritually more relevant' than Schlegelian Romantic Irony since he does not see that the former is only one aspect of the latter, his thesis makes it clear that even in this one aspect Romantic Irony is a basic element in modern literature as a whole. If we add only that an understanding of Romantic Irony is relevant to an understanding of the predicaments of self-conscious art and the self-conscious artist in the modern world we shall not lessen its importance.

Though we may find some of the elements of Romantic Irony in such earlier writers as Chaucer, Shakespeare, and Cervantes, it is not until the later eighteenth century that the full development of Romantic Irony, in practice as well as theory, becomes historically possible. It is then that one finds a number of new ways of looking at things – new attitudes, new values, and new political situations – coming together to provide the right compost both for Romanticism (in all its varieties) and for Romantic Irony. There are three of these that seem, for our purposes, to be of particular importance.

In the first place, since Romantic Irony was born in Germany, there is the historical situation at the end of the eighteenth century. For Germany, as for the rest of Europe, the French Revolution was a deeply disturbing experience; but in Germany with its hundreds of territorial sovereignties there was no possibility of a political revolution. Blocked in that direction, Germany had, however, both scope and means for an intellectual revolution; the only possible German empire at that time was an empire of speculative thought. In 1798 Schlegel wrote:

> The French Revolution, Fichte's *Wissenschaftslehre* and Goethe's *Meister* are the greatest trends [Tendenzen] of our epoch. Anyone who takes exception to my putting these on the same level, anyone who cannot regard a revolution as important unless it is clamorous and materialist has not yet risen to the high and comprehensive point of view the history of mankind requires.[35]

Heine makes the same point though in a somewhat different manner:

> German philosophy is a serious matter, of concern to all mankind. Our remotest descendants alone will be able to judge whether we are to be blamed or praised for having first produced our philosophy and then our revolution. But it seems to me that a methodical people like the Germans had to commence with the Reformation. Thereafter they could occupy themselves with philosophy, and only when they had completed that task, were they in a position to pass on to political revolution. I find this sequence very reasonable. The heads which philosophy used for reflection could be chopped off by the revolution, for its own purposes. But philosophy could never have used these heads if the revolution had first chopped them off. Don't worry, German republicans – your German revolution will be no gentler or milder because it has been preceded by the *Critique* of Kant, the transcendental idealism of Fichte, and even the philosophy of nature.[36]

Secondly, as a result of this ferment of intellectual speculation with its multiplicity of new and daring ideas, there was developed and made acceptable both the concept of the positive value of change, change as dynamic and progressive, and the concept of the normalness of contradiction and paradox in human affairs, in other words the adoption of the open ideology discussed in the previous chapter and of the belief that there are certain fundamental contradictions in the human conditions, in human nature, and in the nature of art which cannot be resolved in one total metaphysical answer. Both these concepts are implicit in Friedrich Schlegel's theory of Romantic Irony. We find him saying, 'Die romantische Poesie ist eine progressive Universalpoesie,' 'Ironie ist gleichsam die ἐπίδειξις der Unendlichkeit,' and 'Ironie ist die Form des Paradoxen.'[37]

This new concern with contradiction and paradox was reflected in the practice as well as the theory of art. In eighteenth-century aesthetics harmony was a dominant principle; in Romantic aesthetics (that is to say, in the aesthetics of the period following the French revolution), though poets and critics still, for the most part, made and spoke of the need for making harmonies, the emphasis had shifted. Harmony became a harmony of opposites, *concordia discors*. Home was still a classicist in speaking of avoiding extremes; Schlegel's advice was to combine extremes. And they will be extremes that combine in a fruitful tension from which, as later in the dynamic Hegelian dialectic, something new is produced. In an article on 'Novalis et le Principe de Contradiction', Jean Wahl says, 'L'esthétique de Novalis sera dominée par cette idée de la contradiction nécessaire et féconde.'[38] And he collects from Novalis a remarkable number of contrarieties: man is a bundle of contradictions, gaiety and seriousness, childishness and wisdom, an ordered chaos and finite infinity; a true poem will be complex and simple, determined and free, dynamic and at rest; it will contain enthusiasm and reason, the strange and the familiar, clarity and mystery, order and disorder, truth that elevates and illusion that flatters; and the poetry of the future will be at once epic, hymn, and drama, tragedy and comedy. One might quote Victor Hugo's *Preface to Cromwell* (1827) to much the same effect:

If we were entitled to say what, in our opinion, the style of dramatic poetry should be, we would declare for a free, outspoken, sincere verse, which dares say everything without prudery, express its meaning without seeking for words; which passes naturally from comedy to tragedy, from the sublime to the grotesque; by turns practical and poetical, both artistic and inspired, profound and impulsive, of wide range and true; . . . lyric, epic, dramatic, at need; capable of running through the whole gamut of poetry, of skipping from high notes to low, from the most exalted to the most trivial ideas, from the most extravagant to the most solemn, from the most superficial to the most abstract, without ever passing beyond the limits of a spoken scene; in a word, such verse as a man would write whom a fairy had endowed with Corneille's mind and Molière's brain. It seems to us that such verse would be *as fine as prose*.[39]

Music too, in the Romantic period, not only becomes 'open, free, indefinite', but makes a much bolder use of dissonances to express, as Chantavoine says, the romantic hero's sense of being out of harmony with nature, with society and with himself.[40]

Thirdly, there was the growth of self-awareness, the increasing extent to which men become conscious of being conscious, and this was of immense importance to the development of Romantic Irony. What I have in mind is not simply self-awareness as a mental activity and not only self-consciousness as an inhibiting or embarrassed state of mind but principally the awareness of the *self* as 'a permanent subject of successive and varying states of consciousness' in which sense the word 'self' seems first to have been used in 1674 ('self-consciousness' was first used in 1690, by Locke). Upon this topic, the mind's turning in upon itself, a great deal might be said without becoming irrelevant. One might, for example, speak of the growth of religious introspection, not confining oneself to English Protestantism or German Pietism (which latter Brüggemann sees as leading up to Romantic Irony). Certainly no less relevant would be the epistemological emphasis in philosophy from Descartes to beyond Kant, Descartes finding his initial certainty in his own mind, Berkeley holding that no object exists apart from Mind (ours or God's), Fichte holding that the Ego is the only ultimate reality.

One result of giving the self or the mind greater existential status, of seeing the mind as much more than an instrument one uses, unconsciously, for dealing with the world, is the setting up of a duality of mind and world or ego and non-ego, a duality which, like other dualities, tends to become polarized into opposites. To some degree it replaces the older dualities of soul and body and of God and the world. When Shaftesbury imagined God as alternatively a transcendent or an immanent *Mind* he showed himself to be hesitating mid-way between that 'closed-world' belief in a transcendent personal God and the Romantic worship of the creative mind of man: God the creator is becoming Mind the creator. For Blake the true God or true man was what he called 'Poetic Genius', and he was not the only Romantic for whom the creative mind attracted a degree of religious feeling. Wordsworth's attitude to the mind was a religious one:

> So prayed, more gaining than he asked, the Bard –
> In holiest mood. Urania, I shall need
> Thy guidance, or a greater Muse, if such
> Descend to earth or dwell in highest heaven!
> For I must tread on shadowy ground, must sink
> Deep – and, aloft ascending, breathe in worlds
> To which the heaven of heavens is but a veil.
> All strength – all terror, single or in bands,
> That ever was put forth in personal form –
> Jehovah – with his thunder, and the choir
> Of shouting Angels, and the empyreal thrones –
> I pass them unalarmed. Not Chaos, not
> The darkest pit of lowest Erebus,
> Nor aught of blinder vacancy, scooped out
> By help of dreams – can breed such fear and awe
> As fall upon us often when we look
> Into our Minds, into the Mind of Man –[41]

Feuerbach expressly referred religion to the mind: religion is 'nothing else than the consciousness of the infinity of the consciousness; or, in the consciousness of the infinite, the conscious subject has for his object the infinity of his own nature'.[42] The old concept of the artist as a god was adopted by the Germans from Shaftesbury's characterization of the true poet as 'a second *Maker*; a just Prometheus under Jove' and it became one of the leading ideas of German literary theory. As such it was a good deal more than an illuminating analogy; eighteenth-century philosophy having begun to empty the objective world, God's creation, of all human content, the artist had to take the place of God and by his imagination create a new reality.

The compost from which Romantic Irony grew may be summarily characterized as a combination of an intellectual ferment, a dynamic *Lebensanschauung*, a heightened self-awareness (from the conjunction of these last two emerges the peculiarly German emphasis upon the will), and a recognition and acceptance both of the complexity and contradictoriness of the world and of the obligation to come to terms with such a world. Implicit in all this are both the irony of the world against man (the general ironic predicaments he is in) and the irony of man against the world (the solution available to him through irony). As an individual, man was seen as a finite creature in a seemingly infinite and endless world whose fathomless complexities he could never penetrate, whose sheer contradictions he could never reconcile, and whose infinite possibilities he could never realize. 'Think of a finite formed within an infinite,' says Schlegel, 'and you will be thinking of a man.'[43] From this point of view, man is a tiny flash of light in 'the great cold the great dark', but a light nevertheless that feels an obligation to comprehend the darkness.

It is possible, however, to reverse this picture and say, not altogether implausibly, that it is man who is infinite and the world that is finite or at least existentially inferior to man. Behind the theory of Romantic Irony is the subjective idealism of Fichte, professor of philosophy at Jena. The doctrine of subjective idealism is that the Ego is the only ultimate reality and posits or op-posits the non-Ego. According to Bertrand Russell, 'the Ego as a metaphysical concept easily became confused with the empirical Fichte'. Whether or not this was so for Fichte, for Schlegel at least the metaphysical Ego seems to have become the individual ego and in particular the ego as artist. Such a view makes it possible to believe that through the mind man can achieve a degree of independence of the world; the long-recognized creative power of

the imagination seems to demonstrate this: 'Only the Poet,' wrote
Sidney,

> disdaining to be tied to any such subjection [to Nature], lifted up with
> the vigour of his own invention, doth grow in effect another nature,
> in making things either better than Nature bringeth forth, or, quite
> anew, forms such as never were in Nature, as the Heroes, Demi-
> gods, Cyclops, Chimeras, Furies, and such like: so as he goeth hand in
> hand with Nature, not enclosed within the narrow warrant of her
> gifts, but freely ranging only within the zodiac of his own wit.

To look upon the Ego as free, God-like, creative, dynamic, progressive, infinite, and vital is to regard the non-ego as static, finite,
and dead. The creative imagination, Coleridge said, 'is essentially
vital, even as all objects (*as* objects) are essentially fixed and dead'.[44]
It is the mind that creates value and meaning.

Placing these two pictures side by side we get a composite
image of man as infinite and free in imagination and reflection but
finite and limited in understanding and action. In other words, we
see the real ironizing the ideal, or more precisely, the ineluctable
realities of life ironizing man's compelling need to reach towards
perfection (and this can be recognized and expressed with bitter or
despairing irony); but conversely, the ideal can ironize the real,
that is, man can express his spirit's independence of the world with
disdainful or insouciant irony. Albert Béguin, probably following
Brüggemann, finds in a work as early as Karl-Philipp Moritz's
Anton Reiser (1785–90), the view that since life *vis-à-vis* our deepest questionings and strongest desires is so fearful and terrible, the
only thing one can do is to make a plaything of the world and so
demonstrate the sovereignty of the mind.[45] And Goethe was to
say something similar: 'Art is the individual's attempt to preserve
himself against the destructive power of the whole.'[46]

This, as I see it, was the basic irony facing the theorists of Romantic Irony, an ironic predicament that one could in some sense
come to terms with by recognizing it and responding with irony.
We must now add that this irony in man's relation to the world
at large has a parallel in the artist's relation to his work, and that
both these ironies enter into the complex concept of Romantic
Irony.

We have already seen that in the Romantic period there was both a keen awareness of the paradoxical and the contradictory in life and a recognition of the need to take account of this. According to Lovejoy, the Romantic ideal, at least in Germany, was an art

> which so far from desiring simplification, so far from aiming at the sort of harmony in art and life which is to be attained by the method of leaving out, should seek first fullness of content, should have for its program the adequate expression of the entire range of human experience and the entire reach of the human imagination.[47]

A. W. Schlegel compares the Greeks and the moderns from this point of view:

> The ancient art and poetry rigorously separate things which are dissimilar; the romantic delights in indissoluble mixtures; all contrarieties: nature and art, poetry and prose, seriousness and mirth, recollection and anticipation, spirituality and sensuality, terrestrial and celestial, life and death, are by it blended together in the most intimate combinations. As the oldest lawgivers delivered their mandatory instructions and prescriptions in measured melodies; as this is fabulously ascribed to Orpheus, the first softener of the yet untamed race of mortals; in like manner the whole of the ancient poetry and art is, as it were, a *rhythmical nomos* (law), an harmonious promulgation of the permanently established legislation of a world submitted to a beautiful order, and reflecting in itself the eternal images of things. Romantic poetry, on the other hand, is the expression of the secret attraction to a chaos which lies concealed in the very bosom of the ordered universe, and is perpetually striving after new and marvellous births; the life-giving spirit of primal love broods here anew on the face of the waters. The former is more simple, clear, and like to nature in the self-existent perfection of her separate works; the latter, notwithstanding its fragmentary appearance, approaches more to the secret of the universe. For Conception can only comprise each object separately, but nothing in truth can ever exist separately and by itself; Feeling perceives all in all at one and the same time.[48]

And elsewhere he says of Shakespeare that he,

> unites in his soul the utmost elevation and the utmost depth; and the
> most opposite and even apparently irreconcilable properties subsist
> in him peaceably together.[49]

The English Romantic poets believed in and successfully trusted
in the power of the imagination to effect a reconciliation and to
put, as Hazlitt says, 'a spirit of life and motion into the universe'.
Or as Coleridge says:

> The poet, described in ideal perfection, brings the whole soul of man
> into activity, with the subordination of its faculties to each other
> according to their relative worth and dignity. He diffuses a tone and
> spirit of unity that blends, and (as it were) *fuses*, each into each, by
> that synthetic and magical power, to which I would exclusively
> appropriate the name of Imagination. This power, first put into
> action by the will and understanding, and retained under their
> irremissive, though gentle and unnoticed, control, *laxis effertur
> habenis*, reveals itself in the balance or reconcilement of opposite or
> discordant qualities; of sameness with difference; of the general with
> the concrete; the idea with the image; the individual with the
> representative; the sense of novelty and freshness with old and
> familiar objects; a more than usual state of emotion with more than
> usual order; judgment ever awake and steady self-possession with
> enthusiasm and feeling profound or vehement; and while it blends
> and harmonizes the natural and the artificial, still subordinates art
> to nature; the manner to the matter; and our admiration of the poet
> to our sympathy with the poetry.[50]

For Friedrich Schlegel, the reconciliation of opposites was not
so simple a matter. It was to be achieved not by a synthesizing intensity but, if at all, only by a kind of irony (the term 'Socratic
Irony', in what follows, is used in a very wide sense, almost equivalent to Romantic Irony):

> Socratic Irony is the only form of dissimulation which is throughout
> both instinctive and deliberate. It is as impossible to affect it as to
> betray it. He who does not possess Socratic Irony will find it still a
> riddle even after the most open explanation. It should deceive only
> those who think it is deception and either take pleasure in the splendid

roguery of getting the better of the whole world or become furious when they suspect, all of a sudden, that they themselves might well be part of the joke. In this irony everything should be in fun and everything in earnest, everything naïvely open and everything deeply dissimulated. Socratic Irony rises out of a union of the sense of life as an art and the spirit of learning and science [wissenschaftlichem Geist], out of a conjunction of perfected natural philosophy [Naturphilosophie] and perfected philosophy of art [Kunstphilosophie]. It contains and inspires a sense of the unresolvable conflict between the absolute and the contingent, between the impossibility and the necessity of full and complete communication. It is the freest of all licenses because it enables one to transcend oneself, and yet it is also what one is most bound by, because it is absolutely essential. It is a very good sign when the unreflective and uncomplicated have no idea whatsoever how they should take this continual self-parody and just go on now believing and now disbelieving until they become giddy and take the joking seriously and the earnestness as a joke.[51]

A comparison of these two passages shows us that Coleridge, his thought dominated by concepts of subordination, reconciliation, and unity, has not fully emerged from the 'closed world', whereas Schlegel with his ironies of 'unresolved conflicts' is quite evidently governed by a concept of 'open-mindedness'. For Coleridge, the function of the imagination is, as it were, to enclose the chaotic world in a perfect harmonious sphere: For Schlegel, its function is to present the chaos and transcend it, and then to present the transcendence and transcend that, substituting for Coleridge's circle an upward and forward pointing arrow.

The impossibility of comprehending the world in its vastness, its complexity, and its dynamic quality is, we see, an impossibility that confronts the work of art. How can a work of art, which of its nature is something that can be finished, and therefore something finite and static, express the infiniteness of life? Even the novel, which the Romantic Ironists regarded as the literary form with the greatest potential, and which, as Thomas Mann says, 'scarcely knows how to begin except with the very beginning of all things and does not want to end at all',[52] even *Joseph and his*

Brothers, could not hope to be co-extensive with the world it represents. Regarded as a form of self-expression, art finds itself in the same impossible situation. How can an artist ever fully express his freedom and infiniteness? Because he himself is 'for ever voyaging through strange seas of thought', what he creates he must leave behind him, in time and in itself necessarily fixed and finite.

The answer given by the Romantic Ironists was that the work of art should itself acknowledge its limitations, and by doing so with irony it would take on the dynamic quality that life has and which art should therefore express. The first step the artist must take is to recognize that he cannot 'preserve himself against the destructive power of the whole' by retreating into pure subjectivity, for to content oneself with the outpourings of individual inspiration is to lack a sense of the universal. 'A poet,' said Goethe:

> ... deserves not the name while he expresses nothing but his few subjective emotions. Only when he can appropriate to himself, and express the world, is he a poet.[53]

Schelling too said that artists are supposed to imitate the whole of nature. Subjectivity, however, is not to be abandoned for objectivity but to be supplemented by objectivity. As Solger says, a novelist is taken hold of by his 'idea' but the idea should also be mastered by the novelist. Or as Adam Müller says, an artist should be able to give himself to his work but should also be able to return to himself. Friedrich Schlegel expressed himself at length on this topic:

> In order to be able to write well on any subject one must no longer be completely absorbed in it. The thought that one would express with all deliberation must already be wholly in the past, and not really concern one at the time. As long as the artist is at the inventive and inspired stage he is, at least as far as communication is concerned, in a state neither of being free nor of allowing freedom [in einem illiberalen Zustande]. At this stage he will want to say everything; but this is the mistake of young men of genius or the prejudice typical of old bunglers. But that way they fail to grasp the value and worth of self-limitation which is, however, for the artist as for all men, the first consideration and the last, the most necessary and the highest. It is the most necessary because wherever a man does not

impose limitations upon himself the world will do it for him and so make a slave of him. It is the highest because it is possible to limit oneself only in those points and aspects where one has unlimited power of self-creation and self-annihilation. Even a conversation among friends which could not at any moment be freely and quite arbitrarily broken off has something narrow, intolerant and unfree about it [etwas Illiberales]. Much more deplorable is the state of a writer who wishes simply to have his say and is in a position to have it, who keeps nothing back and will say everything he knows. There are only three mistakes one has to guard against. First, whatever is completely arbitrary and so seems or should seem to be either nonsense or 'supersense' must yet basically be plainly necessary and rational as well; otherwise what is caprice becomes self-will, narrow-mindedness emerges, and [instead] of self-limitation comes self-destruction. Secondly, one must not rush too hastily into self-limitation but first allow room for autonomous creation, invention and inspiration while it is ready and forthcoming. Thirdly, one must not overdo self-limitation.[54]

With this we might compare Goethe's 'In limitation only is the master manifest' and Thomas Mann's 'What would literature be, if not irony, self-discipline and liberation?'[55] Elsewhere Schlegel says that a work is perfected,

> when it is limited at every point, yet within its borders is without limitation and inexhaustible, when it is quite truly itself, everywhere homogeneous and yet exalted over itself.[56]

Implicit in these quotations are two quite striking ideas: one, that a work of art should present itself, that is, art should represent art; the other, that an artist should objectify his subjectivity. The first is based upon the recognition that a work of art exists both as a communication (or representation) and as the thing communicated (or represented); the second upon the fact that an artist works both consciously and unconsciously. The aim in either case was to introduce into art the dynamic of life. A work of art was no longer simply to be there, simply dumped in the public's lap. It was to be art conscious of itself. Of *Wilhelm Meister*, Schlegel says:

o

One must perhaps both judge and refrain from judging it, and this appears to be no easy task. Fortunately it is precisely one of the books which judges itself and consequently saves the critic the trouble. Indeed, not only does it judge itself, but it also presents itself.[57]

It was art raised to a higher power, poetry squared, the poetry of poetry; as (ordinary) poetry takes the world as its subject, irony takes poetry. Art is now to present life as art *and* to present art as life. Tieck's *Puss-in-Boots*, for example, is a play whose subject is the nature of plays; it is a dramatic illusion of dramatic illusion. The dramatic illusion at one level is broken to be re-created again but at a higher level. In *Les faux-monnayeurs*, Gide's hero-novelist who is also writing *Les faux-monnayeurs*, says:

> What I want is to represent reality on the one hand, and on the other that effort to stylize it into art . . . I invent the character of a novelist, whom I make my central figure; and the subject of the book, if you must have one, is just that very struggle between what reality offers him and what he himself desires to make of it.[58]

Just as one can protect oneself against the overpowering objectivity of the world with irony, by not taking it altogether seriously, so an artist can, indeed should, protect himself against his work. If he did not adopt an ironical attitude towards his work (and his authorship) he would be imprisoned in its finiteness, limited by its limits. *Vis-à-vis* his work the artist is a god – free to create or destroy at his mere pleasure; and this freedom is to be expressed in his work as irony. He is free too, not to create at all, and Schlegel speaks of a certain 'divine idleness'. If I might venture to express the artist's ironical relationship to his work in the form of an analogy which would serve as an elaboration of Schlegel's characterization of irony as '*transzendentale Buffonerie*' – and would run the same risk of being interpreted in the shallowest way possible – I would say that the ironist is like the circus clown on the tight-rope. First the ordinary tight-rope walker performs his feats seriously. Then the clown, sent aloft by the ring-master, pretends to be afraid of heights, pretends to fall, perhaps falls, but the wire catches him by one of his enormous buttons, recovers himself and runs the rest of the way so as to get across quickly; but all the time he is much more skilful than his fellow acrobat.

He has raised tight-rope walking to a higher power, in that he is performing at two levels simultaneously – as a clown and as a tight-rope walker, and demonstrating at the same time both the possibility and the impossibility of tight-rope walking.

The Romantic Ironist, likewise, puts himself into his work but simultaneously indicates his detachment from it. This simultaneous immanence and transcendence of the author, and in this respect his resemblance to God, was a frequent theme with the theorists. The effect is not only to enrich the work with an additional dimension, the dynamic, authorial dimension but also to transform it. *Tom Jones*, to take a simple example, is much more than the story plus Fielding's presence. There is a constant interaction and mutual enrichment. In *Joseph and his Brothers*, Thomas Mann writes:

> Should he [the narrator] appear at all, save as anonymous source of the tale which is being told or is telling itself, in which everything is by virtue of itself, so and not otherwise, indisputable and certain? The narrator, according to this view, should be in the tale, one with it, and not outside it, reckoning and calculating. But how is it with God, whom Abram thought into being and recognized? He is in the fire but He is not the fire. Thus He is at once in it and outside it. Indeed, it is one thing to be a thing, quite another to observe it. And yet there are planes and spheres where both happen at once: the narrator is in the story, yet is not the story; he is its scene but it is not his, since he is also outside it and by a turn of his nature puts himself in the position of dealing with it. I have never tried to produce the illusion that I am the source of the history of Joseph. Before it could be told, it happened, it sprang from the source from which all history springs, and tells itself as it goes. Since that time it exists in the world, everybody knows it or thinks he does – for often enough the knowledge is unreal, casual, and disjointed. It had been told a hundred times, in a hundred different mediums. And now it is passing through another, wherein as it were it becomes conscious of itself and remembers how things actually were with it in the long-ago, so that it now both pours forth and speaks of itself as it pours.

This passage is not, as one might have expected, taken from the introduction and therefore outside the work. It is in, but digresses

from, Chapter IV of Book III (*Joseph in Egypt*). Musil, also, is both
inside and outside his *Man Without Qualities*. His hero, Ulrich,
whose biography resembles Musil's, has taken a year off from life
in order to think things out. The result is evidently the (unfin-
ished) work we read. The fact that Musil took twenty years *not*
to complete his work is an irony of another kind. Writing of
Wilhelm Meister, Schlegel says:

> The author himself seems to take the characters and incidents so
> lightly and whimsically, scarcely ever mentioning his hero without
> irony and smiling down upon his masterpiece itself from the height
> of his spirit. But one should not let oneself be deceived by this into
> supposing that he is not religiously in earnest . . . One should not
> therefore judge this altogether new and unique book, which one can
> learn to understand only from itself, by a concept of the novel which
> has been developed and stuck together out of traditional assumptions
> and beliefs, random experiences and arbitrary demands. To do so
> would be to behave like a child trying to grasp the moon and stars
> in his hands and put them in his little box.[59]

Much of this echoes what Schlegel was saying in his *Fragments*:
'We must raise ourselves above our own love and be able to destroy in thought what we worship'; and '. . . the frame of mind
or spirit which surveys all things and endlessly raises itself above
all limited things, even over our own art, virtue, or genius'.
Schlegel's word 'destroy' is to be understood in the context of the
German commitment, at this time, to a philosophy of dynamic
and dialectic progress; the destruction is in the service of recreation.
Romantic Irony is not negative; it does not, for example, negate
subjectivity by objectivity, the imaginative by the critical, the
emotional by the rational. Nor does it steer a middle course between them: 'Ironie ist Analyse der These und Antithese.'[60]
Schlegel's meaning is that irony does not take sides but regards
both sides critically. The Romantic Ironist will be consciously
subjective, enthusiastically rational, and critically emotional. His
aim is expressed in what Coleridge says of Shakespeare: 'A nature
humanized, a genial understanding directing self-consciously a
power and an implicit wisdom deeper even than our consciousness.'[61] We can say that the theory of Romantic Irony aimed even

higher; perhaps 'more widely' would be a better way of putting
it. 'Romantische Poesie' was to be universal, uniting all the genres
of poetry, mixing poetry and prose, combining with music and
painting and even with philosophy and science: 'All art must be
science [*Wissenschaft*] and all science must be art.'[62]

> The more poetry becomes scholarship and science [Wissenschaft]
> the more it also becomes art [at the highest level]. If poetry is to
> become art, if the artist is to have a thorough insight into and
> knowledge of his aims and purposes as well as of the subjects proper
> to poetry and the obstacles incident to it, he will have to philosophize
> about it. If he is to be not simply an inventive and skilful craftsman
> but also a master in his field really capable of understanding his
> fellow-citizens in the realm of art, he will have to become a scholar
> and a lover of words [ein Philolog].[63]

The attraction for the Romantics of these antitheses was that
they lent themselves to dialectic development. Identification is
static and sterile; contradiction is dynamic and fruitful. Schlegel
speaks of 'the incessant and self-creating alternation of two contradictory thoughts', 'the marvellous eternal alternation of enthusiasm and irony'.[64] Caught between his aspirations for an ideal
he knows is beyond his reach and his limitations of which he is
equally aware, the only possibility for the ironist is a continual
dialectic process of ironic affirmations and negations. Such a process seems to be implicit in self-consciousness itself and perhaps in
irony too. Once a man has become self-conscious he can hardly
not take the next step and become conscious of being self-conscious and then conscious of being conscious of being self-conscious . . . And once a man has become ironical he would be a
rather shallow ironist if he did not direct his irony against himself
and against himself as an ironist as Schlegel does in the following
passage which itself is not without irony but at the same time not
wholly ironical:

> Lastly the irony of irony: generally speaking the most thorough
> irony of irony is the fact that one becomes weary of it if one is offered
> it everywhere and all the time; but what we would here chiefly have
> understood as irony of irony arises in more than one way: When a
> man talks of irony unironically, as I have just been doing; when he

talks of irony ironically but without noticing that he is, at this very
time, the victim of another, much more obvious irony; when he can
no longer find a way out of irony as seems to be the case with this
essay on unintelligibility; when the irony becomes mannered and so
turns round, as it were, and ironizes the writer; when a man has
promised irony for one table-book too many without first checking
his stock and now must be ironical against his inclinations like an
actor with the belly-ache; when a madness takes irony and it can no
longer be governed.[65]

These situations, of course, rapidly become unreal, but nevertheless the concept of infinite regression has a place in literary theory
and in literature. In *Tristram Shandy* we had digressions within digressions within digressions, in *Jacques le fataliste* stories within
stories within stories, in Tieck's *Puss-in-Boots* a theatre within a
theatre within a theatre; in *Les faux-monnayeurs* Gide breaks into
his novel to comment on his characters one of whom is a novelist
writing a novel called *Les faux-monnayeurs* for which purpose he
keeps a journal, extracts from which are presented. Two years
later Gide published his own *Journal des faux-monnayeurs*. Waugh's
Ordeal of Gilbert Pinfold ends with the hero sitting down to write
The Ordeal of Gilbert Pinfold. In Muriel Spark's *The Comforters* the
heroine, who is writing a book called *Form in the Modern Novel*,
hears voices 'something like a concurrent series of echoes' – 'it is
as if a writer on another plane of existence was writing a story
about us'.

It is true that stories within stories within stories are to be found
in folk-lore and in Oriental literature, and perhaps *The Arabian
Nights* may in this respect have had some influence upon 'form in
the Romantic and modern novel', though it shows no awareness
of the ironic potential of its form. There is certainly, moreover, a
kind of mind that is particularly attracted by paradoxes of this
kind. None the less these infinite regressions and infinite transcen-
dencies were especially attractive to some Romantics and again to
some twentieth-century writers and are perhaps to be connected
with the concept of the infinite elusiveness of reality. The hero of
Tieck's *William Lovell* (1795–6) after having conceived of himself
as the only reality, in which belief he treats the rest of the world as

toys to be played with and broken at will, comes to realize that all
the time he himself was only the plaything of a strange old man
who in turn wonders whether he too has not been the toy or tool
of some figure at a yet higher level. Claude-Edmonde Magny, in
her *Histoire du roman français depuis 1918*, calls this kind of novel
the 'sur-roman ouvert'.[66] In a brief discussion of the 'mise en
abyme' effect of works by Balzac, Gide, Proust, and Joyce she
draws attention to the similar nature of such puzzles in philosophy
as 'What is the philosophic value of the statement: One cannot
philosophize without submerging oneself in a reality which is
such that one cannot utter statements of the kind: One cannot
philosophize without, etc. etc.', puzzles which can be solved only
by distinguishing between 'first-order' and 'second-order' statements.

Schlegel relates this conception of infinite progression to the
very nature of Romanticism:

> Romantic poetry is progressively universal [eine progressive
> Universalpoesie]. Its ordained function is not simply that of re-
> uniting all the separate genres of literature and of bringing poetry
> into contact with philosophy and rhetoric; its true and proper aim
> is to join (sometimes by mixing and sometimes by amalgamating)
> poetry and prose, creative spontaneity and criticism, the poetry of
> art and the poetry of nature, to make poetry alive and companionable
> and life and society poetic, to inspire wit with the spirit of poetry,
> and to fill and saturate all forms of art with solid knowledge and
> educational material [Bildungsstoff] of all kinds and animate them
> with the pulsations of humour. It encompasses everything that is at
> all poetic from the organization of art itself in the widest sense (this
> in turn containing within itself other systems) to the sigh and the
> kiss which the child-poet breathes out in artless song. It can so lose
> itself in what it portrays that one might think its whole concern was
> [objectively] to depict imaginary individuals of every kind. And yet
> there has not been until now any kind of imaginative literature so
> adapted for expressing in full the [individual, subjective] mind of the
> author; so that many an author who intended only to write a novel
> has unexpectedly depicted and revealed himself. Only Romantic
> poetry can, like the epic, become a mirror of the whole world round

about, an image of the times. And yet, more than all other kinds of
literature, it can, being free from all commitment to the real and the
ideal, hover on the wings of poetic reflection midway between the
artist and the artefact, raising this reflection to a higher power and a
higher still and multiplying it as in an endless series of mirrors. It is
capable of developing the highest and most versatile of forms,
working not only outwards from [the part] within but also inwards
from [the whole] without, organizing each and every part on the
analogy of the whole it is intended they shall produce, and thereby
opening the way for the achievement of a classicism that is endless in
growth potential. Romantic poetry is among the arts what wit is to
philosophy and what sociability, social intercourse, friendship and
love are to life. Other forms of literature have reached completion
and can now be analysed to the last detail. The Romantic mode of
poetry is still in the making. This indeed is its real essence, that it can
forever only develop and never reach completion. No theory can
ever exhaust it, and only intuitive [divinatorische] criticism could
dare to say what its ideal really is. It alone is endless as it alone is free,
acknowledging as its first law that the poet's complete freedom of
action can tolerate no higher law. The Romantic mode of poetry is
the only one that is more than a mode of poetry, since it is, so to say,
poetry itself; for in a certain sense all poetry is or should be romantic.[67]

What I have said about Romantic Irony can all be confirmed by
the novels of Thomas Mann. Erich Heller has in fact said that
Schlegel's praise of *Wilhelm Meister* may be more aptly applied to
the *Magic Mountain*. Mann's *Doctor Faustus* is an even better example of Romantic Irony. Before speaking of that work, however, I should like as an introduction to begin with something
fairly simple, the following passage from *Northanger Abbey*. Mr
Tilney has been introduced to Catherine Morland:

After chatting for some time on such matters as naturally arose from
the objects around them, he suddenly addressed her with – 'I have
hitherto been very remiss, madam, in the proper attentions of a
partner here; I have not yet asked you how long you have been in
Bath; whether you were ever here before; whether you have been
at the Upper Rooms, the theatre, and the concert; and how you like
the place altogether. I have been very negligent – but are you now at

leisure to satisfy me in these particulars? If you are I will begin directly.'

'You need not give yourself that trouble, sir.'

'No trouble I assure you, madam.' Then forming his features into a set smile, and affectedly softening his voice, he added, with a simpering air, 'Have you been long in Bath, madam?'

'About a week, sir,' replied Catherine, trying not to laugh.

'Really!' with affected astonishment.

'Why should you be surprized, sir?'

'Why, indeed!' said he, in his natural tone – 'but some emotion must appear to be raised by your reply, and surprize is more easily assumed, and not less reasonable than any other. – Now let us go on. Were you never here before, madam?'

'Never, sir.'

'Indeed! Have you yet honoured the Upper Rooms?'

'Yes, sir, I was there last Monday.'

'Have you been to the theatre?'

'Yes, sir, I was at the play on Tuesday.'

'To the concert?'

'Yes, sir, on Wednesday.'

'And are you altogether pleased with Bath?'

'Yes – I like it very well.'

'Now I must give one smirk, and then we may be rational again.'

Catherine turned away her head, not knowing whether she might venture to laugh.[68]

This little scene may be interpreted as in part presenting, in part implying, several stages in the development of the art of conversation each of which stages has an approximate analogue in the development of art in general.

Stage 1. Natural, spontaneous conversation. The equivalent in art would be the, perhaps hypothetical, stage at which a dance or ballad or piece of music is composed with complete spontaneity and un-selfconsciousness.

Stage 2. 'Making conversation', saying the right things on acceptable topics. The equivalent in art is the work consciously but not self-consciously composed within an acceptable tradition.

Stage 3. Being unable to make conversation through being conscious of the unnaturalness of pretending to converse naturally. An artist inhibited by his consciousness of the essential 'artificiality' of art is in a similar position. Madame de Staël says:

> [In Germany] the arts are analysed even before they are felt, and it is useless to say afterward that analysis should be abandoned: one has already tasted the fruit of the tree of science and the innocence of genius is lost. . . . studies . . . whose only goal is to explain genius [will, if] pushed too far, stifle invention. The artist is impeded by the memory of everything that has been said of every masterpiece; he senses between himself and the object he wants to portray a swarm of treatises . . . and he is no longer alone with nature.[69]

Stage 4. A way out of this impasse is available to the person of strong feelings, to such a one as Marianne Dashwood for example:

> It was only necessary to mention any favourite amusement to engage her to talk. She could not be silent when such points were introduced, and she had neither shyness nor reserve in their discussion.

When her sister, with mild irony, comments upon 'such extraordinary despatch of every subject for discourse', she says:

> I see what you mean. I have been too much at my ease, too happy, too frank. I have erred against every common-place notion of decorum; I have been open and sincere where I ought to have been reserved, spiritless, dull, and deceitful: – had I talked only of the weather and the roads, and had I spoken only once in ten minutes, this reproach would have been spared.[70]

The equivalent in art is the *Sturm und Drang* genius or the Shelleyan intensity that sweeps away all inhibition.
Stage 5a. But the artist, when possessed by creative fervour, is, as we have seen Schlegel saying, in an unfree condition. To recover his freedom he must impose upon his work the self-limitation of irony. Heine's 'Ocean-Wraith' in *The North Sea* shows us the poet abandoning himself to a romantic reverie and then withdrawing himself.

> But I, the while, leant over the gunwale,
> With rapt eyes dreamily gazing,
> Far down through the water clear as crystal,
> Still gazing deeper and deeper –

Till, deep in the sea's abysses,
First like a glimmering dawn-cloud,
But ever growing clearer in colour,
Domes of churches and towers loomed upward;
And soon, as clear as day, a city entire.

An infinite longing, deepest sorrow
O'ersteals my heart,
My scarcely healèd heart; –
I feel as though its wounds were gently
Kissed open by belovèd lips,
And set once more a-bleeding –
Blood-drops, warm and crimson,
Fall slowly, slowly dripping fall,
On a grey old house below there,
In the deep sea-city,
On an old and steeply-gabled house,
Tenantless now, and melancholy;
Save at the basement window
A maiden sits,
And leans her head on her arm,
Like a poor and forsaken child –
And I know thee, thou poor forsaken child!

So deep, so ocean-deep, then,
Thou hiddest thyself from me
In childish ill-humour,
And ne'er couldst again come up,
But strange must dwell in a land of strangers,
These centuries long;
And all the while, with soul full of grief,
O'er the whole wide world have I sought thee,
For ever have sought thee,
Thou ever-belov'd one,
Thou long, long lost one!
But now I have found thee –
Ay, now I have found thee again, and gaze in
Thy own sweet face,

Those eyes, so grave and loyal,
That smile so tender –
And never, never again will I leave thee,
And I come to thee, down to *thee*.
And with arms outstretched to enfold thee
Down will I plunge to thy heart!

Just in the nick of time here
The wideawake skipper gripped my foot,
And pulled me back from the bulwark,
And cried, maliciously laughing:
'Devil come for you, Doctor?'[71]

Stage 5b. An alternative means of regaining the power of speaking
or writing freely, a means involving neither a self-regardless blind
intensity nor a violent 'illusion-breaking' anticlimax, is exemplified in Henry Tilney's parody of artificial conversation which destroys artificiality through artificiality and so becomes free at a
higher level. This, on a much greater scale and in a much more
subtle manner, is in general the method of Thomas Mann: 'In
matters of style I really no longer admit anything but parody.'

The whole development, from Stage 1 to Stage 5, is summed
up in a phrase Thomas Mann quotes twice from Merezhkovsky,
'the transition from unconscious creation to creative consciousness'.[72] Creative consciousness was what the Romantic critics
praised Shakespeare for. To Coleridge Shakespeare was, as we
have just seen,

a nature humanized, a genial understanding directing self-consciously
a power and implicit wisdom deeper even than our consciousness.

Coleridge does not see this as irony, but it is not far from Schlegel's demand for both objectivity and subjectivity – 'Every good
poem must be at the same time wholly conscious and wholly instinctive' – and for both irony and enthusiasm – 'Nothing is more
trivial than the empty form of irony without enthusiasm and
without tension between the real and the ideal.'[73] I turn now to
Mann's *Doctor Faustus*, seeing it as a work whose principal theme
is precisely the possibility of creative consciousness. This, or
something like it, was, in fact, the theme of his *Tonio Kröger*

(1903) and several of his subsequent works. In *Doctor Faustus*, however, Mann explores all the complexities of the theme, and additionally, all the complexities of a mode of writing which has to be brought into being in order to treat such a theme.

Doctor Faustus: The Life of the Composer Adrian Leverkühn (1947) is a fictional biography whose explicit intellectual theme is the impasse of music in our hypertrophically self-conscious age and the struggle to break through it. But in writing about music Mann is at the same time writing about all the arts (including his own problems as a novelist), about modern culture in general, and about the position of Germany in Europe. The subject of this 'biography' was born in 1885 and died in 1940, but the work itself takes in the whole period from Luther, the birth of polyphonic music, and the first Faust story to the utter collapse of Nazi Germany. The last paragraph identifies Leverkühn with Germany and both with the damned soul in Michelangelo's *Last Judgement* 'clung round by demons, a hand over one eye, with the other staring into horrors'.

There is material for ironic exploitation in the very form of *Doctor Faustus*. The work is a novel in the form of a biography, fictional narrative pretending to be the relation of actualities. But Zeitblom, the 'biographer', soon discovers that successfully to relate actualities he must obey the rules of art and practise self-limitation, and not, for example, blurt out everything at once. But then to shape one's work and so become a creative artist implies the need to distance oneself from one's subject: 'For a man like me it is very hard, it affects him almost like wanton folly, to assume the attitude of a creative artist to a subject which is dear to him as life and burns him to express.'[74] Later he says:

> What is lacking is distance, contrast, mere differentiation between the material and the hand that shapes it. Have I not said more than once that the life I am treating of was nearer to me, dearer, more moving than my own? And being so near, so moving and so intimate, it is not mere 'material' but a person, and that does not lend itself to artistic treatment. Far be it from me to deny the seriousness of art; but when it becomes serious, then one rejects art and is not capable of it.[75]

Thomas Mann is saying this of his own work as well as making
Zeitblom say it of his, and saying it seriously. But saying it ironically too since he *has* distanced himself, having chosen as his
spokesman a *persona* who is relatively very one-sided and limited.
Some things, however, can only be said seriously by saying them
ironically. Leverkühn's letter to Zeitblom relating his adventure
in the brothel is written in Lutheran German in order that the
writer can say, as if jokingly but really in earnest, what could not
be said at all in modern German – 'Herewith amen – and pray for
me.' Zeitblom comments, 'There could be no better example of
the quotation as disguise, the parody as pretext.'[76] But the whole
of *Doctor Faustus* is parody and quotation and should be enclosed
in quotation marks. It is ironical again that Mann has chosen
fictional form (which none the less pretends not to be fiction but
biography) in order to question the very possibility of fiction. His
hero writes:

> '[History] no longer tolerates pretence and play, the fiction, the self-
> glorification of form, which censors the passions and human
> suffering, divides out the parts, translates into pictures. Only the non-
> fictional is still permissible, the unplayed, the undisguised and un-
> transfigured expression of suffering in its actual moment. Its
> impotence and extremity are so ingrained that no seeming play with
> them is any longer allowed.'[77]

Ironical too that Mann has chosen to present an enormous topic,
the situation of the arts and Germany in modern civilization, in the
form of a biography of an individual, while questioning again
whether this can be done. 'The claim to consider the general har-
monically contained in the particular contradicts itself.'[78]

Adrian Leverkühn was born in one farmhouse (Buchel) and
ended his life as a composer in another (Pfeiffering) so much like
the first that one might think it the same. In between came the
'medieval' town Kaisersaschern, the 'Lutheran' and 'Faustian'
University of Halle-Wittenberg, Leipzig, the great publishing
and musical centre, and Munich, the cultural centre and the city of
Hitler. Nor did he leave these places behind him as he moved on
but took them with him; at least this is said specifically and twice
of Kaisersaschern and there is reason to think it no less true of the

others. For there is a clear parallel between Leverkühn's wander-
ings and the history of music; his own composition, the *Apo-
calypse*, we are told:

> takes in the life-history of music, from its pre-musical, magic,
> rhythmical, elementary stage to its most complex consummation;[79]

and the book itself is largely about the development of music
from polyphonic objectivity (the simplest form of which is the
round as sung by the Buchel stable-girl with the young Leverkühn and Zeitblom) through harmonic subjectivity and sophisticated self-consciousness to a second-order naïvety (of which
Pfeiffering is the symbol):

> To remain on the height of intellect; to resolve into the matter-of-
> course the most exclusive productions of European musical develop-
> ment, so that everybody could grasp the new; to make themselves
> its master, applying it unconcernedly as free building material and
> making tradition felt, recoiled into the opposite of the epigonal; to
> make technique, however high it had climbed, entirely unimportant,
> and all the arts of counterpoint and instrumentation to disappear and
> melt together to an effect of simplicity very far from simplicity, an
> intellectually winged simplicity – that seemed to be the object and
> the craving of art.[80]

There are many such passages in *Doctor Faustus*. Taken together
they argue a very thorough assimilation, on Thomas Mann's part,
of the ideas of Friedrich Schlegel and a very close sympathy with
them, although being a modern, he is a good deal less optimistic;
Schlegel would not have suggested that art can only be redeemed
at the expense of the artist's damnation. As in Schlegel, so in *Doctor Faustus*, one finds an endless dialectic of freedom and order –
freedom binding itself in the interests of greater freedom, freedom
abandoning conventional artifices only to find in the organicism
that replaces them an order that is pre-ordained. Where Schlegel
saw something 'illiberal' in the liberation of unreflective subjectivity, in the unrestrained pourings-out of inspired creation,
and called for self-limitation and self-restraint, Leverkühn speaks
of freedom, 'the relaxing of all objective obligations', as 'a mil-
dew upon talent' and adds:

But freedom is of course another word for subjectivity, and some fine day she does not hold out any longer, some time or other she despairs of the possibility of being creative out of herself and seeks shelter and security in the objective. Freedom always inclines to dialectic reversals. She realizes herself very soon in constraint, fulfils herself in the subordination to law, rule, coercion, system – but to fulfil herself therein does not mean she therefore ceases to be freedom.

In art, at least, the subjective and the objective intertwine to the point of being indistinguishable, one proceeds from the other and takes the character of the other, the subjective precipitates as objective and by genius is again awaked to spontaneity, 'dynamized', as we say; it speaks all at once the language of the subjective. The music conventions today destroyed were not always so objective, so objectively imposed. They were crystallizations of living experiences and as such long performed an office of vital importance: the task of organization. Organization is everything. Without it there is nothing, least of all art. And it was aesthetic subjectivity that took on the task, it undertook to organize the work out of itself, in freedom.[81]

If the naïvely subjective artist is limited through self-ignorance, the self-conscious artist is in a far worse position, inhibited from creation through knowing too much. Writing to his master Kretschmar, Leverkühn expresses doubts about a musical career for himself:

I must disclaim the robust *naïveté* which . . . pertaineth to the nature of the artist. In its place my lot is a quickly satisfied intelligence, . . . I am embarrassed at the insipidness which is the supporting structure, the conditioning solid substance of even the work of genius, at the elements thereof which are training and common property, at use and wont in achieving the beautiful.[82]

And then after a sympathetic appreciative analysis of what is clearly a lovely composition he says: 'Why do I have to laugh? . . . Why does almost everything seem to me like its own parody? Why must I think that almost all, no, all the methods and conventions of art today *are good for parody only*?' Kretschmar replies that this is as it ought to be; his pupil is expressing 'a collective feeling for the historical exhaustion and vitiation of the means and appliances of art, the boredom with them and the search for new ways'.[83]

The next question is whether art as well as being a mere trick is not also a lie in its relation to modern society:

> Whether at the present stage of our consciousness, our knowledge, our sense of truth, this little game is still permissible, still intellectually possible, still to be taken seriously; whether the work as such, the construction, self-sufficing, harmonically complete in itself, still stands in any legitimate relation to the complete insecurity, problematic conditions, and lack of harmony of our social situation, whether all seeming, even the most beautiful, even precisely the beautiful, has not today become a lie.[84]

Art, Leverkühn says, can no longer condone itself:

> Pretence and play have the conscience of art against them today. Art would like to stop being pretence and play, it would like to become knowledge.[85]

One is reminded of Schlegel saying, 'Je mehr die Poesie Wissenschaft wird, je mehr wird sie auch Kunst.' This same idea of the impossibility of the continuance of art is expressed also by the devil in his visit to Leverkühn. Composing itself has got too hard; emancipated art rejects the traditional; clichés of harmony shock worse now than discords; the very concept of art is distasteful. The importance of this idea is underlined by its reappearance in the very next chapter. This time it is Spengler the painter who points to the ever-narrowing gap between what can be done and what cannot be done because it has been done already:

> He delivered himself at that time of the remark that occupation with these songs [Leverkühn's Brentano song-cycle] ended by spoiling one, quite definitely and almost dangerously. Afterwards one could hardly find pleasure in anything in that field. Said other quite good things about being spoiled, of which the needy artist himself was in the greatest danger, it seemed: it might be disastrous for him. For with every finished work he made life harder for himself, and in the end impossible. Spoilt by the extraordinary, his taste ruined for anything else, he must at last deteriorate through despair of executing the impossible. The problem for the highly gifted artist was how,

P

despite his always increasing fastidiousness, his spreading disgust, he could still keep within the limits of the possible.[86]

We come perhaps to the end of this line with the dialogue between Samuel Beckett and Georges Duthuit:

From *Dialogue I*:

B. The only thing disturbed by the revolutionaries Matisse and Tal Coat is a certain order on the plane of the feasible.

D. What other plane can there be for the maker?

B. Logically none. Yet I speak of an art turning from it in disgust, weary of its puny exploits, weary of pretending to be able, of being able, of doing a little better the same old thing, of going a little further along a dreary road.

D. And preferring what?

B. The expression that there is nothing to express, nothing with which to express, nothing from which to express, no power to express, no desire to express, together with the obligation to express.

From *Dialogue II*:

B. The malady of wanting to know what to do and the malady of wanting to be able to do it.

From *Dialogue III*:

B. The situation is that of him who is helpless, cannot act, in the end cannot paint, since he is obliged to paint. The act is of him who, helpless, unable to act, acts, in the event paints, since he is obliged to paint.

D. Why is he obliged to paint?

B. I don't know.

D. Why is he helpless to paint?

B. Because there is nothing to paint and nothing to paint with.[87]

What the theory of Romantic Irony achieved, if I may summarize this last section, was a (highly generalized) programme for modern literature, a *modus vivendi* for the writer and for writing in the modern 'open' world. It both saw and answered the basic questions with which a modern *Weltanschauung* confronts the artist.

It recognized, to begin with, man's ironic predicament as a finite being, terrifyingly alone in an infinite and infinitely complex and contradictory world of which he could achieve only a finite understanding, and in his art only a finite presentation, but a world for which he, and particularly the artist, the artist as God since there was no other, had nevertheless to accept responsibility and give it meaning and value. It went on to recognize that implicit even in the artist's awareness and acceptance of his limitations there lay the possibility, through the self-irony of art, of transcending his predicament, not actually yet intellectually and imaginatively.

The theory of Romantic Irony taught that an open, 'progressive', constantly becoming world could be mastered only by an open, 'progressive' art. The old way of harmonious resolutions in art could no longer result in anything but sentimental falsification and pretence. Of the alternatives, there could be no worthy future in either a recourse to pure subjectivity (though some nineteenth-century artists certainly took this direction) or an adoption of a nihilistic standpoint in which all art would be destroyed (as in certain art-movements of our own day). Wishing to keep open the place of art in an open world, the theorists of Romantic Irony prescribed a 'dynamic' literature which would ironically accept and ironically express within itself the general ironies of art and of the human predicament at large and so preserve itself against 'the destructive power of the whole'.

VIII

IRONY AND THE IRONIST

1 · *The Ironist's Stance*

In this chapter I leave in abeyance, for a time at least, the concept of the Romantic Ironist as presented in the last chapter, and return to the ironist as the 'ironical man', the 'General Ironist' whose character or education has led him always or generally to look at the world through irony-coloured spectacles. The concept of detachment has long been closely associated with irony. When we use the term 'ironic detachment' we may have in mind any one of three different things: (*a*) the factual, logical, dispassionate, urbane, or insouciant manner that some ironists adopt, even though they may be motivated to irony by contempt, indignation, hatred, or disgust; (*b*) the factor of control that enables such ironists to pretend to be disinterested or impartial or even sympathetic, enthusiastic, or ingenuous; (*c*) either a real absence or deficiency of feeling behind the façade of amused indifference or the ability actually to suspend judgement. It is this third class of detachment that characterizes the 'ironical man', the man whose irony truly expresses his character or his view of life. Ironists who could be detached in this way were apparently not recognized by Thirlwall since we find him saying:

> But where irony is not merely jocular, it is not simply serious, but earnest. With respect to opinion it implies a conviction so deep, as to disdain a direct refutation of the opposite party: with respect to feeling, it implies an emotion so strong, as to be able to command itself, and to suppress its natural tone, in order to vent itself with greater force.[1]

A view so simple as Thirlwall's could not have been taken by his contemporaries in Germany. I have once before quoted Goethe as saying:

A poet deserves not the name while he expresses nothing but his few subjective emotions. Only when he can appropriate to himself, and express the world, is he a poet.

It is equally remote from Thomas Mann's concept of irony as objectivity:

The novel scarcely knows how to begin except with the very beginning of all things and does not want to end at all; for the novel, the poet's line holds true: 'The fact that you cannot end is what makes you great.' But its greatness is mild, restful, serene, wise – 'objective'. It keeps its distance from things, *has* by its very nature distance from them; it hovers over them and smiles down upon them, regardless of how much, at the same time, it involves the hearer or reader in them by a process of weblike entanglement. The art of the epic is 'Apollinian' art as the aesthetic term would have it; because Apollo, distant marksman, is the god of distance, of objectivity, the god of irony. Objectivity is irony and the spirit of epic art is the spirit of irony.

Here you will be startled and will ask yourselves: how is that? Objectivity and irony – what have they to do with one another? Isn't irony the opposite of objectivity? Isn't it a highly subjective attitude, the ingredient of a romantic libertinism, which contrasts with classic repose and objectivity as their opposite? That is correct. Irony can have this meaning. But I use the word here in a broader, larger sense, given it by romantic subjectivism. In its equanimity it is an almost monstrous sense: the sense of *art* itself, a universal affirmation, which, as such, is also a universal negation; an all-embracing crystal clear and serene glance, which is the very glance of art itself, that is to say: a glance of the utmost freedom and calm and of an objectivity untroubled by any moralism. This was the glance of Goethe who was to that extent an artist that he uttered the strange and unforgettable characterization of irony: 'Irony is that little grain of salt which alone renders the dish palatable.' Not for nothing did he remain all his life such a great admirer of Shakespeare; for in the dramatic cosmos of Shakespeare this cosmic irony of art actually prevails, rendering his work so objectionable to such a moralist as Tolstoy took pains to be. I speak of this cosmic irony of art when I speak of the ironic objectivity of the epic.[2]

This last quotation gives me my principal theme for this section, the objectivity of the ironical observer and what, typically, it implies as to the observer's relationship and attitude to what he observes. The ironist and the object or victim of his irony are related as observer and observed. This accords with the basic duality of irony and with its basic opposition as well. The opposition of points of view which the irony presents is paralleled by a tension between the ironist's sense of his own position, that is, his attitude and his feelings as an observer, and his sense of the victim's position. The word 'observer' itself connotes both detachment and objectivity: a person is necessarily outside of and at a distance from what he observes; seeing is accounted the most intellectual of the senses and therefore the most objective (all this Thomas Mann coalesced into three words, 'Objectivity is irony'). Detachment and objectivity in turn connote disengagement, freedom, dispassion, a critical attitude. It is not, however, a scientific detachment and objectivity, since the attitude of the ironical observer is always coloured by his consciousness of the victim's confident unawareness. In other words, the ironist is never completely detached.

The ironist's awareness of himself as the unobserved observer tends to enhance his feeling of freedom and induce a mood perhaps of serenity, or joyfulness, or even exultation. His awareness of the victim's unawareness invites him to see the victim as committed where he feels disengaged; bound or trapped where he feels free; swayed by emotions, harassed, or miserable, where he is dispassionate, serene, or even moved to laughter; trustful, credulous, or naïve where he is critical, sceptical, or content to suspend judgement. And where his own attitude is that of a man whose world appears real and meaningful, he will see the victim's world as illusory or absurd.

There is no difficulty in documenting the ironist's feeling of being lifted up, unburdened, and liberated. Jean Paul Richter, for example, says that:

one could call the irony of Plato (and sometimes that of Galiani) . . . a universal irony, which, singing and playing, soars not only above errors but above all knowledge (for Plato does not raise himself only above the stupidities of men); and this irony resembles a free flame,

consuming and delighting at the same time, a flame which is the very
spirit of agility and rises only towards the heavens.[3]

And Goethe says that irony raises a man 'above happiness or un-
happiness, good or evil, death or life'[4] to a position which might
remind us of Verlaine's line about Nature's throne 'de splendeur,
d'ironie, et de sérénité'. Amiel compares 'the feeling which makes
man earnest [with] the irony which leaves them free', and Thomas
Mann, as we have just seen, speaks of irony as:

> an all-embracing crystal clear and serene glance, which is the very
> glance of art itself, that is to say: a glance of the utmost freedom and
> calm and of an objectivity untroubled by any moralism.

Speaking of his *Doctor Faustus* he couples the ironic spirit with
'artistic playfulness', 'gaiety in the sense of being beyond jest and
earnestness'.[5] There is also no difficulty, as we shall see later, in
documenting the ironist's view that what he sees from on high is
the contrary of his own position; the duality of observer and observed inevitably develops into a polarity.

The possibility of taking an ironical view may be directly derived from something as fundamental as the uniquely human
capacity for using language 'symbolically'. To be able to sub-
stitute words for things means being able to emerge, partly
though not entirely, from the mere flux of the purely subjective,
from the levels of mere feeling, mere experience, and merely instinctive action. Language implies abstraction and reflection,
which is to say, a transcending of the immediate and the experiential and an escape from the tyranny of the sequential. To see
someone as a victim of irony is to see him as being, relative to oneself, still submerged in unreflective subjectivity. What Ian Watt
says of the relationship to irony of the language of the eighteenth
century is relevant here:

> The analytic, generalizing tendency of the eighteenth-century
> vocabulary may itself be regarded as ironigenic . . .; partly because
> it lacks connotation, excludes the normally attendant feelings and
> evaluations with which its concrete referent is usually associated;

and partly because generalized diction has its own kind of connota-
tion, always suggesting a cool, unemotional and hence sceptical
evaluation of what it describes.[6]

But if man alone can be ironical only men can be ironized. One
can, it is true, see animals in ironic situations but only by a kind of
pathetic fallacy; if we laugh at the cat who looks behind the looking-glass for the cat reflected in it, it is because we mistakenly im-
pute to her the ability to avoid being so deluded. To see men as
victims of irony, to see them objectively, means seeing them as
objects, turning them into objects, or animals, seeing them as not
human, but at the same time imputing to them the human capacity to avoid being victims. This is the ironic view of men that
has found expression in animal fables from Aesop to Kafka. The
creatures we laugh at or pity in these fables are animals in that they
do not have or can only parody the intellectual potential that
distinguishes men, the power to see oneself and transcend one's
circumstances. At the same time they must also be *like* men, symbols of human nature, in order that we may pass judgment upon
their failure to exercise this power. The ironic view is totally un-
accommodating but perfectly just. The ironist, as I have said, cannot help feeling as a man, but irony itself is a matter of seeing not
feeling: it is based on intellect not sentiment.

There are certain 'basic situations' which, from their nature as
dualities of a *de haut en bas* kind (for the most part), tend to function
as ready-made containers, so to speak, for irony. These are the
dualities of God and man (or heaven and earth), audience and
play, puppet-master and puppet, artist and work of art, man and
animal (or machine), giant and pigmy, aristocrat and bourgeois,
rich and poor, traveller and native, present and past, waking and
dreaming. It will be difficult to talk about these one by one because of their interrelations and overlappings: God may be
thought of as the spectator of the *theatrum mundi*, or as the dreamer
of the dream we live; giants may be travellers, and native inhabitants may be animals; the novelist may be the god of his fictional
world. What I should like to make clear, by way of a selection of
passages and references, is that these dualities tend to produce
similar sets of ironic polarities: disengaged/involved; free/en-

slaved; dispassionate/emotional; serene/wretched; real/illusory; critical/credulous; meaningful/absurd.

The pure or archetypal ironist is God, 'the Aristophanes of heaven', as Heine calls him – 'He that sitteth in the heavens shall laugh: the Lord shall have them in derision.' He is the ironist *par excellence* because he is omniscient, omnipotent, transcendent, absolute, infinite, and free. In Solger's view:

> Supreme Irony reigns in the conduct of God as he creates men and the life of men. In earthly art Irony has this meaning – conduct similar to God's.[7]

The archetypal victim of irony is man, seen, *per contra*, as trapped and submerged in time and matter, blind, contingent, limited, and unfree. His status as the archetypal victim is well expressed by the self-evident futility of his recent plea, 'Stop the world! I want to get off!' The world stops only for those who have already got off: 'Sometimes I imagine,' says Renan, 'that if everyone arrived at our philosophy, the world would stop.'[8]

He that sitteth in the heavens or finds himself there has every inducement to laugh not simply because of what he sees but because of his elevated position. Conversely, if one wants to laugh heaven is the place to go to. There are many texts illustrating laughter from on high at the darkness and misery of a world the laughers have escaped. One reads in Lucretius:

> But this is the greatest joy of all: to stand aloof in a quiet citadel, strongly fortified by the teaching of the wise, and to gaze down from that elevation on others wandering aimlessly in a vain search for the way of life, . . . O joyless hearts of men! O minds without vision! How dark and dangerous the life in which this tiny span is lived away![9]

Pompey's spirit in Lucan's *Pharsalia*, Scipio in the *Somnium Scipionis*, Dante in the *Paradiso*, Troilus's ghost in *Troilus and Criseyde*, the gods of Tennyson's 'Lotus Eaters' all look down from heaven or near it and laugh or smile at what they see, so bearing out the truth of Jean Paul's statement:

> If man, like ancient theology, glances down from the world beyond on the terrestrial world, the latter looks small and vain.[10]

Amiel says much the same:

> When once a man has touched the absolute, all that might be other than what it is seems to him indifferent. All these ants pursuing their private ends excite his mirth. He looks down from the moon upon his hovel; he beholds the earth from the heights of the sun; he considers his life from the point of view of the Hindoo pondering the days of Brahma; he sees the finite from the distance of the infinite [sous l'angle de l'infini], and thenceforward the insignificance of all those things which men hold to be important makes effort ridiculous, passion burlesque, and prejudice absurd.[11]

The aeroplane in Waugh's *Vile Bodies*, on the other hand, fails to rise beyond the reach of despair to the realm of ironic laughter; we see the meaningless scurry of insignificant life but the bitterness is an index of the author's continuing involvement.

The concept of the *theatrum mundi* with the gods *in* the gods as 'the sharp judicious spectators' is too well known to need much illustration. When Macbeth no longer has an interest in the world, life has become for him only an empty mechanical repetition (tomorrow and tomorrow and tomorrow) of a performance signifying nothing. There are several ways in which we can see the drama of life as ironic. Claudel speaks of 'this very interesting drama, written by an infinitely wise and good author, a drama in which we have an essential role but in which it is impossible to know in advance the smallest peripeteia'.[12] A more familiar view is that which sees men as actors who can do and say only what has been set down for them though behaving as if they had free will:

> d'humbles marionnettes
> Dont le fil est aux mains de la Nécessité[13]

as Sully-Prudhomme puts it. To this we may add that our aware-ness of stage-life as an illusion enables us to imagine our own life as illusory. In *The Man Without Qualities* Ulrich, looking out from the Palais Leinsdorf upon a somewhat half-heartedly riotous mob, sees first the street and then the room he is in as a stage:

> And these people under the window here, at whom Ulrich was still staring down, spellbound, without taking any notice of Count Leinsdorf – they too were only staging a farce! . . . 'No,' he thought,

'what they are up to is a performance much more like a ritual act, a consecrated play with affronted emotions of the profoundest kind, some half-civilised, half-savage vestige of communal actions that the individual does not need to take seriously down to the very last detail.' He envied them. 'How pleasant they are even now, at this stage, when they are trying to make themselves as unpleasant as possible!' he thought . . . But at the same time he felt behind him the presence of the room, with the big paintings on the wall, the long Empire desk, the stiff perpendicular lines of the bell-ropes and the curtains. And that in itself now had something of the quality of a little stage, on which he stood right in front, in the opening between the curtains, while outside, on the greater stage, the drama went past; and these two stages had a peculiar way of uniting, without regard for the fact that he stood between them.[14]

From an ironic standpoint, life may be seen as a tapestry (the web of life), as a painting (or canvas), and as a narrative; Tennyson and Shakespeare called it a tale of little or no meaning. That it is more frequently called a drama is, I think, not or not only because plays are more frequently ironical than narratives. There is irony in *Tom Jones* and yet even there Fielding speaks of 'the great theatre of nature'. The reason is that only in the theatre does the observer actually see not only real men without free will (as actors they have resigned it) but also embodied fictions behaving as if they had free will. And only in the theatre does the observer watch actual people who *cannot* know they are being watched. It is true that a character in a novel can only say what the novelist wrote for him and that he cannot be aware that he is only being read about; but, not being embodied in an actor, he cannot appear to us as we might appear to Hardy's Spirit Ironic or some other extra-terrestrial observer.

The ironical relationship between the artist and the work of art cannot simply be that of observer and observed, the work not being independent of the artist. We shall find ourselves talking rather of the artist's power, objectivity, and freedom, and of the illusory nature of the work. The concepts of the artist as a god (as in Scaliger, Sidney, and Shaftesbury) and of God as an artist (as in Goethe, Schelling, and Friedrich Schlegel) are of greater antiquity

than the names I have mentioned. But it was not until they combined with the growing self-consciousness of the artist (the
eighteenth-century novelist in particular) and the emphasis, in
late eighteenth-century and Romantic literary theory, on the
artist's creative processes that the gap between the artist and his
work became wide enough for the artist to be thought of as 'He
that sitteth in the heavens', with all the attitudes towards his work
that accompany the God's-eye view. An interesting statement of
the artist's god-like relation to his work is to be found in Thirlwall:

> The dramatic poet is the creator of a little world, in which he rules
> with absolute sway, and may shape the destinies of the imaginary
> beings to whom he gives life and breath according to any plan he
> may choose . . . From this [mimic] sphere [of his creating] . . . he
> himself stands aloof. The eye with which he views his microcosm,
> and the creatures who move in it, will not be one of human friend-
> ship, nor of brotherly kindness, nor of parental love; it will be that
> with which he imagines that the invisible power who orders the
> destiny of man might regard the world and its doings.[15]

The ironist is potentially capable, perhaps inclined by nature, to
look at the real world with the same eye. A. R. Thompson, in his
Dry Mock, writing of Ibsen, says:

> In a poem of the late 'fifties, 'On the Heights', he describes how the
> young artist learns to live 'above life's line of snow' and watch his
> home burn down, his mother buried, his sweet-heart wed to another,
> without emotion except for the aesthetic effect of the pictures . . .
> 'Up here on the fells must be freedom and God, / Men do but grope,
> in the valley.'[16]

Thomas Mann's Tonio Kröger says:

> [The curse of literature] begins by your feeling yourself set apart, in
> a curious sort of opposition to the nice, regular people; there is a gulf
> of ironic sensibility, of knowledge, scepticism, disagreement, be-
> tween you and the others.[17]

And in *Lotte in Weimar* he presents Riemer explaining Goethe to
Lotte:

'You are wrong,' said he, 'it is not furor. It is something else, I know not what; something higher, perhaps, let us say. He is illumined. But inspired he is not. Can you imagine the Lord God being that? He is the object of our fervour; but to Him it is of course foreign. One ascribes to Him a peculiar coldness, a destructive equanimity. For what should He feel enthusiasm, on whose side should he stand? For He is the whole, He is His own side, He stands on His side, His attitude is one of all-embracing irony. I am no theologian, my good friend, and no philosopher. But my experience has often led me to speculate upon the relation between, yes, the unity of the All and the Nothing, *nihil*. And if it is allowable to derive from this sinister word a cult, a system, a mental attitude towards the world, then one may justly go on to equate the all-embracingness and the nihilism. It follows that it is wrong to conceive of God and the Devil as opposed principles; more correctly, the diabolic is only one side – the wrong side, if you like – of the divine. If God is All, then He is also the Devil; and one cannot approach to the godlike without at the same time approaching to the diabolic – so that, in a manner of speaking, heaven looks at you out of one eye, and the hell of the iciest negation and most destructive neutrality out of the other. But whether they lie close together or far apart, it is two eyes, my dear lady, that make up one gaze. So now I ask you: what sort of gaze is that wherein the horrifying contradiction of the two eyes is united? I will tell you, tell you and myself: it is the gaze of absolute art, which is at once absolute love and absolute nihilism and indifference, and implies that horrifying approach to the godlike-diabolic which we call genius.'[18]

The duality of the subjective, shadowy, and irrational dream and the relatively objective, definite, and rational waking state has long provided an analogy for the duality of an illusory world and a real heaven:

> He hath awakened from the dream of life –
> 'Tis we, who lost in stormy visions, keep
> With phantoms an unprofitable strife,
> And in mad trance, strike with our spirit's knife
> Invulnerable nothings.

Nothing more easy than to exploit the irony of this and see all our triumphs and defeats as equally the dream of an extra-terrestrial being such as Hardy's:

> ... dreaming, dark, dumb Thing
> That turns the handle of this idle show!

> ... a fixed foresightless dream
> Is Its whole philosopheme.[19]

The voice is that of the Spirit Ironic. The last irony in Mark Twain's *Mysterious Stranger* is the revelation that nothing exists but the solipsist's dream. José Ferrater Mora, in his book on Unamuno, brings out the parallels between literary creation and dreaming and between the novelist and God, who in dreaming us creates a 'kind of cosmic novel'.[20]

Typically, as we have seen, the ironist from his safe seat on high watches the victim wandering aimlessly down below. But the ironist's freedom may be expressed by mobility as well as by a secure and joyful elevation above the pull of gravity. If he is not in a position where he can, 'with extensive view / Survey mankind from China to Peru', he may be found as a traveller to or from China or Peru, not wandering aimlessly but freely journeying. As a Turkish spy or a Persian nobleman in Paris, an Englishman in Lilliput, a picaresque perambulator, or a time-machine traveller from the future, the ironist retains his detachment and his power of seeing with fresh eyes what superstition, custom, and prejudice have obscured for the stay-at-home victims. This physical mobility of the traveller is the outward and visible sign of the ironist's spiritual or mental agility (as physical elevation is the sign of spiritual or mental superiority); and a sign of his (relative) invulnerability too, as the ironical philosopher Hume suggests:

> How complete must be *his* victory who remains always, with all mankind, on the offensive, and has himself no fixed station or abiding city which he is ever, on any occasion, obliged to defend?[21]

It is not uncommon to find '*de haut en bas*' irony combined with 'mobile' irony. Gulliver is a giant in Lilliput as well as a stranger. In Lesage's *Le Diable Boiteux* Don Cléofas is elevated above

Madrid by the devil Asmodée who removes the roofs of the houses they visit so that, without being seen, they can see the spectacle of life, much as in a modern theatre the stage appears to the onlookers as a room with one wall removed. We might notice in passing, as a fact not without significance, that the British periodicals of the eighteenth century had for the most part titles that suggested the detachment and objectivity of either the mobile or the elevated observer: *The Rambler*, *The Idler*, *The Adventurer*, *The World*, *The Lounger*, *The Bee*, *The Spectator*, *The Examiner*, *The Mirror*, *The Observer*, *The Looker-on*, *The Connoisseur*.

The relationship in irony between the observer and the observed can take many different forms. But whether the difference between them is presented as 'cosmological', from Heaven to Earth, or geographical, from Persia to Paris or from mountain to valley (or Magic Mountain to lowlands), or physical, from giant to pigmy, or biological, from man to penguin, or social, from dandy to boor, or aesthetico-psychological, from spectator to play, the laughter that tends to arise at the spectacle of insignificance, wretchedness, vanity, stupidity, or littleness is fundamentally the laughter of freedom at enslavement. The ironist tends to laugh because by comparison he feels free. In order to be able to laugh he presents his victim as not free.

Boswell quotes Johnson as saying, 'All theory is against the freedom of the will; all experience for it.' Diderot says much the same:

> On est fataliste, et à chaque instant on pense, on parle, on écrit comme si l'on persévérait dans le préjugé de la liberté. . . . On est devenu philosophe dans ses systèmes et l'on reste peuple dans son propos.[22]

It is in fact a commonplace that subjectively we feel free, but what we see objectively, from outside, we cannot see as anything but determined. Descartes' discovery of himself as a free thinking mind was arrived at by a subjective, experiential process; what he discovered objectively was that animals were soulless machines. In Voltaire's *Micromégas* the gigantic visitors from Sirius and Jupiter supposed at first that the humans they came across were

too small to have souls; what made them reverse this natural supposition were the microscope and the megaphone that raised these
insects to the status of rational beings. Bergson's theory of the
laughable is based upon the possibility of seeing men as merely
mechanical:

> The attitudes, gestures and movements of the human body are
> laughable in exact proportion as that body reminds us of a mere
> machine.

> We laugh every time a person gives us the impression of being a
> thing.[23]

Albert Cook's *The Dark Voyage and the Golden Mean* takes a
similar view:

> When men are represented comically as beasts, we laugh because
> we know that inasmuch as they are bestial we can be successful by
> predicting them . . . Tragedy reveals the soul of the individual hero;
> comedy represents the all-too-human under the rational subguise of
> beast or machine.[24]

God, as the ultimate 'outsider', again provides an analogy for
the ironist. Theology, like philosophy, raises doubts about free
will precisely because it posits an abstracted, detached point of
view. We read, for example, in Boethius's *Consolations of Philosophy* (Book V, Prosa 6) that God inhabits a never-ending present;
past, present, and future are simultaneously present to His omniscience, as in a map here, there, and yonder can all be seen at once.
Boethius believed in free will, but having once posited God's
complete foreknowledge his attempt to persuade us by logic that
this does not preclude free will is laborious and unconvincing.
Theologians of other centuries have felt the same sharp stone in
their shoes, as well they might – only people who wear shoes get
stones in them. As long as there is a transcendent observer, what
he observes will appear 'fixed', and only a god who has come
down to earth and has been made man can redeem men and set
them free from the old law. But it's no good his going back
again.

Similarly, the man who, as we say, 'stops to think' emerges to some degree from the flux of time; whereas to be wholly engaged in something is to lose track of time. The novelist, accordingly, whose work is not a mere adventure story or a mere fictionalized day-dream but a composition, something apart from himself which he reflects upon, may play down the element of time as a sequential quality and in its place emphasize the structural or spatial quality, or alternatively, the randomness of events. In either case his characters will tend to figure as the victims of destiny or chance and hence as potential if not actual victims of irony.

Already in an earlier chapter (see p. 31) I had very briefly remarked that ironists are themselves vulnerable to irony. We are now in a position to elaborate this a little. What the ironist objectively sees is, to put it in the most basic terms, a soulless slave mechanically performing meaningless acts in a meaningless world while being confidently unaware that he is anything but a rational self-determining person behaving purposefully in a meaningful world. This induces in the ironist the feeling that he is everything that the victim is not. But the situation the ironist feels and assumes himself to be in is precisely the same situation as the victim mistakenly assumes that *he* is in. The only difference is that the ironist is looking at a victim; the result, however, of his focusing his attention in this direction is that he leaves his rear exposed. This close resemblance of ironist and victim of irony can perhaps be brought out more clearly by the curious fact that a portrait of someone smiling, but not smiling at anything represented in or implied by the portrait, may be interpreted either as a portrait of someone smiling ironically or as an ironical portrait of someone smiling with foolish self-satisfaction. Evelyn Waugh evidently felt the truth of this since he speaks of 'the sly, complacent smile of la Gioconda'.[25]

Looking at this in another way, we can say that the terms 'elevated', 'detached', 'free', and so on which seem so inevitably and naturally applicable to the ironist are not entirely unequivocal. The German Romantic Ironists were on occasion inclined to exult in the freedom that irony gave them to soar above the earth, that 'dim spot that mortals call the world'. But some later explorers and exploiters of this free space were to find out that 'above' and 'below' became less and less meaningful and they began to wonder whether the infinite heavens were not after all only the bottomless pit, and whether the archetypal ironist were not the Devil instead of God.

So it is a question whether this gaiety and serenity of the ironic spirit can be maintained. No doubt there is something exhilarating in the destructive powers of irony, and Heine can attack the un-ironical *King Oedipus* of Count Platen with splendid verve:

> There is nowhere in this work a trace of that profound world-destructive imagination which underlies every Aristophanic comedy, from which, as from a fantastic, ironic, magic tree, bloom the rich branches of thought, with their nests of singing nightingales and clambering apes. This loftiness of conception, with its death-jubilation and its fireworks of destruction, we cannot, of course, expect from the poor Count.[26]

But if irony really is world-destructive, the magic tree may wither, the nightingales may fly away, and only a wilderness of chattering apes may remain.

This nihilism of irony finds a perfect image in the echo in the Marabar caves of *A Passage to India*:

> The echo . . . is entirely devoid of distinction. Whatever is said, the same monotonous noise replies, and quivers up and down the walls until it is absorbed into the roof. 'Boum' is the sound as far as the human alphabet can express it, or 'bou-oum', or 'ou-boum', – utterly dull. Hope, politeness, the blowing of a nose, the squeak of a boot, all produce 'boum'.
>
> The echo began in some indescribable way to undermine her hold on life. Coming at a moment when she chanced to be fatigued, it had managed to murmur, 'Pathos, piety, courage – they exist, but are identical, and so is filth. Everything exists, nothing has value.' If one had spoken vileness in that place, or quoted lofty poetry, the comment would have been the same – 'ou-boum'. . . . The Marabar . . . robbed infinity and eternity of their vastness, the only quality that accommodates them to mankind.[27]

But whether irony, taken far enough, necessarily ends in nihilism and world-destruction is a matter for argument. I reserve the question for the following section in which the morality of irony is discussed.

I have tried in this section to present only what has seemed to me archetypally, essentially, or generally true of the 'ironical man' in his relationship to and his attitude towards what he observes ironically. In practice, of course, these relationships and attitudes will vary to the degree that ironists are various. But while it is for the critic to characterize merely individual differences, there are grounds for thinking that the ironist's position as such tends to generate certain other feelings and attitudes, besides those I have already spoken of.

If we bear in mind that the ironist is continually confronted by oppositions between pleasant appearances and harsh realities, we shall not think it surprising that his irony should frequently be coloured by feelings of melancholy and compassion. It is, however, chiefly among writers in French that we find an awareness of a relationship between these feelings and irony. Amiel recognized:

> in [his] ironical and disillusioned being . . . a child, a simple heart, a saddened and a guileless spirit believing in ideals, in love, in holiness.[28]

Georges Palante, glossing a passage from Remy de Gourmont, writes:

> It is from among the sentimental that ironists are recruited. These endeavour to free themselves from their sentimentalism employing irony as their weapon. But the sentimentalism resists and can still be heard faintly through the ironical intention. Some take pleasure in their sentimentalism; they cherish it and would not, for anything in the world, tear out and throw away the delicate flower of sentiment. They use irony to cover up sentiment. It is the modesty-veil of passion, tenderness, and regret.[29]

A few years later Raphaël Cor, in a book on Anatole France, uses the same words: 'Among the sensitive, irony is often only the modesty of tenderness.'[30] Chevalier, also writing with Anatole France in mind, says:

The Ironist's mind keeps pace with the pioneers of his time, embracing eagerly each new discovery, ever open and on the alert for whatever science, erudition and criticism may bring to light. His emotions, on the other hand, will haunt the deserted, leaf-strewn avenues of the past, feeding upon vanished realities.[31]

And Jankélévitch in his *L'Ironie, ou la bonne conscience*:

Irony is the somewhat melancholy gaiety which the discovery of a plurality inspires in us.[32]

One might rather think irony was apt to develop a bad conscience to judge from a certain tendency in some ironists to soften its essential mercilessness with compassion or love. There is the well-known passage in Anatole France:

The more I reflect upon human life, the more I believe that it should be given, as witnesses and as judges, Irony and Pity, just as the Egyptians on behalf of their dead called upon the goddess Isis and the goddess Nephtys. Irony and Pity are two good counsellors; the one, in smiling, makes life agreeable for us; the other, weeping, makes it sacred. The irony I invoke is not cruel. It mocks neither love nor beauty. It is mild and benevolent. Its laughter calms anger, and it is this irony that teaches us to make fun of the fools and villains whom otherwise we might have been weak enough to hate.[33]

And in Thomas Mann's 'Art of the Novel':

In all of this you must not think of coldness and lovelessness, contempt and scorn. Epic irony is rather an irony of the heart, a loving irony; it is greatness filled with tenderness for little things.[34]

2 · The Morals of Irony

There are three uses of irony which do not call for any special justification. Irony may be used as a rhetorical device to enforce one's meaning. It may be used, in any of the Four Modes, as a satiric device to attack a point of view or to expose folly, hypocrisy, or vanity. It may be used as an heuristic device to lead one's readers to see that things are not so simple or certain as they seem, or perhaps not so complex or doubtful as they seem. It is probable that most irony is rhetorical, satirical, or heuristic. In such cases it is the end that must justify the means.

Beyond this point the morality of irony becomes questionable, which, however, is not to suggest there may be no answer. Few would wish to have so restricted a view as that of Settembrini in *The Magic Mountain*:

> 'Don't you believe them, Engineer, never believe them when they grumble. They all do it, without exception, and all of them are only too much at home up here. They lead a loose and idle life, and imagine themselves entitled to pity, and justified of their bitterness, irony, and cynicism. "This pleasure resort," she said. Well, isn't it a pleasure resort, then? In my humble opinion it is, and in a very questionable sense too. So life is a "sell", up here at this pleasure resort! But once let them go down below and their manner of life will be such as to leave no doubt that they mean to come back again. Irony, forsooth! Guard yourself, Engineer, from the sort of irony that thrives up here; guard yourself altogether from taking on their mental attitude! Where irony is not a direct and classic device of oratory, not for a moment equivocal to a healthy mind, it makes for depravity, it becomes a drawback to civilization, an unclean traffic with the forces of reaction, vice, and materialism.'

> 'Imagine,' he [Castorp] said to himself, 'he talks about irony just as he does about music, he'll soon be telling us that it is politically suspect – that is, from the moment it ceases to be a "direct and classic device of oratory". But irony that is "not for a moment equivocal" – what kind of irony would that be, I should like to ask, if I may make so bold as to put in my oar? It would be a piece of dried-up pedantry!' Thus ungrateful is immature youth! It takes all that is offered, and bites the hand that feeds it.[35]

Irony that is not simply rhetorical, satirical, or heuristic must be more or less self-regarding, or self-regarding as well as satirical or heuristic. It may be self-regarding, self-protective, or evasive to such an extreme degree that we would do better to call it sometimes hoaxing, sometimes hypocrisy. On the other hand, there are circumstances in which we would readily sympathize with

and even approve of self-regarding or self-protective irony. It
may be the only or the natural or the best way of dealing with
certain real difficulties.

Renan is a case in point. He was, André Hallays tells us, a man
with divided loyalties to two opposed attitudes, each fundamental
to his personality. There were, Hallays says, two Renans:

> The Renan who loved stories of the past retained in daily life the
> priestly virtues and attitudes; the Renan who believed quite un-
> reservedly in the future of science placed reason and methodology
> above everything and pursued unwearyingly his great critical work.
> The first Renan recommended to the second reserve and respect for
> people's feelings. The second, with the light-heartedness of an honest
> workman, mocked the first, smiling at his romanticism and his
> seriousness. Thence attenuations, reticences and, where necessary, the
> stratagem of the paradox. Therein lies all the irony of Renan.[36]

Much more common is the irony of a suspended judgement. A
man may be unable to take sides in some controversial question
either because he sympathizes with both sides or because, sym-
pathizing with neither, he can see no third alternative. In such a
case we might not think it improper for him to express himself
ironically and so protect himself against the danger of a premature
judgement. Irony, Jankélévitch says, practises 'l'art d'effleurer',

> adopting, one after another, an infinity of points of view in such a
> way that they correct each other; thus we escape all one-sided
> *centrismes* and recover the impartiality of justice and reason.[37]

Amiel's view of Renan's manner, not essentially different from
that of Hallays, is expressed differently; for him Renan is a man
unable to accept or reject opposed points of view:

> In the last analysis he is a free-thinker, but one whose flexible
> imagination permits itself the delicate epicureanism of religious
> emotion. He looks on the man who does not lend himself to these
> graceful fancies as vulgar, and on the man who takes them seriously
> as limited. He amuses himself with the variations of conscience as
> with a kaleidoscope, but he is of too subtle a mind to laugh at them.
> The true critic neither concludes nor excludes; his pleasure is to

understand without believing and to profit from works of enthusiasm
while still remaining detached and free of illusion. This behaviour
might be thought double-dealing; but it is no more than the pleasant
irony of a highly cultivated mind that wishes neither to be ignorant
of anything nor to be taken in by anything.[38]

Irony, again, may be not merely the natural or merely the best
way but perhaps the only way to deal with life. The detached
point of view of an inhabitant of China or Saturn that an eighteenth-century ironist temporarily adopted may become a necessity. As Amiel says:

> One needs to be a Japanese to recognize the farcical contradictions
> of the Christian civilization. One needs to be an inhabitant of the
> moon fully to comprehend the stupidity of man and his state of
> perpetual illusion.[39]

One must separate oneself from a world which is dead, illusory,
unmanageable, contradictory, or absurd. But unless one commits
suicide, one must also accept it. Accept it therefore ironically. For
Goethe irony was 'that little grain of salt which alone renders the
dish palatable'.[40] For Kierkegaard 'no authentic human life was
possible without irony' [that is, 'mastered' irony, not Romantic
Irony].[41] For Anatole France 'the world without irony would be
like a forest without birds'.[42] The alternative might be despair,
Bertrand Russell's conviction that 'only on the firm foundation
of unyielding despair can the soul's habitation henceforth be safely
built'.[43] Parallel with but at a much higher level than all those
writers of the turn of the century (see Albérès *L'aventure intellectuelle du xxᵉ siècle*) who felt they must escape from the sterilities of
intellectualism into life as pure experience, is Thomas Mann saying in his *Meditations of a Non-Political Man*:

> Irony and radicalism – this is an alternative and an Either–Or. An
> intelligent man has the choice (*if* he has it) to be either ironical or
> radical. There is, in all decency, no third possibility. Which he is
> depends upon the argument he accepts as ultimately and absolutely
> valid: life or spirit . . . For the radical man life is no argument. *Fiat
> spiritus, pereat vita!* But the words of irony are: 'Can truth be an
> argument if it is a matter of life?'[44]

And a few years later he speaks of:

> that irony which glances at both sides, which plays slyly and
> irresponsibly – yet not without benevolence – among opposites, and
> is in no great haste to take sides and come to decisions; guided as it
> is by the surmise that in great matters, in matters of humanity, every
> decision may prove premature; that the real goal to reach is not
> decision but harmony, accord. And harmony, in a matter of eternal
> contraries, may lie in infinity.[45]

Kenneth Burke relates this 'negative capability', this ability to
accept contradictions, to other twentieth-century phenomena:

> Irony, novelty, experimentalism, vacillation, the cult of conflict –
> are not these men [Mann and Gide] trying to make us at home in
> indecision, are they not trying to humanize the state of doubt?[46]

After so long an age of faith in a world accepted as ultimately
meaningful the state of doubt is intolerable, but it is perhaps a
state we must learn to live with. In Musil's *Man without Qualities*
we have this brief exchange:

> [Ulrich] had been talking the way one does when, in a moment of
> uncertainty, one sums up the result of decades of certainty . . . 'And
> so,' Walter retorted sharply, 'you think we ought to do without any
> meaning in life?' Ulrich asked him what he really needed a meaning
> for. One got along all right without it, he commented.[47]

Irony as a means of avoiding decisions in situations in which a
decision is either impossible or clearly unwise is, though self-
protective, usually heuristic as well. There are, however, cases in
which irony is more purely self-regarding. One may, for example,
be determined to tell the truth, to satisfy one's own conscience, in
circumstances in which telling the truth is dangerous. 'If men,'
says Shaftesbury, 'are forbid to speak their minds seriously on
certain subjects, they will do it ironically.'[48] To this end one may
as a 'private ironist' put on an antic disposition and pretend to be
a fool or a simpleton, or speak equivocally or ambiguously, or
employ the device I have called 'irony by analogy'. This is how
Heine explained one aspect of Goethe's irony:

Just as Cervantes at the time of the Inquisition took refuge in humorous irony to present his thoughts without exposing himself to the clutches of the familiars of the Holy Office, so Goethe expressed in tones of humorous irony that which he dared not say openly, since he was a courtier and a minister of state. Goethe never suppressed the truth, but where he could not show her naked, he dressed her in humour and irony.[49]

To recognize an irony in the incompatible demands of the individual and society is, in a sense, to raise oneself above these demands though one still remains both an individual and a member of society. This ironic acceptance of an incompatibility can then be the basis, can at least be proposed as a basis for a way of living that reconciles the assertive and submissive, the seclusive and the gregarious instincts. There is in Knox an excellent account of Shaftesbury's advice to himself on how to live ironically:

> The second irony inherent in Shaftesbury's ideas would be that pervasive irony of manner which is a fusion of modest self-abnegation, a kind of gravity, and an apparent tolerance of all things behind which hide reservations about all things . . . The motive is to defend one's soul against prying by the world, to defend oneself from one's own temporal interests and passions, and yet to seem to live in accommodation with the society one belongs to. It is a constant way of life which is not intended to issue in verbal warfare; indeed the reservations beneath the tolerance are hidden to all except the acutest observer, the general effect being one of simple and true, though slightly peculiar, character.[50]

In *Marius the Epicurean* the hero protects himself by an ironical manner while accommodating himself to the demands of society:

> He was become aware of the possibility of a large dissidence between an inward and somewhat exclusive world of vivid personal apprehension, and the unimproved, unheightened reality of the life of those about him . . . To move . . . in that outer world of other people, as though taking it at their estimate, would be possible henceforth only as a kind of irony.[51]

And later we read again of:

the irony which lay beneath that remarkable self-possession, as of one taking all things with a difference from other people, perceptible in voice, in expression, and even in his dress. It was, in truth, the air of one who, entering vividly into life and relishing to the full the delicacies of its intercourse, yet feels all the while, from the point of view of an ideal philosophy, that he is but conceding reality to suppositions, choosing of his own will to walk in a day dream, of the illusiveness of which he at least is aware.[52]

The passage from Knox presents Shaftesbury as using irony to defend himself from his own temporal interests and passions. In societies where it is not the thing for a man openly to express his feelings he may by parodying them express them nevertheless. Where conventional behaviour is conventionally despised a man may use irony to protect himself against contempt as Mr Donne does in Ivy Compton-Burnett's *Elders and Betters*:

> 'Well, my daughter,' said Mr Donne, embracing Anna in a conventional but ironic manner, and introducing these qualities into his speech; 'so we are united once again.'[53]

Different again is the genuinely prophylactic self-irony that runs through *Doctor Faustus*. An ambitious, greatly gifted, but at the same time highly self-conscious writer, like Thomas Mann, is inevitably in a false position the moment he undertakes a major work; obviously one cannot plan greatness in all seriousness. In his *Genesis of a Novel* he says:

> To propose that a work be big in every sense, to plan it so from the start, was probably not right – neither for the work nor for the state of mind of the author. Therefore I must introduce as much jesting, as much ridicule of the biographer, as much anti-self-important mockery as possible.[54]

Self-protective irony may be an expression of prudence or wisdom in the face of a world full of snares or a world in which nothing is certain. But thin partitions divide the bounds of prudence and timidity. In the following passage, Jeffrey, the editor of the *Edinburgh Review*, is seen both as ironically aware of the fact that nothing is simple and as laughing for fear of being laughed at:

I am almost as great an admirer [of Wordsworth] as Sharpe. The only difference is, that I have a sort of consciousness that admirers are ridiculous, and therefore I laugh at almost everything I admire, or at least let people laugh at it without contradiction. You must be in earnest when you approve, and have yet to learn that everything has a respectable and a deridable aspect.[55]

Victor Brombert points out that Stendhal uses irony to protect himself and his heroes (whom nevertheless he ironizes on his own account) against the obtuse or vulgar reader, and he quotes from Stendhal's *Promenade dans Rome*: 'Quelle duperie de parler de ce qu'on aime! Le premier sot ne viendra-t-il pas, par un mot plaisant, salir votre souvenir?'[56] And yet Brombert finds Stendhal's irony 'défensive, et pour ainsi dire timide'.[57]

Timid, Stendhal may be, but so long as there is something worth protecting, the ironist has our sympathy. It is a different matter when irony is used as a means to have one's cake and eat it, or to camouflage emptiness or mere negation, or to disguise weakness as strength and then by this false show of strength to intimidate others (not that one need sympathize with the intimidated). Ironies of these kinds are related to a number of other protective devices: in order to be right whatever the outcome, the oracles protected themselves by equivocal utterances ('If Croesus goes to war he will destroy a mighty empire'); in order to prevent the gods from thinking him more fortunate than a mortal should be, Caesar, it is said, permitted his soldiers to sing ribald songs about him in his triumphal processions; in order to placate his angry superiors, Dr Panna Lal, the apothecary in *A Passage to India*, behaves before them like a buffoon. Fulke Greville, casting about for some way of publishing his treatise, *The Declination of Monarchy*, whose faults he recognized though he was reluctant or unable to mend them, writes:

A new counsell rose up in me, to take away all opinion of seriousnesse from these perplexed pedigrees; and to this end carelessly cast them into that hypocriticall figure *Ironia*, wherein men commonly (to keep above their workes) seeme to make toies of the utmost they can doe.[58]

Such procedures lend themselves to the charge of cowardice and trickery as well as hypocrisy. It is possible, for example, to see in what Hume says an irony against irony:

> How complete must be *his* victory who remains always, with all mankind, on the offensive, and has himself no fixed station or abiding city which he is ever, on any occasion, obliged to defend?[59]

Amiel felt the world to be a burden and a limitation upon his spirit; his true life was in contemplation: 'La virtualité pure, l'équilibre parfait est mon refuge de prédilection. Là je me sens libre, désinteressé, souverain.'[60] But he was aware of this refuge as a temptation; and worse:

> This eternal smile of unfeeling criticism, this supercilious, bowelless mockery which corrodes and demolishes everything, opts out of all personal duty and all vulnerable affection, and cares only to understand but not to act, this ironical contemplation, how maleficent, how infectious and unwholesome! At bottom I find it immoral like pharisaism, for it does not preach by example, and it imposes on others the burdens it refuses for itself. It is insolent as well for it pretends to be knowledge while it is only doubt.[61]

More recently Benjamin De Mott, writing of the 'sick' comedians of America, says:

> The ['sicknik'] ironist steps forth as a self-protecting man; fearing quick assessment he seeks a manner that will convey that he is more complicated than any words he utters can suggest.

> [The new irony] must begin in gestures that create an elite group; it must end not in positions but in universal hostility – hostility to *all* positive assertion, rejection of any lines of intelligence available to ordinary men. The one truth the new irony has to tell is that the man who uses it has no place to stand except in momentary community with those who seek to express a comparable alienation from other groups. The one conviction it expresses is that there are really no sides left: no virtue to oppose to corruption, no wisdom to oppose to cant. The one standard it accepts is that on which the simple man – the untutored non-ironist who fancies (in his dolthood) that he knows what good and bad should mean – is registered as the zero of our world, a cipher worth nothing but uninterrupted contempt.[62]

Such irony, on De Mott's showing, can move only in the direction of nihilism. It becomes the irony of the devil, 'the spirit of eternal negation'. Excluded for ever from participation in the world, unable to love (or hate if it is true that one can only hate what could be loved) his glacial indifference can find expression only in irony. A similar train of thought led Maurras to say that Heine, 'grimace l'ironie quand il se voit exclu du lyrisme supérieur'.[63] (I am far from suggesting that the reader accept so simple an explanation of Heine's irony: Maurras doubtless had his reasons which reason would not recognize.) The link between Jeffrey's 'sort of consciousness that admirers are ridiculous', and 'the spirit of eternal negation' can be found in a sentence of Jacques Barzun: 'To admire nothing at all, for fear of being duped, is a progressive disease of the spirit.'[64]

Barzun in a later work blames the novel:

Where have intellectuals learned, together with their anti-intellectualism, these diffident gestures of the spirit? The answer is: in the novel. The novel from its beginnings in *Don Quixote* and *Tom Jones* has persistently made war on two things – our culture and the heroic . . . The novel . . . has been the textbook of increasingly plain manners, a manual of resentful self-consciousness . . . Two centuries of geniuses have shown us that every moral attitude betrays an immoral urge, every virtue its complementary vice, every institution the evil it is meant to restrict. No wonder modern man has grown suspicious of himself and others, devious, ironic.[65]

It is likewise the novel that provides Wayne C. Booth with examples of the irresponsible irony that so easily intimidates even the most reputable critics:

When Lionel Trilling confessed recently his inability to decide, in reading Nabokov's controversial *Lolita*, whether the narrator's final indictment of his own immorality is to be taken seriously or ironically, he hastened to explain that this ambiguity made the novel better, not worse. 'Indeed, for me one of the attractions of *Lolita*,' he says, 'is its ambiguity of tone . . . and its ambiguity of intention, its ability to arouse uneasiness, to throw the reader off balance' and, by urging 'moral mobility', to represent peculiarly well 'certain aspects

of American life'. The argument is clear. Our life is morally
ambiguous; this book makes it seem even more so – it throws us even
more off balance, presumably, than we were before – and hence its
very lack of clarity is a virtue.

In short, we have looked for so long at foggy landscapes reflected
in misty mirrors that we have come to *like* fog. Clarity and simplicity
are suspect; irony reigns supreme. [It is now] something which in
itself is desirable. In a recent book on irony in the drama, we read
that *because* Fielding was a 'greater ironist', he is probably a greater
novelist than Richardson. Though no responsible critic has ever
argued that all ambiguities resulting from irony are good ambiguities, it is astonishing to see how reluctant we have become to
discriminate, to point to this or that particular difficulty springing
from irony and say, 'This is a fault.' After all, we say, it is only the
enemies of literature who ask that its effects be handed to the reader
on a platter. And yet we all know that our lines of communication
have been fouled, and that this is not a good thing.[66]

The real import of the last four or five pages is that the morality
of irony is questionable, not simply because certain ironists abuse
irony and, by employing it to cover up their weaknesses, irre-
sponsibly destroy its efficacy or render it suspect, but because irony
by its nature seems to have a power to corrupt the ironist. This it
does by offering him both a refuge from life and a means of sub-
jecting it to his own ego, in short, by providing for him, free of
charge, a 'womb with a view', to borrow a phrase of Cyril Con-
nolly's.

The most thorough-going presentation of the self-defeat of the
ironical man is in Kierkegaard's *Concept of Irony*. Kierkegaard saw
Romantic Irony as a dissolution of objectivity in the interest of a
preservation of subjectivity, a process which involves in the end
the reduction of all reality to the bare self-consciousness of the
completely bored ironist. In Romantic Irony, according to Kierkegaard, 'all historical actuality was negated to make room for a
self-created actuality'.[67] The ironist refused, for example, to accept
the past as something that once given cannot be ignored. His ego,
inhabiting the timeless present of pure subjectivity, can at will
lend absolute validity to any historical period; that is, he can take

fourth-century Athens as his standpoint from which to ironize any other period, and when he has exhausted its potentiality he can transfer this gift of absolute validity to, say, the Middle Ages. This treatment of historical periods, validating and invalidating them at pleasure, can be equally well applied to religious and to philosophical systems. It can be applied to one's own life: the ironist can adopt and lend absolute validity to the role of the beggar or the magistrate, the man of feeling or the stoic, the child or the sage, the peasant or the aristocrat, and he can do this with some (temporary) plausibility since irony directs our attention away from the standpoint and towards the deficiencies of what is being ironized. Then 'because the ironist poetically produces himself as as well as his environment with the greatest possible poetic licence, because he lives completely hypothetically and subjunctively, his life finally loses all continuity. With this he wholly lapses under the sway of his moods and feelings.'[68] But moods and feelings are as ironizable as roles and so in time, as they lose all content, the existence of the ironist is reduced to a mere thread of boredom conscious of nothing but itself.

> Irony is free, to be sure, free from all the cares of actuality, but free from its joys as well, free from its blessings. For if it has nothing higher than itself, it may receive no blessing, for it is ever the lesser that is blessed of a greater.[69]

This, one imagines, would be the state of the archetypal ironist, whether God or Devil; but Kierkegaard does not allow his thoughts to stray in that direction.

It is difficult not to feel the force of these arguments. There is no doubt that for some men the habit of irony may be a corrosive and paralysing disease of the spirit or that an ironical attitude *might* result in perpetual ennui or nihilism. But one is not convinced that this must be so for all 'ironical men'.

Against Kierkegaard one may raise three points. First, that his condemnation of the 'Romantic Ironist' is too theoretical and does not sufficiently recognize that the world will not allow a man to treat everything ironically. Where Kierkegaard does recognize this it is only to scoff at the ironists, this time for not being ironical:

One or another youthful ward of the Young Germany and France would long ago have died of boredom [induced by their habit of irony] had not their respective governments been so fatherly as to arrest them in order to give them something to think about.[70]

Kierkegaard himself arranged to be born too late to be burnt for heresy. One may say that in general his view of irony too closely resembles those frequent prophecies of the imminent collapse of civilization which moralists see as the inevitable result of this or that deplorable divergence from established custom. In theory, the world is always going very rapidly to the dogs; in practice, the dogs seem to have the essential characteristic of a mirage. So Kierkegaard's perpetually ironical man has all the signs of a thorough scapegrace except that he has so far had the grace not to emerge definitively from theory.

Secondly, Kierkegaard has misrepresented Romantic Irony, as both Beda Allemann and Ingrid Strohschneider-Kohrs have pointed out. Romantic Irony in Friedrich Schlegel's sense was not essentially negative and destructive but, as I have tried to show, progressive and recreative. Nor was it essentially subjective in the sense that it sought detachment *in the interests of* personal freedom since it taught that the ironist should be immanent in his work as well as transcendent. The Romantic Ironist was not the simple and typical ironist, the heaven-dwelling observer, I was presenting in the previous section. He was aware of being himself inextricably involved in the contradictions of life. This awareness, exemplified in our own time by Mann and Musil, operates to prevent the ironist both from taking his irony too far in Kierkegaard's sense (and so becoming a victim of irony through ironizing everything out of existence, including most of himself) and from not taking his irony far enough and stopping short of self-irony of a more fruitful kind. Heine, Mann, and Musil, though pretty thorough-going ironists, escaped the fate Kierkegaard foretold for the ironist.

As there may be scientists who botanize upon their mothers' graves, so there may be ironists who find in Auschwitz only material for a flippant anti-semitic joke. But I see no reason to suppose that the habit of irony prevents ironists from being serious when seriousness is called for. Socrates, on trial for his life, was ironical towards his accusers. But he was prepared to die rather than capitulate and afterwards make ironical jokes about the relative values of life and honesty. Voltaire did not take a detached ironical view of the Calas case. Nor did Heine merely ironize Prussian illiberalism, or Anatole France the Dreyfus affair. Thomas Mann did not make ironical jokes about Hitler; his irony, wideranging as it is, is in the long run ethically motivated, and the central chapter of *The Magic Mountain*, the Snow chapter, culminates with a biblical allusion: 'For the sake of goodness and love, man shall let death have no dominion over his thoughts.' Even Musil, a more 'open' ironist than Mann, makes his hero (indistinguishable from himself) say, in a sentence 'that astonished him less by its substance than by its total lack of irony', 'I'm seeking instruction in the ways of the holy life.'[71]

The third and most important point against Kierkegaard I shall postpone for a while, returning to the general charge, which is also Kierkegaard's, that irony leads to nihilism. As against those who make this charge, claiming to judge irony by its fruits, one must insist that they examine the whole crop not just the windfalls. We know that power corrupts but also that it would be stupid to propose that no one should exercise power; we know what evil is done in the name of virtue and what dangers lie in self-righteousness, but these are not reasons for becoming a blackguard. There are also dangers in earnestness, in not having a sense of irony. Nothing is safe from attack if one can choose the evidence.

Those who attack irony should also examine the fruits of their own trees. Attacking irony is not a way of establishing the superior validity of any other attitude; one may be throwing stones from glass houses. While I hold no brief at all for merely timid or evasive irony and applaud Wayne Booth's attack upon foggy ambiguities and the easy ironies of shallow minds, I think we ought to be suspicious of the general charge that irony is rocking the boat. It is the function of irony to point out that it is the waves that are doing the rocking and that this is only to be expected when one is at sea and not on dry land. It is the function of irony to ask whether we have any reason to suppose we inhabit a world

R

whose meaningfulness irony could destroy rather than a world
whose meaninglessness irony might make clear.

This is precisely the third point against Kierkegaard. The real
basis of his objections to irony is his commitment as a Christian
to a closed-world ideology. Though he was himself a superb ironist and could employ a wide range of ironic strategies with great
verve, subtlety, and originality, he could not take an ironical, that
is, open view of the totality of existence. Since he was a believer,
there was one direction in which he could not be ironical; since
he believed in God it followed that irony had to be subordinated
to the ethical and the religious. The business of irony is to see
clearly and ask questions. Its victims are the blind; its enemies
those who do not wish to be pressed for answers. Irony, mobile
and disengaged, has always been an object of suspicion in the eyes
of established authority and those who feel a need for its blessing.
Socrates was accused, Xenophon says, of causing those who con-
versed with him to despise the established laws and of teaching
children to show contempt for their parents. It was not only because Heine was a Jew that the Nazis attacked his works. The following passage from Franz Koch's *Geschichte deutscher Dichtung*
(1937) may be taken as representing the Nazi view of Heine
as a totally irresponsible writer, without fundamental beliefs
and essentially alienated from the true spirit of the German
people:

> Much greater [than the damage done by Heine's lyric poetry] is the
> damage done by such works of his as 'Atta Troll' or 'Deutschland,
> ein Wintermärchen' or by his prose, writings which, like poison or
> acid, ate into everything round them, the effect of this being to make
> a German feel inwardly insecure.[72]

It is not the ironist, however, but the man who does not wish to
see or enquire, who incites men to war or establishes a totalitarian
state. When Anatole France complained that martyrs lacked a
sense of irony he might have added, with at least as much point,
that a sense of irony did not characterize those who felt a need to
martyr them. The theories of Marx and Freud encouraged relativistic thinking and are therefore compatible with the openness of
irony. But communism and psychoanalysis when rigidified into

dogmas and systems cannot tolerate irony any more than a bishop can.

We live in a world which imposes upon us many contradictory pressures. Stability is a deep human need, but in seeking stability we run the risk of being imprisoned in the rigidity of a closed system, political, moral, or intellectual. We need the reinvigoration that change brings but not a drifting from one novelty to another. We cannot wish never to feel or always to be swept by emotions. We wish to be objective but we cannot treat men as objects. We behave instinctively when we should be rational and rationally when instinct would serve us better. Those who close their eyes to the ambivalences of the human condition – the proponents and adherents of systems, the sentimental idealists, the hard-headed realists, the panacea-mongering technologists – will naturally find an enemy in the ironist and accuse him of flippancy, nihilism, or sitting on the fence.

Though some ironists may be guilty of these charges, irony is properly to be regarded as more an intellectual than a moral activity. That is to say, the morality of irony, like the morality of science, philosophy, and art, is a morality of intelligence. The ironist's virtue is mental alertness and agility. His business is to make life unbearable for troglodytes, to keep open house for ideas, and to go on asking questions.

REFERENCES

The reader is advised that the notes have no other function but that of locating references and quotations.

CHAPTER ONE (pp. 3–13)

1. *The Well Wrought Urn* (London, 1949, 1960 reprint), p. 191.
2. Ann Arbor, 1964, p. 13.
3. *A Course of Lectures on Dramatic Art and Literature*, trans. John Black, revised A. J. W. Morrison (London, 1861), p. 370.
4. Friedrich Schlegel, Lyceums-Fragment 23, *Kritische Ausgabe*, II, ed. Hans Eichner (Paderborn, 1967), 149.
5. Trans. Lee M. Capel (London, 1966), p. 292.
6. C. Wallace-Crabbe, 'The Habit of Irony? Australian Poets of the Fifties', *Meanjin Quarterly*, XX (1961), 164.
7. A. D. Pryor, 'Juvenal's False Consolation', *AUMLA*, 18 (November 1962), 167–80.
8. See, e.g. Kathleen Williams, *Jonathan Swift and the Age of Compromise* (Lawrence, 1958), pp. 154–209.
9. H. L. Koonce, 'Moll's Muddle: Defoe's use of irony in *Moll Flanders*', *E. L. H.*, XXX (December 1963), 377–94.
10. *The Well Wrought Urn*, pp. 153–62.
11. London, 1924 (1945 reprint), p. 250.
12. 'The Poetry of Andrew Marvell', *The Pelican Guide to English Literature*, ed. Boris Ford (London, 1956, 1962 reprint), III, 193.
13. 'Pure and Impure Poetry', Mesures Lecture, Princeton, 1942, printed in *Critiques and Essays in Criticism 1920–1948*, ed. R. W. Stallman (New York, 1949), p. 101.

CHAPTER TWO (pp. 14–39)

1. *The Poetry and Prose of Heinrich Heine*, ed. Frederic Ewen, 2nd edn (New York, 1959), pp. 355–6.
2. Ibid., p. 457.

3. Trans. Jacques Barzun, in *Rameau's Nephew and other Works* (New York, 1956), p. 62.
4. *Gods and their Makers*, (London, 1897, reissued 1920), pp. 209–21.
5. Hugo Von Hofmannsthal, 'Two Essays: I – The Irony of Things', *London Mercury*, IX (1923).
6. New York, 1932, p. 42.
7. London, 1953, 1961 reprint, pp. 29–30.
8. University Microfilms, Ann Arbor, 1957, pp. 11–13.
9. *Renaissance and Modern Studies*, VI (1962), 113.
10. *The Decline and Fall of the Roman Empire*, ed. J. B. Bury, 3rd edn (London, 1901), II, 472.
11. *Northanger Abbey*, ed. R. W. Chapman, 3rd edn (Oxford, 1933), p. 43.
12. London, 1950, p. 122.
13. Jane Austen, *Pride and Prejudice*, ed. R. W. Chapman, 3rd edn (London, 1932), p. 7.
14. Choderlos de Laclos, *Les Liaisons Dangereuses*, trans. P. W. K. Stone (London, 1961), p. 111.
15. Ibid., pp. 109–10.
16. *The Writings of Mark Twain* (New York, 1899), XIV, 52.

CHAPTER THREE (pp. 40–63)

1. Stephen Crane, *The Red Badge of Courage*, ed. R. W. Stallman (New York, 1951), pp. vii–viii.
2. *Pride and Prejudice*, ed. R. W. Chapman, 3rd edn (London, 1932), pp. 67–68.
3. *Middlemarch*, Book I, Chapter vii.
4. G. G. Sedgewick, *Of Irony, Especially in Drama*, 2nd edn (Toronto, 1948), p. 11.
5. Trans. Thomas Twining (London, Everyman, 1943), p. 22.
6. In *Tragedy; Modern Essays in Criticism*, eds Laurence Michel and Richard B. Sewell (New Jersey, 1963), p. 34.
7. London, 1910, p. 26.
8. *The Ironic Temper*, p. 42.
9. Norman Knox, *The Word IRONY and its Context 1500–1755* (Durham, N. C., 1961), p. 60.

10. *The Works of Henry Fielding*, ed. Leslie Stephen (London, 1882), I, 283.

11. Thomas Babington Macaulay, 'Lord Bacon', *Edinburgh Review*, No. 132 (July 1837), 428.

12. *Institutio Oratoria*, VIII, vi, 54, trans. H. E. Butler (London, 1922, 1959 reprint).

13. F. R. Leavis, 'The Irony of Swift', *Scrutiny*, II (1934), 364–78; A. E. Dyson, 'Swift: the Metamorphosis of Irony', *Essays and Studies*, new series, XI (1958), 53–67.

14. Jane Austen, *Pride and Prejudice*, p. 68.

15. *Life of Sidney* (Oxford, 1907), pp. 153–4.

CHAPTER FOUR (pp. 64–98)

1. 'How to Tell a Story', *The Writings of Mark Twain* (New York, 1899), XXII, 8.

2. 'On Some of the Old Actors', *Essays of Elia*.

3. *The Guardian*, No. 40.

4. *Collected Poems* (London, 1965), pp. 185–6.

5. *A Tale of a Tub with Other Early Works*, ed. Herbert Davis (Oxford, 1957), p. 147.

6. 'L'ironie', *Revue Politique et Littéraire*, 4ᵉ Série, IX (23 April 1898), 517.

7. Hilaire Belloc, 'Godolphin Horne', *Selected Cautionary Verses* (London, 1950), p. 29.

8. *An Essay of Dramatic Poesy*, ed. Thomas Arnold, 3rd edn (Oxford, 1946), p. 103.

9. *Life and Works of Arbuthnot*, ed. George A. Aitken (Oxford, 1892), pp. 468–70.

10. *The Decline and Fall of the Roman Empire*, II, 11–12.

11. Knox, op. cit., p. 121.

12. 'The Encyclopedia', trans. Ralph H. Bowen, in *Rameau's Nephew and Other Works*, pp. 310–11.

13. *Candide, or Optimism*, trans. John Butt (London, 1947, 1956 reprint), p. 31.

14. William Lecky, *History of European Morals*, 6th edn revised (London, 1884), p. 344.

15. *The Genesis of a Novel*, trans. Richard and Clara Winston (London, 1961), p. 47.
16. *The Works of Alexander Pope*, ed. W. L. Bowles (London, 1806), VI, 313.
17. *The Works of Henry Fielding*, I, 126.
18. Trans. A. T. Hatto (London, 1965), p. 235.
19. *Pudd'nhead Wilson*, in *The Writings of Mark Twain* (New York, 1899), XIV, vii.
20. *Selected Works*, trans. Michael Grant (London, 1960), pp. 52–53.
21. *Encounter* (June, 1959), p. 60.
22. *British Pamphleteers*, Vol. II, ed. Reginald Reynolds (London, 1951), p. 68.
23. *Plato and his Dialogues* (London, 1947), p. 24.
24. Plato, 'Euthyphro', trans. F. M. Stawell in *Socratic Discourses, Plato and Xenophon*, introd. A. D. Lindsay (London, 1910, 1937 reprint), pp. 318–20.
25. John M. Major, 'The Personality of Chaucer the Pilgrim', *PMLA*, LXXV (June 1960), 160.
26. Ed. J. Dover Wilson (Cambridge, 1935), p. 99.
27. St Thomas Aquinas, *Summa Theologiae*, ii. Q. xi. Article IV.
28. *The Works of Henry Fielding*, IX, 51.

CHAPTER FIVE (pp. 99–115)

1. *Reisebilder* (1828), *The Poetry and Prose of Heinrich Heine*, p. 735.
2. Trans. Eithne Wilkins and Ernst Kaiser (London, 1953, 1961 reprint), I, 332–3.
3. George Meredith, *The Egoist* (London, 1915), pp. 17–28.
4. A. J. Arberry, *Tales from the Masnavi* (London, 1961), p. 48.
5. Trans. E. F. Watling (London, 1953), pp. 115–16.
6. 'Le récit de Thésée', *Australian Journal of French Studies*, II (1965), 175, 176.
7. London, 1954, pp. 202–3.
8. Ulrich Von Hutten et. al., *Epistolae Obscurorum Virorum*, ed. and trans. F. E. Stokes (London, 1909), p. 371.
9. *The Writings of Mark Twain*, XX, 29–31.
10. Samuel Butler, *The Fair Haven* (London, 1913), pp. 13–15.
11. Berlin, 1959, pp. 94–132.

12. John Stuart Mill, *On Liberty* (London, 1929, 1938 reprint), pp. 35–36.

13. Connop Thirlwall, 'On the Irony of Sophocles', *The Philological Museum* (Cambridge, 1833), II, 490.

CHAPTER SIX (pp. 119–158)

1. *The Concept of Irony*, p. 271.
2. 'L'ironie: étude psychologique', *Revue Philosophique de la France et de l'étranger* (Feb. 1906), p. 153.
3. *The Modern Theme*, trans. James Cleugh (New York, 1931, 1961 reprint), p. 54.
4. George Chapman, *The Tragedy of Charles, Duke of Byron*, Act V, Sc. iii, 189–92.
5. *Mustapha*, in *Poems and Dramas of Fulke Greville*, ed. Geoffrey Bullough (Edinburgh, 1939), II, 136.
6. *The Spectator*, No. 253.
7. *Conversations with Eckermann*, 16 December 1828.
8. Joseph Spence, *Observations, Anecdotes, and Characters of Books and Men* (Oxford, 1966), p. 462.
9. *The Prelude*, Book III, 59–63 (1850 version).
10. 'On the Limits of the Beautiful' (1794), *The Aesthetic and Miscellaneous Works*, trans. E. J. Millington (London, 1849), p. 418.
11. *The Man without Qualities* (London, 1953–4, 1961 reprint), I, 271–2.
12. 'Glosa a Ramiro de Maeztu', *Glosario*, 1911. Translated from R. M. Albérès, *L'aventure intellectuelle du xxe siècle* (Paris, 1959), p. 73.
13. *The Man without Qualities*, I, 361–2.
14. Ibid., I, 254.
15. *The Poetry and Prose of Heinrich Heine*, pp. 195–7.
16. G. R. G. Mure, *A Study of Hegel's Logic* (Oxford, 1950), p. 257.
17. *The Babylonian Talmud*, ed. L. Epstein (London, 1938), Seder Mo'ed, I, trans. H. Freedman (Shabbath 153a), 781.
18. *War and Peace* (Book IX, Chapter I), trans. Louise and Aylmer Maude (London, 1941, 1958 reprint), II, 259.
19. *The Man without Qualities*, II, 288.
20. *Oeuvres Romanesques*, ed. Henri Bénac (Paris, 1962), p. 529.

21. 'A Dialogue between the Soul and the Body', *The Poems of Andrew Marvell*, ed. Hugh Macdonald (London, 1952), p. 15.
22. *The Romantic School* (1836), *The Poetry and Prose of Heinrich Heine*, p. 612.
23. *The Nature of the Universe*, trans. R. E. Latham (London, 1951), p. 166.
24. Bartholomew Griffin, in *Elizabethan Lyrics*, ed. Norman Ault, 3rd edn (London, 1949), p. 228.
25. *Fragments d'une Journal Intime*, ed. Bernard Bouvier (Paris, 1931), II, 31.
26. From 'The Grumbling Hive', *The Fable of the Bees*, ed. F. B. Kaye (Oxford, 1924), p. 36.
27. *Parables for the Theatre*, trans. Eric Bentley (Minneapolis, 1965), pp. 91–92.
28. *Pascal's Pensées*, ed. H. F. Stewart (London, 1950), p. 90.
29. Paris, 1902, pp. 13–14.
30. Ibid., p. 196.
31. Ed. Henry D. Aiken (New York, 1948, 1965 reprint), pp. 40–41, 78–79.
32. London, 1926, pp. 16–21.
33. *The Complete Short Stories of Mark Twain*, ed. Charles Neider (New York, 1958), pp. 608–11.
34. London, 1914, p. 8.
35. *Reisebilder* (1830), *The Poetry and Prose of Heinrich Heine*, p. 382.
36. *Confessions* (1854), *The Poetry and Prose of Heinrich Heine*, p. 488.
37. London, 1923 (1925 reprint), p. 304.
38. Thomas Mann, *The Magic Mountain*, p. 338.
39. Samuel Beckett, *Waiting for Godot* (London, 1959, 1964 reprint). p. 44.
40. *Encounter* (November 1965), pp. 48–49.
41. *The Man without Qualities*, II, 229, 231–2.
42. T. S. Eliot, *The Cocktail Party* (London, 1950, 1958 reprint), pp. 118, 122, 158.
43. Aldous Huxley, *Point Counter Point* (London, 1947, 1954 reprint), pp. 554–5.
44. *The Man without Qualities*, I, 295.
45. *Journals*, ed. Alexander Dru (London, 1938, 1959 reprint), p. 50.

46. Quoted from Theodore Weiss, 'How to end the Renaissance',
    Sewanee Review, LXXIII (1965), p. 644.

CHAPTER SEVEN (pp. 159–215)

1. *A History of Modern Criticism; II: The Romantic Age* (London, 1955,
   1961 reprint), p. 14.
2. *Friedrich Schlegel: Literary Notebooks, 1797–1801*, ed. Hans Eichner
   (Toronto, 1957), pp. 114, 62.
3. Thomas Mann, *Tonio Kröger*, trans. H. T. Lowe-Porter (London,
   1955, 1962 reprint), p. 152.
4. *Mme de Staël on Politics, Literature and National Character*, trans. and
   ed. Morroe Berger (London, 1964), p. 242.
5. *Four Tales*, trans. Michael Bullock (London, 1962), pp. 16–17.
6. Schlegel, *Notebooks*, p. 84.
7. *Collected Poems* (Chicago, 1963), p. 3.
8. *The Complete Greek Drama*, eds Whitney J. Oates and Eugene
   O'Neill, Jr. (New York, 1938), II, 919–20.
9. *Point Counter Point*, p. 409.
10. Scarron, *Le roman comique*, ed. Emile Magne (Paris, n.d.), p. 5.
11. Machado da Assis, *Epitaph of a Small Winner*, trans. William L.
    Grossman (London, 1953), p. 190.
12. *Salon de 1767* (Paris, 1875–9), XI, 136, quoted from Kurt Weinberg,
    Henri Heine, 'Romantique défroqué' (Paris, 1954), p. 43.
13. 'The Self-Conscious Narrator in Comic Fiction before *Tristram
    Shandy*', *PMLA*, LXVII (March 1952), 163–85.
14. *The Defence of Poetry*, ed. H. F. B. Brett-Smith, 2nd edn (Oxford,
    1923, 1929 reprint), pp. 53–54.
15. 'Rapports', *Cahiers du Sud*, XVI (1937), 20.
16. *Jacques le fataliste et son maître*, p. 493.
17. Ibid., p. 537.
18. Ibid., p. 495.
19. Ibid., p. 505.
20. Ibid., pp. 718, 777.
21. Ibid., p. 778.
22. Ibid., pp. 513–14.
23. Ibid., p. 653.
24. Ibid., pp. 515–16.

25. Ibid., p. 527.
26. Trans. Geoffrey Skelton (London, 1965), pp. 38–39.
27. Ibid., p. 6.
28. Paris, 1958, p. 149.
29. *Notebooks*, p. 64.
30. See the bibliography.
31. *The Prose of Christopher Brennan*, eds A. R. Chisholm and J. J. Quinn (Sydney, 1962), pp. 379–95.
32. *Notebooks*, pp. 84, 137, 69.
33. *The Aesthetic and Miscellaneous Works*, p. 220.
34. University Microfilms (Ann Arbor, 1957), p. 2.
35. Athenäums-Fragment 216, p. 198.
36. *Religion and Philosophy in Germany* (1835), *The Poetry and Prose of Heinrich Heine*, pp. 759–60.
37. Athenäums-Fragment 116, p. 182; 'Philosophische Lehrjahre', 1796–1806, *Kritische Ausgabe*, XVIII, ii (1), ed. Ernst Behler, p. 128; Lyceums-Fragment 48, p. 153.
38. *Cahiers du Sud*, XVI, 1937, p. 194.
39. Quoted from *Harvard Classics*, ed. Charles W. Eliot (New York, 1910), pp. 391–2.
40. J. Chantavoine and J. Gaudefroy-Demombynes, *L'ère romantique: le romantisme dans la musique européenne* (Paris, 1955), pp. 353–8.
41. *The Excursion*, Preface to the edition of 1814.
42. Ludwig Feuerbach, *The Essence of Christianity*, trans. Marian Evans, 2nd edn (London, 1881), p. 3.
43. Ideen, 98, p. 266.
44. *Biographia Literaria*, Chapter XIII (London, 1906, 1952 reprint), p. 146.
45. *L'âme romantique et le rêve, essai sur le romantisme allemand et la poésie française* (Marseilles, 1937), p. 72.
46. *Sämtliche Werke* (Stuttgart and Berlin, 1902), XXXIII, 16.
47. Arthur O. Lovejoy, 'On the Discrimination of Romanticisms', *English Romantic Poets, Modern Essays in Criticism*, ed. M. H. Abrams (New York, 1960), p. 15.
48. *Lectures on Dramatic Art and Literature*, pp. 342–3.
49. Ibid., p. 368.
50. *Biographia Literaria*, Chapter XIV, pp. 151–2.
51. Lyceums-Fragment 108, p. 160.

52. 'The Art of the Novel', *The Creative Vision*, eds H. M. Block and H. Salinger (New York, 1960), p. 88.

53. *Conversations with Eckermann*, 29 January 1826. Quoted from Rose F. Egan, 'The Genesis of the Theory of "Art for Art's Sake" in Germany and England', *Smith College Studies in Modern Languages*, V (April 1924), 25.

54. Lyceums-Fragment 37, p. 151.

55. 'Anzeige eines Fontane-Buches', *Gesammelte Werke* (Frankfurt a.M., 1960), X, 580.

56. Athenäums-Fragment 297, p. 215.

57. 'Über Goethes Meister', *Kritische Ausgabe*, II, 133.

58. André Gide, *The Coiners*, trans. Dorothy Bussy (London, 1950, 1952 reprint), p. 207.

59. 'Über Goethes Meister', p. 133.

60. Ibid., p. 131; Lyceums-Fragment 42, p. 152; *Notebooks*, p. 93.

61. 'Literary Reminiscences', *Coleridge's Literary Criticism*, ed. J. W. Mackail (London, 1921), p. 186.

62. Lyceums-Fragment 115, p. 161.

63. Athenäums-Fragment 255, pp. 208–9.

64. Ibid. 121, p. 184; 'Gesprach über die Poesie', *Kritische Ausgabe*, II, 318–19.

65. 'Über die Unverständlichkeit', *Kritische Ausgabe*, II, 369.

66. Paris, 1950, I, 269.

67. Athenäums-Fragment 116, pp. 182–3.

68. *Northanger Abbey*, pp. 25–26.

69. *Mme de Staël on Politics, Literature and National Character*, pp. 251–2.

70. Jane Austen, *Sense and Sensibility*, ed. R. W. Chapman (Oxford, 1933), pp. 47–48.

71. Trans. John Todhunter, *Heine's Prose and Poetry* (London, 1934, 1962 reprint), pp. 60–62.

72. 1. 'Anna Karenina' (1939), *Essays of Three Decades*, trans. H. T. Lowe-Porter (New York, 1947), p. 179; 2. 'The Art of the Novel', (1939), pp: 88–89.

73. *Notebooks*, p. 113.

74. Trans. H. T. Lowe-Porter (London, 1954), p. 5.

75. Ibid., p. 176.

76. Ibid., p. 145.

77. Ibid., p. 240.

78. Ibid., p. 241.
79. Ibid., p. 394.
80. Ibid., p. 321.
81. Ibid., p. 190.
82. Ibid., pp. 132–3.
83. Ibid., pp. 133–5.
84. Ibid., p. 180.
85. Ibid., p. 181.
86. Ibid., p. 259.
87. Quoted from Hugh Kenner, *Samuel Beckett, a Critical Study* (London, 1962), pp. 30–31.

CHAPTER EIGHT (pp. 216–247.)

1. 'On the Irony of Sophocles', p. 484.
2. 'The Art of the Novel', pp. 88–89.
3. *Vorschule der Ästhetik*, VIII, 38, in *Werke*, ed. Norbert Miller (Darmstadt, 1962), V, 156.
4. Quoted from Erich Heller, *The Ironic German: A Study of Thomas Mann* (London, 1958), p. 236.
5. *The Genesis of a Novel*, p. 23.
6. 'The Ironic Tradition in Augustan Prose from Swift to Johnson', in *Restoration and Augustan Prose* (Third Clark Library Seminar, July 1956) (Los Angeles, n.d.), p. 28.
7. Josef Budde, *Zur romantischen Ironie bei Ludwig Tieck* (Bonn, 1907), p. 24, quoted from G. G. Sedgewick, *Of Irony*, p. 17.
8. *Dialogues Philosophiques* (Paris, 1876), p. 30, quoted from Chevalier, *The Ironic Temper*, p. 63.
9. *The Nature of the Universe*, p. 60.
10. *Vorschule der Ästhetik*, VII, 33, in *Werke*, V, 129.
11. *Amiel's Journal*, trans. Mrs Humphry Ward, 2nd edn (London, 1889, 1904 reprint), p. 215.
12. Paul Claudel, *Positions et propositions* (Paris, 1934), translated from Albérès, *L'aventure intellectuelle du xxᵉ siècle*, p. 52.
13. 'Un Bonhomme', *Oeuvres de Sully Prudhomme, Poésies 1866–1872* (Paris n.d.), p. 31.
14. II, 410, 412.
15. 'On the Irony of Sophocles', pp. 490–1.

16. Berkeley and Los Angeles, 1948, pp. 204–5.
17. *Tonio Kröger*, pp. 153–4.
18. Trans. H. T. Lowe-Porter (London, 1940, 1947 reprint), pp. 63–64.
19. *The Dynasts*, pp. 524, 517.
20. Unamuno, *A Philosophy of Tragedy*, trans. Philip Silver (Berkeley and Los Angeles, 1962), pp. 37–39.
21. *Dialogues concerning Natural Religion*, p. 56.
22. *Oeuvres Complètes*, éd. Assézat et Tourneux (Paris, 1875–7), II, 373. Quoted from I. H. Smith, 'Diderot's *Jacques le fataliste*', *AUMLA*, 8 (May 1958), 18.
23. Bergson, *Laughter*, ed. Wylie Sypher, *Comedy* (New York, 1956), pp. 79, 97.
24. Cambridge, Mass., 1949, p. 47.
25. *Brideshead Revisited* (London, 1949), p. 188.
26. *Reisebilder* (1830), *The Poetry and Prose of Heinrich Heine*, p. 379.
27. E. M. Forster, *A Passage to India* (London, 1936, 1961 reprint), pp. 145, 147.
28. *Journal Intime*, I, 284.
29. *L'ironie: étude psychologique*, p. 151.
30. M. *Anatole France et la Pensée Contemporaine* (Paris, 1909), p. 69.
31. *The Ironic Temper*, p. 79.
32. Vladimir Jankélévitch, *L'Ironie, ou la Bonne Conscience* (Paris, 1950), p. 29.
33. 'Le Jardin d'Epicure', *Oeuvres Complètes* (Paris, 1948), IX, 450.
34. 'The Art of the Novel', p. 88.
35. *The Magic Mountain*, pp. 281–2.
36. 'L'ironie', *Revue Politique et Littéraire*, No. 17, 4e Série, IX (23 April 1898), 517.
37. *L'Ironie, ou la Bonne Conscience*, p. 23.
38. *Journal Intime*, I, 277–8.
39. Ibid., II, 166.
40. Quoted from Thomas Mann, 'The Art of the Novel', p. 88.
41. *The Concept of Irony*, p. 338.
42. 'Rabelais', *Oeuvres Complètes*, VII, 43.
43. 'A Free Man's Worship', *Mysticism and Logic* (London, 1917, 1959 reprint), p. 48.
44. Quoted from Erich Heller, *The Ironic German*, pp. 236–7.

45. 'Goethe and Tolstoy', *Essays of Three Decades*, p. 173.
46. *Counter Statement*, 2nd edn (California, 1953), pp. 104–5.
47. *The Man Without Qualities*, I, 255.
48. *Characteristics*, ed. J. M. Robertson (Gloucester, Mass., 1963), I, 50.
49. *The Romantic School* (1836), *The Poetry and Prose of Heinrich Heine*, p. 611.
50. *The Word IRONY and its Context*, p. 52.
51. Walter Pater, *Marius the Epicurean*, 4th edn (London, 1898, 1909 reprint), I, 133.
52. Ibid., I, 212–13.
53. London, 1944, p. 20.
54. *The Genesis of a Novel*, p. 34.
55. Quoted from *Three Oxford Ironies*, ed. George Gordon (London, 1927), p. 13.
56. Quoted from Victor H. Brombert, 'Stendhal: Le romancier des interventions', *Aurea Parma*, Fasc. II (July–December 1950), p. 5.
57. Brombert, *Stendhal et la voie oblique* (New Haven, 1954), p. 157.
58. *Life of Sidney* (Oxford, 1907), pp. 153–4.
59. *Dialogues concerning Natural Religion*, p. 56.
60. *Journal Intime*, I, 233.
61. Ibid., p. 165.
62. 'The New Irony: Sickniks and Others', *The American Scholar*, 31 (Winter, 1961–2), pp. 110–16.
63. Charles Maurras, 'Ironie et Poésie', *Barbarie et Poésie* (Paris, 1925), p. 352.
64. *Romanticism and the Modern Ego* (Boston 1943, 1947 reprint), p. 172.
65. *The House of Intellect* (London, 1959), pp. 74–75.
66. *The Rhetoric of Fiction* (Chicago, 1961, 1965 reprint), pp. 371–2.
67. *The Concept of Irony*, p. 292.
68. Ibid., p. 301.
69. Ibid., p. 296.
70. Ibid., p. 302.
71. *The Man without Qualities* (London, 1960), III, 99.
72. Hamburg, 1937, p. 202.

A SELECTED BIBLIOGRAPHY

With some exceptions, the works listed here are those which discuss the concept of irony or which deal in general terms with the practice of irony. I have included a selection of books and articles on topics which the present work relates to irony.

'ALBÉRÈS, R.-M.' *L'aventure intellectuelle du xxᵉ siècle*, Paris, 1959.

ALCANTER DE BRAHM. *L'Ostensoir des Ironies*, Paris, 1899.

ALLEMANN, BEDA. *Ironie und Dichtung*, Pfullingen, 1956.

AMIEL, HENRI-FRÉDÉRIC. *Fragments d'un Journal Intime*, ed. Bernard Bouvier, 2 vols, Paris, 1931.

Amiel's Journal, trans. Mrs Humphry Ward, London, 1885.

BABBITT, IRVING. *Rousseau and Romanticism*, New York, 1919.

BANULS, ANDRÉ. Ironie und Humor bei Thomas Mann, *Annales Universitatis Saraviensis* (University of Saarland), VIII, i–ii (1959), 119–31.

BARZUN, JACQUES. *Classic, Romantic and Modern*, Boston, 1961.

BAUM, GEORGINA. *Humor und Satire in der bürgerlichen Ästhetik*, Berlin, 1959.

BAUMGART, REINHART. *Das Ironische und die Ironie in dem Werken Thomas Manns*, München, 1964.

BÉGUIN, ALBERT, *L'âme romantique et le rêve, essai sur le romantisme allemand et la poésie française*, Marseilles, 1937.

BENJAMIN, WALTER. *Der Begriff der Kunstkritik in der deutschen Romantic*, in *Schriften*, II, Frankfurt a.M., 1955.

BERTRAND, J.-J. A. *Cervantes et le romantisme allemand*, Paris, 1914.

BILTZ, K. P. *Das Problem der Ironie in der neueren deutschen Literatur, insbesondere bei Thomas Mann*, Diss. Frankfurt a.M., 1932.

BIRNEY, EARLE. English Irony before Chaucer, *University of Toronto Quarterly*, VI (July 1937), 538–57.

BOESCHENSTEIN, HERMANN. Von den Grenzen der Ironie, *Stoffe, Formen, Strukturen: Studien zur deutschen Literatur*, eds Albert Fuchs and Helmut Motekat, München, 1962.

BOOTH, WAYNE C. The Self-Conscious Narrator in Comic Fiction before *Tristram Shandy*, *PMLA*, LXVII (1952), 163–85.

The Rhetoric of Fiction, Chicago, 1961.

BOUCHER, MAURICE. L'Ironie Romantique, in 'Le Romantisme Allemand', *Cahiers du Sud*, Numéro Spécial, XVI, 1937.

K. W. F. Solger, *Esthétique et philosophie de la présence*, Paris, 1934.

BRACHER, FREDERICK. Understatement in Old English Poetry, *PMLA*, LII (December 1937), 915–34.

BRENNAN, CHRISTOPHER. *The Prose of Christopher Brennan*, eds A. R. Chisholm and J. J. Quinn, Sydney, 1962.

BRENNAN, J. G. *Thomas Mann's World*, New York, 1942.

BREWER, E. V. The Influence of Jean Paul Richter on George Meredith's Conception of the Comic, *JEGP*, XXIX (1930), 242–56.

BRIEGLEB, KLAUS. *Ästhetische Sittlichkeit: Versuch über Friedrich Schlegels Systementwurf zur Begründung der Dichtungskritik*, Tübingen, 1962.

BROMBERT, VICTOR H. Stendhal: Le romancier des interventions, *Aurea Parma*, Fasc. II (July–December 1950), 1–13.

Stendhal et la voie oblique: l'auteur devant son monde romanesque, New Haven, 1954.

BROOKS, CLEANTH. Irony as a Principle of Structure, *Literary Opinion in America*, ed. Zabel, Morton, Dauwen. Rev. edn New York, 1951.

Irony and 'Ironic' Poetry, *College English*, IX (1948), 231–7.

Modern Poetry and the Tradition, Chapel Hill, 1939.

The Well Wrought Urn, London, 1949.

BRÜGGEMANN, FRITZ. *Die Ironie als entwicklungsgeschichtliches Moment*, Diss. Jena, 1909.

BÜCHNER, WILHELM. Über den Begriff der Eironeia, *Hermes*, IV (1941), 339–58.

BUDDE, JOSEF. *Zur romantischen Ironie bei Ludwig Tieck*, Diss. Bonn, 1907.

CHANTAVOINE, H. De l'Ironie en Littérature, *Le Correspondant* (10 April 1897), 181–9.

CHANTAVOINE, JEAN and GAUDEFROY-DEMOMBYNES, JEAN. *L'ère romantique: le romantisme dans la musique européenne*, Paris, 1955.

CHEVALIER, HAAKON M. *The Ironic Temper: Anatole France and his Time*, New York, 1932.

S

CLOUGH, W. O. Irony: A French Approach, *Sewanee Review*, XLVII, No. 2 (April–June 1939), 175–83.

COR, RAPHAEL. *Anatole France et la Pensée Contemporaine*, Paris, 1909.

CRANE, R. S. The Critical Monism of Cleanth Brooks, *Critics and Criticism*, ed. R. S. Crane, Chicago, 1952.

The Languages of Criticism and the Structure of Poetry, Toronto, 1953.

DAAB, ANNALIESE. *Ironie und Humor bei Kierkegaard*, Diss. Heidelberg, 1926.

DE MOTT, BENJAMIN. The New Irony: Sickniks and Others, *The American Scholar* (Winter 1961–2), 108–19.

DENHOF, MAURICE. Rapports, in 'Le Romantisme Allemand', *Cahiers du Sud*, Numéro Spécial, XVI, 1937.

DONALDSON, E. TALBOT. Chaucer the Pilgrim, *PMLA*, LXIX (September 1954), 928–36.

DOUMIC, RENÉ. Les inconvénients de l'ironie, *La Vie et les Moeurs*, Paris, 1895.

DULCK, J. Humour et ironie, *Bulletin du Centre d'Études de Littérature générale de Bordeaux*, Fasc. VII, 1959.

DYSON, A. E. *The Crazy Fabric*, London, 1965.

EASTMAN, MAX. *Enjoyment of Laughter*, New York, 1936.

The Sense of Humour, New York, 1921.

EGAN, ROSE F. The Genesis of the Theory of 'Art for Art's Sake' in Germany and in England, *Smith College Studies in Modern Languages*, Vol. II, No. 4, 1921; Vol. V, No. 3, 1924.

EICHNER, HANS. Friedrich Schlegel's Theory of Romantic Poetry, *PMLA*, LXXI (December 1956), 1018–41.

EMPSON, WILLIAM. *Seven Types of Ambiguity*, London, 1930.

Some Versions of Pastoral, London, 1935.

Tom Jones, *Kenyon Review*, 20 (Spring, 1958), 217–49.

ENDERS, CARL. Fichte und die Lehre von der romantischen Ironie, *Zeitschrift für Ästhetik*, 14 (1920), 279–84.

ERNST, FRITZ. *Die romantische Ironie*, Diss. Zürich, 1917.

ESCARPIT, ROBERT. *L'humour*, Paris, 1960.

FOLKIERSKI, WLADYSLAW. *Entre le classicisme et le romanticisme*, Cracow, 1925.

FRANZ, ERICH. *Goethe als religiöser Denker*, Tübingen, 1932.

FREUD, SIGMUND. *The Complete Psychological Works*, ed. James Strachey, 23 vols, London, 1955–64.

FRIEDEMANN, KÄTE. Die romantische Ironie, *Zeitschrift für Ästhetik*, 13 (1919), 270–82.

FRIEDLÄNDER, PAUL. *Plato*, 3 vols, New York, 1958.

FRYE, NORTHROP. *The Anatomy of Criticism*, Princeton, 1957. The Nature of Satire, *University of Toronto Quarterly*, XIV (October 1944), 75–89.

GAULTIER, JULES DE. *Le Bovarysme*, Paris, 1902.

GIBSON, WALKER. Authors, Speakers, Readers, and Mock Readers, *Kenyon Review* (Autumn 1945), 645–52.

GILBERT, K. E. and KAHN, H. *A History of Esthetics*, Revised edn, London, 1956.

GINDIN, JAMES JACK. *Renaissance and modern theories of irony: their application to Donne's Songs and Sonnets*, Ann Arbor Microfilms, 1954.

GOLDBERG, S. L. *The Classical Temper: A Study of James Joyce's Ulysses*, London, 1961.

GUREWITCH, MORTON L. *European Romantic Irony*, Ann Arbor Microfilms, 1957.

HALLAYS, ANDRÉ. L'ironie, *Revue Politique et Littéraire*, No. 17, 4ᵉ Série, Tome IX (23 April 1898), 515–21.

HAMBURGER, KÄTE. *Die Logik der Dichtung*, Stuttgart, 1957.

HASS, HANS EGON. *Die Ironie als literarisches Phänomen*, Diss. Bonn, 1950.

HAYM, RUDOLF. *Die romantische Schule*, Berlin, 1870.

HAZARD, PAUL. *La Crise de la Conscience Européenne 1680–1715*, Paris, 1935. *European Thought in the Eighteenth Century*, London, 1954.

HAZLITT, W. Wit and Humour, *Lectures on the English Comic Writers*, 1819.

HEGEL, G. W. F. *Sämtliche Werke*, ed. Hermann Glockner, 20 vols, Stuttgart, 1958.

HELLER, ERICH. *The Artist's Journey into the Interior*, London, 1966. *The Hazard of Modern Poetry*, London, 1953. *The Ironic German*, London, 1958.

HELLER, JOSEF. *Solgers Philosophie der ironischen Dialektik*, Diss. Berlin, 1928.

HIGHET, GILBERT. *The Anatomy of Satire*, Princeton, 1962.

HUIZINGA, JOHAN. *Homo Ludens: A Study of the Play-Element in Culture*, trans. R. F. C. Hull, London, 1949.

HUTCHENS, ELEANOR N. The Identification of Irony, *ELH*, XXVII (December 1960), 352–63.

Prudence in *Tom Jones*: a study of connotative irony, *Phil. Q.*, 39 (October 1960), 496–507.

IMMERWAHR, RAYMOND. Friedrich Schlegel's Essay *On Goethe's Meister*, *Monatshefte*, XLIX (1957), 1–22.

The Subjectivity or Objectivity of Friedrich Schlegel's Poetic Irony, *Germanic Review*, 26 (1951), 173–91.

The Esthetic Intent of Tieck's Fantastic Comedy, St Louis, 1953.

INGERSLEV, FREDERIK. Romantische Ironie in moderner deutscher Literatur, An Thomas Mann und Jakob Wassermann erläutert; *Edda: Nordisk Tidsskrift für Litteraturforskning*, 30 (1930), 256–68.

JACKSON, HOLBROOK. The Irony of Irony, *Essays of Today and Yesterday*, London, 1927.

JAMES, HENRY. *The Art of the Novel*, New York, 1934.

JANKÉLÉVITCH, VLADIMIR. *L'Ironie, ou La Bonne Conscience*, 2nd (revised) edn, Paris, 1950.

JANCKE, RUDOLF. *Das Wesen der Ironie: Strukturanalyse ihrer Erscheinungsformen*, Leipzig, 1929.

JEPSEN, LAURA. *Ethical Aspects of Tragedy*, Univ. Florida Press, 1953.

JOST, WALTER. *Von L. Tieck zu Hoffmann*, Frankfurt a.M., 1921.

KAHN, GUSTAVE. L'ironie dans le roman français, *La Nouvelle Revue*, Vol. 24 (1903).

KIERKEGAARD, SØREN. *The Concept of Irony, with Constant Reference to Socrates*, trans. Lee M. Capel, London, 1966.

Concluding Unscientific Postscript, trans. David F. Swenson, Princeton, 1944.

Journals, ed. Alexander Dru, New York, 1938.

KNOX, NORMAN. *The Word IRONY and its Context 1500–1755*, Durham, N.C., 1961.

KOYRÉ, ALEXANDER. *From the Closed World to the Infinite Universe*, New York, 1958.

LAFFONT-BOMPIANI. Article on irony [by Maurice Boucher?], *Dictionnaire universel des lettres*, Paris, 1961.

LANGE, VICTOR. Friedrich Schlegel's Literary Criticism, *Comparative Literature*, VII (Fall 1955), 289–305.

LAUFER, ROGER. *Style rococo, style des 'lumières'*, Paris, 1963.

LÉON, XAVIER. *Fichte et son temps*, Paris, 1922–7.

LEWALTER, ERNST. *Friedrich Schlegel und sein romantischer Witz*, Diss. München, 1917.

LOCK, W. The Use of peripeteia in Aristotle's *Poetics*, *Classical Review*, IX (1895), 251–3.

LUSSKY, A. E. *Tieck's Romantic Irony*, Chapel Hill, 1932.

MAGNY, CLAUDE-EDMONDE. *Histoire du roman français depuis 1918*, Paris, 1950.

MAJOR, JOHN M. The Personality of Chaucer the Pilgrim, *PMLA*, LXXV (June 1960), 160–2.

MANDEL, OSCAR. The Function of the Norm in *Don Quixote*, *Modern Philology*, LV (February 1958), 154–63.

MANN, THOMAS. Goethe and Tolstoy, *Essays of Three Decades*, New York, 1947.

The Art of the Novel, *The Creative Vision*, eds Haskell M. Block and Herman Salinger, New York, 1960.

The Theme of the Joseph Novels, Library of Congress, 1963.

MASON, EUDO C. *Deutsche und englische Romantik, Eine Gegenüberstellung*, Göttingen, 1959.

MATENKO, PERCY. *Tieck and Solger*, New York, 1933.

MAURRAS, CHARLES. Ironie et Poésie, *Barbarie et Poésie*, Paris, 1925.

MEREDITH, GEORGE. *An Essay on Comedy*, 1877.

MUDRICK, MARVIN. *Jane Austen: Irony as Defence and Discovery*, Princeton, 1952.

MÜLLER, ADAM. *Vermischte Schriften über Staat, Philosophie und Kunst*, 2 vols, Vienna, 1812.

MUELLER, G. E. Solger's Æsthetics – A Key to Hegel, *Corona: Studies in Celebration of the Eightieth Birthday of Samuel Singer*, ed. A. Schirokauer, Durham, 1941.

NIEBUHR, REINHOLD. *The Irony of American History*, New York, 1952.

ORTEGA Y GASSET, JOSÉ. *The Dehumanization of Art, Notes on the Novel*, trans. Helene Weyl, Princeton, 1948.

The Modern Theme, trans. James Cleugh, New York, 1961.

PALANTE, GEORGES. L'ironie: étude psychologique, *Revue Philosophique de la France et de l'étranger*, Tome LXI (February 1906), 147–63.

PAULHAN, FRANÇOIS. *La Morale de l'Ironie*, Paris, 1909.

PERRY, CHARLES M. *The Ironic Humanist*, Iowa, 1924.

PIRANDELLO, LUIGI. *L'umorismo*, 2nd (enlarged) edn, Florence, 1920.

POUND, EZRA. Irony, Laforgue, and Some Satire, *Literary Essays of Ezra Pound*, ed. T. S. Eliot, London, 1954.

PULOS, C. E. *The New Critics and the Language of Poetry*, Nebraska, 1958.

PULVER, M. *Romantische Ironie und romantische Komödie*, Diss. Freiburg, 1912.

RADER, MELVIN (ed.). *A Modern Book of Aesthetics*, Rev. edn, New York, 1952.

RAMSEY, WARREN. *Jules Laforgue and the Ironic Inheritance*, New York, 1953.

RANSOM, JOHN CROWE. *The New Criticism*, Connecticut, 1941.

REGLER, GUSTAV. *Die Ironie im Werke Goethes*, Leipzig, 1923.

REYNAUD, H. *De l'ironie*, Valence, 1922.

RIBBECK, OTTO. Über den Begriff des εἴρων, *Rheinisches Museum* 31 (1876), 381–400.

RICHTER, J. P. F. [JEAN PAUL]. *Werke*, ed. Norbert Miller, 6 vols, Darmstadt, 1959–63.

RICHARDS, I. A. *Principles of Literary Criticism*, London, 1924.

RODWAY, ALLAN. Terms for Comedy, *Renaissance and Modern Studies*, VI (1962), 102–24.

ROOT, JOHN G. Stylistic Irony in Thomas Mann, *Germanic Review*, XXXV (April 1960), 93–104.

ROSENBERG, E. H. *Melville and the Comic Spirit*, Cambridge, Mass., 1955.

ROUCHE, M. Le romantisme allemand, *Bulletin 13, Centre d'études et de discussions de littérature générale*, Bordeaux, 1954.

ROUGE, J. Culte et culture du moi chez F. Schlegel, *Revue de Métaphysique et de Morale* (April 1934), 205–33.

RUHRIG, HELMUT ERNST. *Heinrich Heine, Beiträge zur Bestimmung seines ironischen Humors*, Diss. Freiberg, 1953.

SARTON, MAY. The Shield of Irony, *Nation* (14 April 1956), 314–16.

SCHAERER, RENÉ. Le Mecanisme de l'Ironie dans ses rapports avec la Dialectique, *Revue de Métaphysique et de Morale*, 48 (1941), 181–209.

SCHASLER, MAX. *Das Reich der Ironie in kulturgeschichtlicher und ästhetischer Beziehung*, Berlin, 1879.

SCHILLER, FRIEDRICH. *Über naive und sentimentalische Dichtung*, 1795.

SCHLAGDENHAUFFEN, ALFRED. *Frédéric Schlegel et son groupe: La doctrine de l'Athenaeum* (1798–1800), Strasbourg, 1934.

SCHLEGEL, AUGUST WILHELM. *A Course of Lectures on Dramatic Art and Literature*, trans. John Black, revised A. J. W. Morrison, London, 1861.

SCHLEGEL, FRIEDRICH. *Literary Notebooks, 1797–1801*, ed. Hans Eichner, Toronto, 1957.
Kritische Schriften, ed. Wolfdietrich Rasch, München, 1956.
The Aesthetic and Miscellaneous Works, trans. E. J. Millington, London, 1849.
Kritische Ausgabe, ed. Ernst Behler, 22 vols, Paderborn, 1958–.

SCHROTTER, KARL. *Die romantische Ironie Friedrich Schlegels als geistesgeschichtliches Phänomen*, Diss. Greifswald, 1924.

SCHUWER, CAMILLE. La part de Fichte dans l'Esthétique Romantique, in 'Le Romantisme Allemand', *Cahiers du Sud*, Numéro Spécial, XVI, 1937.

SEDGEWICK, G. G. *Of Irony, Especially in Drama*, 2nd edn, Toronto, 1948.

SEIDLIN, OSKAR. Ironische Brüderschaft: Thomas Manns *Joseph der Ernährer* und Laurence Sternes *Tristram Shandy*, *Orbis Litterarum*, XII (1958), 44–63.

SHARPE, ROBERT BOIES. *Irony in the Drama: An Essay on Impersonation, Shock, and Catharsis*, Chapel Hill, N.C., 1959.

SIDGWICK, ARTHUR. On Some Forms of Irony, *The Cornhill Magazine* (April 1907), 497–508.

SILZ, WALTER. *Early German Romanticism*, Cambridge, Mass., 1929.

STROHSCHNEIDER-KOHRS, INGRID. *Die romantische Ironie in Theorie und Gestaltung*, Tübingen, 1960.

SZONDI, PETER. Friedrich Schlegel und die romantische Ironie: Mit einem Anhang über Ludwig Tieck, *Euphorion*, 48 (1954), 397–411.

TATE, ALLEN. Tension in Poetry, *The Man of Letters in the Modern World*, London, 1955.

THIRLWALL, CONNOP. On the Irony of Sophocles, *The Philological Museum*, Vol. II, Cambridge, 1833.

THOMPSON, ALAN R. *The Dry Mock, A Study of Irony in Drama*, Berkeley, 1948.

THOMSON, J. A. K. *Irony: An Historical Introduction*, London, 1926.

TIMMER, B. J. Irony in Old English Poetry, *English Studies*, 24 (1942), 171–5.

TURNER, F. MCD. C. *The Element of Irony in English Literature*, London, 1926.

VAN TIEGHEM, PAUL. *L'ère romantique: le romantisme dans la littérature européenne*, Paris, 1948.

VISCHER, FR. TH. *Ästhetik: oder Wissenschaft des Schönen*, Leipzig, 1847.

VOGT, G. *Der Ironie in der romantischen Komödie*, Diss. Frankfurt a.M., 1953.

WAGENER, FERDINAND. *Die romantische und die dialektische Ironie*, Diss. Freiburg, 1931.

WAHL, JEAN. *Études Kierkegaardiennes*, Paris, 1949.
Novalis et le Principe de Contradiction, in 'Le Romantisme Allemand', *Cahiers du Sud*, Numéro Spécial, XVI, 1937.

WALZEL, OSKAR. Methode? Ironie bei Friedrich Schlegel und bei Solger, *Helicon*, I (1938), 33–50.

WARD, HOOVER. Irony and Absurdity in the Avant-Garde Theatre, *Kenyon Review* (Summer 1960), 436–54.

WARREN, ROBERT PENN. Pure and Impure Poetry, *Critiques and Essays in Criticism*, ed. R. W. Stallman, New York, 1949.

WATT, IAN. The Ironic Tradition in Augustan Prose from Swift to Johnson, *Restoration and Augustan Prose*, Los Angeles, 1957 [?].

WEIGAND, HERMANN J. *Thomas Mann's Novel 'Der Zauberberg': a Study*, London, 1933.

WEINBERG, KURT. *Henri Heine, 'romantique défroqué', héraut du symbolisme français*, Paris and New Haven, 1954.

WELLEK, RENÉ. *Confrontations*, Princeton, 1965.
A History of Modern Criticism; II: The Romantic Age, London, 1955.

WERNAER, ROBERT M. *Romanticism and the Romantic School in Germany*, New York and London, 1910.

WERY, LÉON. De l'Ironie, *Le Thyrse*, 1904.

WILLOUGHBY, L. A. *The Romantic Movement in Germany*, London, 1930.

WIMSATT, W. K. and BROOKS, CLEANTH. *Literary Criticism: a Short History*, New York, 1957.

WINTERS, YVOR. *Primitivism and Decadence*, New York, 1937.

WORCESTER, DAVID. *The Art of Satire*, Cambridge, Mass., 1940.

WRIGHT, ANDREW H. Irony and Fiction, *Journal of Aesthetics and Art Criticism*, XII (1953), 111–18.

Jane Austen's Novels: A Study in Structure, London, 1953.

ZEYDEL, E. H. *Ludwig Tieck, the German Romanticist*, Princeton, 1935.

INDEX